PRIDE

PRIDE

THE CHARLEY PRIDE STORY

Charley Pride

with
Jim Henderson

QUILL
William Morrow
New York

It is the policy of William Morrow and Company, Inc., and its imprints and
affiliates, recognizing the importance of preserving what has been written, to
print the books we publish on acid-free paper, and we exert our best efforts to
that end.

Library of Congress Cataloging-in-Publication Data

Pride, Charley.
    Pride: the Charley Pride story / Charley Pride
with Jim Henderson. —
        p.   cm.
    Includes index.
    ISBN 0-688-14232-X
    1. Pride, Charley.   2. Country musicians—United States—
Biography.   I. Henderson, Jim, 1942–   . II. Title.
ML 420.P972A3   1992
782.42'1642'092—dc20   93–34360
    [B]   CIP
                                                           MN

Printed in the United States of America

13 14 15

BOOK DESIGN BY BRIAN MOLLOY/CIRCA 86, INC.

To the memory of Tessie B. Stewart Pride,
a proud and gentle woman,
a wise and tolerant mother
who showed me the way

ACKNOWLEDGEMENTS

Putting one's life on paper is an arduous undertaking and summoning the years of memories can be both painful and joyful. In this effort, I have had the untiring support and encouragement of friends and loved ones and my debt of gratitude to them is large.

Foremost among them is Rozene, my loving, wonderful, understanding, and supportive wife—truly my best friend. She has labored hours and hours helping to make my dreams come true. Without her my life, and this book, would not have been the same.

I would also like to thank . . .

. . . Jim Henderson for his patience and dedication in helping me put this together. In spite of my travels and hours on the golf course, he somehow gathered enough information to make this book a reality.

. . . Hortense Ransom, Nora McNeal, and John Daines in my office for their invaluable assistance and for putting up with my mood swings.

. . . Jerry Lastelick, my attorney, for his editing assistance, and for always being there for me and my family.

. . . Chet Atkins, formerly of RCA Records; Jack Clement,

my first producer; and Jack Johnson, my first manager, for believing in me and helping to make it happen. And Jerry Bradley, who gave unending support, help and friendship during my recording career.

. . . My children, Kraig, Dion, and Angela, who grew up without having a dad around all the time, and my beautiful grandsons, Carlton and Malachi, who have enriched my life in ways that defy words.

. . . My father, who cracked the whip when I was growing up and instilled in me values, strength, work ethics, and the resolve to persist in the face of difficulty.

. . . Bob Sowers and Fred Acciardo, talented pilots who logged many hours keeping me on schedule and who brought us down safely from a mid-air collision.

. . . My good friend Al Donahue and the many DJs and program directors in the United States and abroad who took my music to the world.

. . . Preston Buchanan, a bass guitarist who has been with me longer than anyone, and to all of my many band members and road crew. You are the greatest!

. . . The legion of fans, friends, and colleagues who made it possible for me to take the wondrous journey through the clouds that once teased a small boy's dreams.

C O N T E N T S

Contents

Part 2

P R O L O G U E

Testing the Waters

The Detroit job paid two hundred dollars and all I had to do to earn it was drive 3,200 miles and sing for ten minutes. As much as I needed the money, that wasn't what excited me. Those ten minutes might well be the most important of my life.

"You'll open the show at three o'clock and again at eight," Jack Johnson said.

Jack was my manager. We had been together since 1963, when I first wandered into Nashville trying to get my foot in the door of country music. By late 1966, I had released three singles and an album but the door still wasn't open all the way.

Radio stations across the country had been playing my records for the past year. The first two singles—"Snakes Crawl at Night" and "Before I Met You"-had received generous air play, and "Snakes" had even made it into the Top 40. The third—"Just Between You and Me"—was headed toward the Top 10 and would earn me a Grammy nomination.

But hardly anyone was aware of who I was or what I was. RCA had issued those records with sparse press-release biographies and without the customary publicity photographs. The RCA brass didn't try to deceive anybody about my race, they just didn't advertise it.

They were trying to protect their investment or avoid a controversy. There were no mainstream black performers in country music and never had been. In the 1930s, a black musician named DeFord Bailey appeared regularly on *The Grand Ole Opry* playing harmonica and spoons, but that was a fleeting novelty act. Blacks had never carved out a lasting place in the genre: By the time I came along, DeFord had gone back to shining shoes in Nashville.

Considering the racial climate of the times, it was natural, I suppose, for RCA to proceed with caution. Their strategy was to slip me into the tent and downplay my racial identity until the fans and the industry became accustomed enough to my music to accept me. I had no objection to that. I wanted to stand or fall on my music, not my skin color.

But there were no guarantees that country music, whose roots were in the South, was ready for Charley Pride. It was only a few years earlier that Rozene and I were driving with our son, Kraig, from Memphis to Mississippi to visit our families and I was told to "get out of here" when I tried to buy milk for the baby at the back door of a small whites-only snack bar. If things had changed at all, it could have been for the worse. The South was rife with civil rights sit-ins, demonstrations, and protest marches, and in little mood for tolerance.

If the disc jockeys in Dixie didn't play my records, if the club owners and concert promoters in the South wouldn't book me, if whites in Atlanta and Dallas and a hundred whistle stops in between wouldn't buy my records, my singing career would have the longevity of a corncob in a pig trough. If there was anything the country music business dreaded more than political controversy, it was a bad investment.

As a voice with no face, I made it into the tent with no problems. The success of "Just Between You and Me" pretty well established that my voice was marketable. Jack Johnson only had to convince someone to test market the whole person.

It hadn't been easy.

The promoters of the Detroit concert had put together a strong package, and one that was expensive. The lineup included Red Foley, a venerable figure in country music; Buck Owens, one of the young superstars; and Merle Haggard, one of the hottest new singers in the business. Dick Curless, Lester Flatt, and Earl Scruggs were also on the program. Ralph Emery, the Nashville DJ and probably the most famous country music radio personality in the business, would emcee.

It was not unusual for a newcomer to open a show, but I was not the standard neophyte. From Jack Johnson I learned that there was a lot of debate among the promoters about whether they should gamble on me.

But I couldn't remain a faceless voice forever. Most of Nashville realized I was black and word was getting out to the rest of the country as well. Over the years, some newspaper and magazine articles have reported that for the jacket of my first album I was photographed from the back. Not true. A full frontal photograph graced that album cover. Of course, a lot of radio listeners hadn't seen that album and television exposure was pretty limited in those days.

I heard stories about barroom arguments when one of my songs was played on the jukebox.

"I heard that's a colored guy singing that song."

"The hell it is. Colored guy doesn't sound like that."

Some radio listeners called their local DJs to find out if the rumor they had heard was true: "Is Charley Pride a Negro?"

After "Just Between You and Me" was released and started

to hit, my bookings increased enough that I was able to devote full time to singing, but most of the shows I was doing were small gigs in and around Montana, where I had lived since 1960—nothing that gave me the kind of exposure I would get before ten thousand people in the Olympia Arena.

Over the telephone, Jack Johnson and I talked about what I should say, if anything, when I walked on stage. Should I just start singing or try the standard banter that entertainers sometime engage in to establish a rapport with the audience?

"You need to say something to soften them up," Jack said. "Something brief and not too serious."

We tried out a few lines and agreed on one short sentence that seemed appropriate.

A few days before the Detroit concert, I was scheduled to do a show in Grand Rapids, Minnesota, with Tompall and the Glaser Brothers, who were also just starting out, and their names, like mine, were not exactly household words. That job would pay even less than the two hundred dollars I would get in Detroit.

Rozene and I talked about how I would make the trip—more than 1,600 miles from Helena to Detroit through Grand Rapids and a lot of it on two-lane highway. The interstate highway system was still under construction and open only in patches across western Montana. To fly, I would have to drive to the airport in Great Falls and make at least one connection to Grand Rapids, and another flight or two to get to Detroit. It would be expensive—a lot more than the two or three hundred dollars I would earn from the trip.

Driving was the reasonable option. With the money I had earned singing in taverns, I had bought a 1966 Mustang convertible and I figured it was up to the trip.

Huddled inside the cocoon of that little Mustang, with just the hum of the engine and the wind whistling around the rag top, I had a long solitary drive and a lot of time to think. I felt no apprehension about what I was heading into. I had never dwelt on the negative possibilities of things. I would do the Grand Rapids matinee show, leave immediately for Detroit, and arrive a couple of hours before three o'clock the next day— plenty of time to rehearse with the band. Three songs in the afternoon, three that night: pretty light duty for someone accustomed to solo gigs that lasted four and five hours.

The Mustang was as faithful as sunrise but Grand Rapids was a grand disappointment. No one there knew who Charley Pride or the Glaser Brothers were. There may have been forty people in the audience.

"What are y'all going to do now?" I asked the Glaser Brothers after the show. There were three of them: Jim, Chuck, and Tompall.

"Play golf," Tompall said.

"I'd like to play with you."

"Have you ever played?"

"No . . . but I've hit a baseball coming at me ninety miles an hour. I think I can hit a ball that's just sitting on the ground."

They looked at each other.

"Do you have any clubs?"

"No."

"Come on, you can use ours."

We got out to the golf course and when my turn came I teed the ball up, stepped back, and took a swing at it. *Swoosh.* The ball was still sitting on the tee. I didn't understand how I could have missed it. Embarrassed, I drew back to swing again, thinking, This time I'm going to murder it. *Swoosh.* It was still sitting there.

I thought they were playing some kind of trick on me. I actually thought that and I accused them of it.

"We're not doing anything," they said. "You said you could do it—go ahead."

15

I swung several more times. *Swoosh. Swoosh. Swoosh.* On the last try, the club slipped out of my hand and landed up in a big cottonwood tree.

Throwing other clubs up to dislodge it, we finally got it down, and after a few more tries, I nipped the ball about forty yards or less. We all laughed.

"I guess there's more to this game than I thought," I admitted.

"We wanted to tell you that it wasn't like hitting a baseball," Tompall said, "but decided to see if you could pull it off without our help."

That was my introduction to golf. It cost me valuable time getting to Detroit.

By late Friday night, the Mustang had taken me without a hitch to the outskirts of Chicago and I was too tired to push on. I found a motel, slept for a few hours, and set out early the next morning on the last three-hundred-mile leg to Detroit. No longer was I humming across the wide open spaces. I was ensnared in a maze of highways and unfamiliar landmarks, confusing road signs, and traffic congestion.

I made a few wrong turns and had to stop for directions. I parked at red lights, inched along behind semitrailer trucks, and picked my way slowly around Lake Michigan, through Gary, Indiana, and back up to Kalamazoo and Battle Creek. It was well past noon when I went through Ann Arbor and time was becoming critical. I had seriously miscalculated.

In Detroit, again, I had to stop a couple of times to get directions to the auditorium. Two-thirty came and went. Then two-forty. Finally, I found the Olympia, parked, got my jacket off a hanger and my guitar from the backseat, and walked through the stage door at ten minutes to three.

A guy was standing there watching me. He was a stage manager or something like that. He looked at his watch and then back at me.

"Well, Charley, it's kind of late . . ." he said.

Okay, here we go, I thought. The promoters had made their concerns clear to Jack Johnson and I figured it wouldn't take much of an excuse for them to wiggle out of the commitment. A disastrous golf game and my error in judging the time it would take to drive across half the continent might have given it to them.

The guy facing me stammered some more and looked at his watch again. I was waiting for him to tell me I had blown the most important opportunity of my life.

"You don't have to do the three o'clock show," he said. "You can wait and do the one at eight."

I'm thinking, Well, I don't have to call my manager, but if I don't get to do this three o'clock show, there's going to be a reason why I don't get to do the eight o'clock show.

"I'll be ready in two minutes," I said.

"You don't have time to rehearse with the band. And . . . ah . . ."

"No, I haven't rehearsed, but do they play country music?"

"Yeah."

"Well, I sing country music. We should do just fine."

Merle Haggard's band, The Strangers, would back me up, and even that was not decided without some controversy. Neither Haggard nor Buck Owens wanted their musicians to be the "house" band that played for the performers who didn't have their own. Buck was the bigger star and so he won the argument.

I sat down, tuned my guitar, told The Strangers which songs I would sing, and got ready to go on.

Before introducing me, Ralph Emery asked the audience, "How many here are from the South?" A lot of hands went up. Detroit was the depository of many Southerners who had migrated north over the past two or three decades to work in the auto factories.

Standing in the wings, I watched Ralph try to cushion the crowd for what was coming.

"Well, folks, we've got a young man here from down in Sledge, Mississippi, a good country singer," he said. "I'm sure you've been hearing him on the radio quite a bit. He's had three records—'Snakes Crawl at Night,' 'Before I Met You,' and his latest is 'Just Between You and Me,' which is moving up the charts."

That drew a rowdy applause, since a lot of folks recognized the song. The audience, a good-old-boy crowd from back home, was getting ready to see this singer they knew only as "Country Charley Pride," but they were not really expecting what they were going to see.

Ralph said, "Ladies and gentlemen, from RCA Records, Charrrr-leeeeeey Pride."

Again, the clapping and shouting erupted. The lights went up and I stepped from the shadows. As suddenly as it had begun, the applause faded. It didn't stop—just dropped like volume being turned down on a radio. It settled to a low murmur. I walked across the stage and people looked around as though they were wondering when Charley Pride was going to appear.

I stood in front of the microphone, propped my arms on the guitar hanging around my neck, and spoke the line Jack Johnson and I had chosen.

"Ladies and gentlemen," I said, "I realize this is a little unique . . . me coming out here on a country music show wearing this permanent tan."

That brought another burst of applause and scattered laughter. Evidently, I was saying exactly what they were thinking. I began to feel relaxed and confident. This didn't seem like an audience on the verge of hurling insults or walking out.

"I only have three singles out," I said, "and I am going to try to do those and some Hank Williams and I hope you like it."

That was it.

The band fired up and we hit it, without ever having re-hearsed together. I got through my ten minutes and the crowd was screaming for more. After the show, I went out in front of the stage and stood behind one of those little rope barriers. People pushed and shoved to get autographs and a lot of them wanted to talk. They asked where I was from, how I had learned to sing country—things like that.

The eight o'clock show was a repeat of the first, and the feeling was tremendous. The acceptance and approval were things I would have to earn over and over again in the years to come, but standing there, talking to those folks, I was able to believe it would happen.

A long time ago, growing up in Sledge, Mississippi, I made a decision and informed my father of it.

"I just don't want to be a cotton picker, Daddy," I told him.

"You don't want to pick cotton?" he said, as though that future had already been carved out for me. "Well, what do you think you're going to do?"

I had no idea then or for many years after. But leaving Detroit and heading back for Montana, there was no longer any doubt in my mind. If my luck held, I would never stoop over another row of cotton.

PART

1

CHAPTER ONE

Always a Dreamer

I came from a family of eleven children—eight boys and three girls. The oldest were Bessie and Jonas McIntyre, my mother's from a previous marriage. The rest of us were the sons and daughters of Mack Pride. There would have been more, but three—including twin boys—were stillborn and a fourth was miscarried.

I was my mother's fourth born, behind Bessie and Jonas and Mack Jr., and my father's second. After me came Catherine, Louis, Edward, Joe L., Harmon, Maxine, and Stephen.

My father named me Charl Frank Pride, but the person who typed the birth certificate put an "ey" on the end of "Charl," so officially I was Charley.

In his stubbornness Daddy refused to acknowledge that clerical error and insisted on calling me Charl. When he scolded me, which was often, he used the sterner and more emphatic *"Charl Frank . . .!"*

At the risk of provoking him further, I would interrupt. "Daddy, I'm Charley."

"No you're not," he would snap. "You're Charl. I named you Charl and that's your name. I don't care what anybody says."

We lived in a three-room shotgun house—three rooms in a line front to back—so called because you can "fire a shotgun through the front door and out the back without hitting anything." The children slept three and four to a bed, lying alternately head to foot. Many a time, I was awakened in the night by toes jabbing me in the face, or shivering because the covers had been pulled to the other end. The house was little more than a tin and cracked-wood shack and in wintertime there was no way to keep it warm throughout the night.

Being poor wasn't something we thought about much. It was just a fact of life, and we weren't any worse off than most other folks around us. We scrounged for everything we got and usually we got very little. But we did it together.

Everyone in the family had morning chores before going to school or to the fields. We were awakened before sunrise, and if we lagged, trying to squeeze out one last snooze, Daddy came into the room and pulled the blankets from the bed. Once you are jolted awake by frigid temperatures, it is hard to fall back to sleep.

The girls helped Mother get the dough started for biscuits and the boys had to bring in water and firewood, first for the kitchen stove and then for the potbellied heater.

After the fires were going and Mother's kettle was filled with fresh water, we took burlap sacks outside to fill them with weeds and grasses for the hogs, which had to be fed before we could eat. Daddy would already be in the yard, filing the chopping hoes.

Depending on the season, we headed to school or followed him to the field. If a choice had to be made between work and school, school always won. Mother and Daddy were determined that their kids get an education and they never pulled us out of school to work, the way a lot of families did.

When I was six or seven, fetching the morning water became my job. The pump was fifty or sixty yards from the house. It was scary traipsing through the darkness and the silence, with the light from the kitchen window getting smaller behind me. In winter the chore took longer because the pump had to be drained each night to keep it from freezing up. Some moisture always remained inside and the next morning warm water had to be poured in to unstick the pump sucker.

My cousins made it worse by convincing me they had seen bobcats prowling around the road by our house. Each time I passed the woodpile on my way to the pump, I stopped and listened for any animals that might be hiding there. If someone had said, "Boo!" I would have jumped out of my overalls. But I would have moved on, driven by the bigger fear that Daddy would be waiting with a belt if I dallied too long.

Conquering that fear, I suppose, taught me that you have to walk past a lot of woodpiles in life and most of them do not harbor wild animals.

Mother was a talkative and outgoing person, and I was a lot like her. I used to talk to her about things, even sex, that I should have discussed with my father, but she was so much easier to talk to when she had the time.

She was philosophical and could find something positive in almost every situation, no matter how bad it was. In material ways, we were poor, but Mother always told us that what is important is the way you look at rich and poor. Everyone has something that makes them rich in their own way.

I was looking through a magazine when I was six or seven and saw an advertisement for a new car. It was a blue Ford coupe, about the most dazzling thing I had ever seen. I tried to imagine my mother riding in that car.

"Mama," I said, carrying the magazine over to where she was washing clothes, "if I had a million dollars I could buy that car for you."

"Yeah," she said, looking down at the magazine and then at me. She stopped washing, dried her hands, and sat down with me.

"You're right," she said. "You could buy me that car if you had a million dollars. That's a lot of money . . . a million dollars. But I'll tell you something. There are people who would give up a whole bunch of millions for what you've got."

My eyes became wide. What did I have that was worth a million bucks?

"Hold out your hand," mother said. "See, you've got five fingers on that hand . . . five on the other hand. You've got both your eyes . . . both your legs. Some people don't have those things."

She planted seeds like that and they outlived her. Even now, someone will say, "How are you doing?" and without thinking I'll answer, "Pretty good. I got all my fingers and both eyes."

Daddy was a deacon in the Baptist church, but Mother seemed the more spiritual of the two. I always thought she had a feel for how things worked, things we don't fathom, things unexplainable—in the realm where God fits into things. She always believed the dead knew what the living were doing. Because she believed that, I believe it, too. I believe that she's somewhere with Him watching me and that makes me feel good. I've believed that all these years and I'm not going change my beliefs under any circumstances.

Her influence on me was that strong.

I was always a dreamer, in childhood especially. I used to sit and look up at the clouds and wonder if I could walk on them and where they would take me if I could. I talked about walking on the clouds and the moon, talked about it so much that my brothers and sisters were convinced that the heat had scorched my brain. People thought I was a little strange

26

anyway, and talking about walking on clouds didn't help my image any.

I always wanted to fly—not in the aviation sense, but in terms of branching out, exploring and achieving something. I wanted to absorb everything. I wanted to grow up fast. In movies I would see things I didn't have and places I had never been, and I longed for more than that little world of the Mississippi Delta could give. The Delta was small and there were not many opportunities to experience anything outside of our day-to-day lives.

In some ways we did grow up fast, learning to work and scuffle for ourselves almost as soon as we could walk. In other ways we were pretty sheltered.

I didn't learn where babies came from until I was eleven. Daddy didn't want us to be taught such things and would go to great lengths to keep us from finding out.

When our cow was getting ready to calve, Daddy told the children, "Don't go near the lot." We weren't allowed to ask why, but I was full of curiosity.

My brother and I were playing ball in the yard and I could hear the cow groaning and belching. The ball slipped by me and rolled almost to the lot, giving me a chance to peek at what Daddy didn't want me to see. Looking over the fence, I saw legs sticking out near the back of the cow. The calf was being born breeched, but I had no idea what was going on.

I ran to Daddy and said, "There's a leg sticking out of old Jersey."

"You didn't see nothin', boy. You didn't see nothin'."

"Yes . . . I saw . . ."

He got louder. "You didn't see nothin'."

Until I was eleven years old, the mechanics of birth, animal or human, were a mystery to me. I believed what I was told and so I always believed babies came in those little bags that the midwives carried.

I believed that until Harmon was born. I said something

27

to one of my cousins about the midwife bringing the baby and he laughed at me.

"You stupid idiot," he said, and proceeded to tell me the facts of life.

I probably believed in Santa Claus longer than many kids. Mother and Daddy told me there was a Santa and I was willing—I may have been eager—to believe it until they told me different. Christmas was special and I always looked forward to it. I would go to bed early so Santa could come, although I didn't expect to find a lot of toys under the tree the next morning.

But I always woke up smelling apples and oranges and pecans. To this day, those memories still overwhelm me if I eat apples, oranges, or pecans. As soon as the taste hits my mouth, it's Christmas.

My tendency to daydream and fantasize, along with learning life's little secrets too slowly at home, probably had something to do with my itch to discover what was in the world beyond the Delta.

I had nothing against Mississippi. The inequities of segregation were painful, but that was my home and those were my people. I loved Mississippi and do to this day. When I go there to visit my father, I am still taken by its beauty and bounty. I love to see things grow and growing things is what the Delta does best. Even with the listing, tin-roof shanties, the dirt roads, and the gaping storefronts of bland farm towns, the landscape is as alluring as it is level: acre after acre, mile after mile of corn and soybean and cotton growing fat from soil that never tires. The rainbows that stretch from horizon to horizon after a summer rain are the most spectacular I've ever seen.

But I always had the feeling that there was something else I was supposed to do, something besides following in my father's footsteps and being another sharecropper working another man's land and growing old with a cotton sack around my neck and watching my children do the same.

By my late teens, I left home and got as far as Memphis, sixty miles to the north, where I played baseball and worked odd jobs to supplement the meager salary of the Negro American League. In my spare time I often went downtown and stood on the sidewalk outside a big department store, tucked one leg up behind me, leaned against the wall, and watched people go by.

I tried to guess who they were, what they were thinking, where they were going. Studying others might easily have been a way of trying to answer the same questions about myself. *Who are you, Charley, and where are you going?*

Good question.

CHAPTER TWO

The Rod and the Strap

"Daddy!"

"What?"

"Daddy!"

"Where are you?" Mack Pride stood in the shadows under the peach tree looking from side to side.

"I'm up here."

He peered up through the tangle of branches and leaves, his eyes as penetrating as lasers, the muscles in his jaw set rock hard.

"You get down from there," he commanded.

When Mack Pride commanded, you obeyed or you paid with the flesh of your rump. My own prepubescent backside eternally bore the grapes of his wrath, but something—childish rebellion, maybe, or the need for attention—drove me to defiance.

His arms hung at his sides, his head was bent back, straining the muscles in his neck, and his lips were drawn into thin lines. There was no doubt in my mind that a sound thrashing awaited me down there.

"I'm going to jump," I said.

"You'll do no such thing. Get down from there."

"Yes I am, Daddy. I'm going to jump."

"*Charl Frank!*"

The words cut through me like a cold wind. I clung to my perch and stared back at him, wondering why I had gotten myself into this situation. It made no sense to provoke him without an escape route. There was no hope of making him show anxiety or compassion. If I wanted attention, I was angling for the wrong kind.

All I could be certain of was that I had no intention of jumping. I may have been goofy but I wasn't suicidal.

Realizing there was no other choice, I reached for a lower branch and began making my way down the tree, sure that he would be waiting with a freshly stripped pecan switch when I got to the ground.

He whipped me across the yard and into the house while I tried my hardest not to cry out.

After he left the house, one of my brothers asked me, "Why do you want to make Daddy mad like that?"

My legs and butt stung with new welts while I considered the question. I couldn't think of an answer.

Daddy always said I was the most aggravating of his children. I've never denied that I was mischievous. My brothers and sisters thought I was a little kooky and some of my cousins didn't even want to hang around with me. I would do about anything to get a laugh or get attention, and I didn't always consider that the consequence would be another round with Daddy's belt. I didn't do hurtful things, but I guess I was a nuisance.

For a while, my great-grandpa lived with us and I taunted him mercilessly—harmless teasing but annoying nonetheless. He slept in a long nightgown and before bedtime or in the mornings I would lift the hem of it as though I were going to peek underneath.

"Get away from there," he would snap, pushing me aside

with a bony hand. In a few minutes I would be back. One day he was sitting on the porch and I made several tugs on his gown but jumped back each time before he could swat me. Finally, he grabbed the hem, lifted it almost to his waist, and snapped, "All right, there it is. Look! Look!"

That stopped my pestering him about his nightshirt, but I found other ways. I flipped water on him when he was in the yard or ran up behind him and snapped his suspenders against his back. One day I was teasing him and leading him around a chair. I led him around and around that chair until he got dizzy. Daddy caught me doing it and dealt out the usual punishment.

Looking back on it, I realize I shouldn't have done those things to him. It didn't occur to me then just how much of a pest I was. I loved that old man and probably just wanted him to notice me. I still talk to him. Every once in a while, when I think about him, I look up and say, "Great Granddaddy, I didn't mean nothin'."

When I was about eight, I hit upon the idea of jumping off the barn using an old umbrella as a parachute. I had seen photographs and newsreels of paratroopers in action during World War II and was amazed at how gently they alighted from such heights. It looked like harmless fun.

Ours was not a tall barn and getting on the roof was no trouble. Getting down was. I perched on the edge for a moment and imagined myself gliding softly to earth. Not considering the alternative, I popped the umbrella open and jumped. The umbrella made a *whoosh*ing sound as the ribs bent upward, ripping the fabric as they went. I fell like a plump acorn into a small stack of hay and wood.

I had no idea Mack Pride was anywhere around, but he was beside me almost as soon as I stood up and brushed the dust and hay off myself. I cried as much from Daddy's switch as from the scratches sustained in the fall. I guess I deserved that one, too. I had torn up our only umbrella.

The truth is, I grew up not liking my father very much. I loved him and there was a lot about him that I admired and respected, but I didn't like him.

Our household was a stern environment—too stern. I think the children were terrified of our father to the extent that we were a dysfunctional family. He beat us for the smallest offenses and we learned to read the look in his eyes, to anticipate just what we needed to do to avoid being knocked down. He was never playful with us, seldom praised us for our accomplishments, never hugged us or otherwise expressed affection.

When he decided that something would be a certain way, there was no further discussion. No one in the family could express an opinion or a preference without risking his strap. He was the chief. If we attempted to speak up, we were cut short.

"Daddy, I think . . ."

"Hush, boy. It don't matter what you think."

"But I'd like . . ."

"You just do what you're told."

Aggravating him may have been a way of masking the stark fear he could provoke in me, a way of saying, "I'm a person with my own feelings and opinions. I'm your flesh and your blood but not you and not your property."

I wanted his approval, which was no small ambition. One day he and I were picking cotton and I was determined to weigh in with the heavier sack. We were working side by side, each pulling two rows. I stayed right beside him but when we got to the scales his sack weighed more.

"What's going on here?" I asked him.

He said, "Come here," and led me back down the rows I

had picked. He turned over a leaf to expose a boll. "You missed that one." Another leaf. "That one, too." Cotton opens under leaves as well as above them. He was getting everything and I was getting only what I could see.

He said, "There's an art to everything, son," and went back to work.

Mother sometimes tried to talk to him, tell him he was too rough on us, but she rarely sided openly with the children against him. She may have felt that it was not the proper thing to do or that it would have been futile anyway.

She was not afraid of him as we were. Many nights I fell asleep listening to them argue and awoke the next morning to the same battle sounds. Though she stood up to him, I doubt that she won many arguments.

Some of my father's severity may have been dictated by the harsh way we had to live. Poverty alone was an impairment to a normal family life, demanding too much time just for survival and leaving too little for being together, for talking and understanding.

Living in the country also meant certain dangers were ever present and children had to be disciplined to avoid them. I had a knack for finding them.

Watching a small crop-dusting plane, something like a Piper Cub, looping and rolling over the fields around our house one afternoon, I realized something was wrong. The engine stalled out and the plane started down and the pilot was in trouble. I watched the plane until it dropped into a cornfield and out of sight. I started up a tree to get a better vantage point. Scooting up that tree, not thinking about anything but that plane, I ran smack into a fully occupied wasp nest. They swarmed out and attacked. By the time I got back to the ground, my head was covered with stings and swollen from the venom.

That many stings could kill an adult, but I survived them as well as the spanking I got for not being more careful.

With so many kids to tend to, and so much work to get done every day, Mother and Daddy didn't have time to stand over each one of us all the time. Rules were simply laid down and we were expected to obey them. More than my brothers and sisters, I had trouble with rules.

A quarter of a mile or so from our house was Pluid Lake, which would cover over with thin ice during the winter. Daddy constantly warned us, "Do not go to that lake." One morning when the ground was too frozen to work, Ed and Catherine and I were outside playing—skating, without skates, where ice had formed in ruts and wheel tracks from many wagons. We skated our way right out to Pluid Lake.

We were having a good time, slipping and sliding and skipping acorns across the ice, unaware of the danger, unaware of Mack Pride.

"*Awright!*" I heard Daddy yell. He had followed us, and since I was the oldest, he held me responsible for disobeying his order. He whipped all three of us with dedication but stayed close behind me as I slipped and stumbled all the way home.

"Don't you fall, Charl Frank," he barked. "If you go down I'm going to keep you down." The last thing I wanted was more of his belt and somehow I made it home upright.

That whipping we deserved. If one of us had fallen through the ice with no one there to help, it would have been fatal. Daddy is convinced to this day that his discipline kept me from killing myself. Maybe it did, but at the time the punishment always seemed excessive for the crime.

Although I liked school, I acted up there almost as much as at home and spent a lot of time in the principal's office, where the whippings were as ferocious as any Daddy could dish out.

The principal, or whoever was administering the treatment, would recruit two boys to help him. One took you by the arms, the other by the feet, and held you face up in a horizontal position. The principal swung his strap so that it came up underneath your rump with pounding force. Using the two student aides served another purpose: It allowed them to witness what was in store if they, too, got out of line.

Schools had the authority to do that in those days, but one of our principals got into trouble for going a bit too far. He tried to intensify the whipping by putting little pieces of wire on the end of the strap. It would turn young flesh into bloody pulp.

Most of what got me into trouble was not serious—just goofy stunts aimed at my classmates, but occasionally, and regrettably, at adults. One of my favorite tricks was to walk out of the school building, collapse on the ground, roll my eyes back, and hold my breath. The other kids would gather around and poke at me, but I wouldn't move. They'd smack me and I wouldn't even flinch. Then they'd yell to the teachers for help.

"Something's wrong with Charley . . . Charley ain't breathing . . . Charley's dead."

When I had held my breath as long as I could, I would jump up laughing and try to get away before a teacher or the principal showed up. It worked a few times, until everyone in school was wise to me. After that, I could have collapsed for real and died on that school ground and the others would have stood around snickering at me.

Probably the worst whipping I took was from a Professor Gresham—a big, ruddy-faced teacher who could swing a leather strap the way George Herman Ruth swung ash wood. It was the result of one of my brilliant impulses.

In the school yard, near the lunchroom window, was an artesian well with a pressure pump. By holding your hand over one part of the valve, you could cause the water to squirt higher and you could aim it in any direction—even through a lunchroom window.

Inside, a woman was cleaning up and putting dishes away.

She stopped in front of the window with some cups and saucers in her hand. I looked at the well pump and back at her. There was no way I could get away with it, but the temptation was too strong to let that deter me. I directed a stream of water through the window, startling the woman enough that she dropped the dishes she was holding.

Later that afternoon, Professor Gresham took me by the arm, picked two volunteers to accompany us, and escorted me from the classroom. I watched him retrieve the strap from the hook where it hung on the principal's office wall. The professor was icy-eyed and humorless, a huge man who looked like he could kill a hog with his bare hands and eat it in one sitting. It would have been appropriate if a preacher had come in with a Bible and my last meal.

Suspended above the floor in the firm grasp of two friends, I closed my eyes and waited.

Whack! My butt felt like it had been seared with a flatiron.

Whack! I squirmed and squinched and gritted my teeth.

Whack! Lord, don't let me wet my pants.

Whack! Whack! Whack!

Daddy was in town after school that day and bumped into the principal.

"We had to give Charley a bustin' today," the principal told him.

Daddy snorted and said, "Yeah, well, who hasn't?"

Over time, I have come to realize that Daddy was not unfeeling; he was just unable to express his emotions in the normal way. I never saw him cry. But he must have. I believe everybody cries.

If he couldn't express his affection in words, he sometimes did it with subtle gestures. I can recall times when he drove the cotton to be ginned and on the way back he would stop and buy ice cream for us kids. He drove the wagon as fast as he could to get home before the ice cream melted.

He showed concern for his children by using the strap to keep us on a straight and narrow path and he showed tenderness by protecting us and caring for us. We all survived the hardships of our youth and turned out to be reasonably solid citizens.

When I was about six years old, I went out to bring the cow into the barn. She bolted and started back down the pasture. Trying to cut her off, I got pinned between her and the barbed-wire fence and ended up with a long, deep gash down the right side of my face. My whole jaw was laid open.

Rather than hugging and comforting me, Daddy's first reaction was to shake and smack me. "You're going to be scarred for the rest of your life," he said, as though I had intentionally cut my face. I didn't realize it then, but he probably was frightened that I would be disfigured from the accident. Scolding me was the only way he knew to express his concern.

But he took me straight to the house, got a can of coal oil, and cleaned the cut. Then he scraped soot from the chimney and packed it into the wound. That was one of those home remedies that actually worked. We had no bandages and as the soot fell out, he repacked it. He tended to my face constantly for two weeks, and when it healed there was barely a scar showing.

As I have grown older, I have tried to rationalize the way he was. He, too, was from a dysfunctional family and suffered physically at the hands of his mother and father. With a tiny house packed with kids, eight of them boys, maybe he had to rule with an iron hand to maintain discipline. However I account for him in my own mind, it doesn't change one thing—how much I regret that there was no warmth or tenderness between us.

CHAPTER THREE

"Mississippi Cotton Pickin' Delta Town"

It had rained off and on for a couple of days and the ground was charcoal muck. Winter was coming on and Mother and Daddy were trying to get the last cotton out of the field. I was only about five years old and not much help with the crops, especially on a day like that. When the ground was wet, you had to fold your cotton sack up and carry it rather than drag it behind you.

So Mother went to pick cotton with Daddy and left me and Mack Jr., who was seven, at home to look after our sister, Catherine and baby brother, Louis. As young as we were, we knew how to take care of ourselves. When you grow up in the country, you learn self-reliance early. You are conditioned to watch for snakes or listen for bobcats or other animals. You learn their behavior and how to deal with them.

Some animals, though, are less predictable than others.

Late in the morning, Junior and I took Catherine and Louis outside. We were playing in the yard when I saw a car creeping along the narrow, muddy road that ran by our house. There were two men inside—white men. The car stopped at our yard and from the way the two men looked us over we sensed this was not a friendly visit. We stood motionless and stared at them. They pointed at us and laughed and yelled things I didn't really understand.

Then one of them held up a set of false teeth in one hand, snapped them open and shut, and grinned at us. I had never seen false teeth before, had no idea what they were, but didn't like the looks of them.

"These are your uncle Sam Scott's teeth," the man said, grinning, clicking them again and again.

Pure horror spread through me. Oh, Lord, they've killed my uncle and cut out his teeth, I thought.

Junior and I stood frozen by fear.

I heard one of the men say, "Get that little one."

The other said, "No, get that little big-headed one over there."

They jumped out and sprinted toward Junior. He and I might have been able to outrun them, but that would have meant leaving Catherine and Louis behind. If we screamed, no one would hear us. In an instant, they grabbed Junior, tossed him into the backseat, and drove away.

All I could think of was getting to Mother and Daddy. I left Catherine and Louis alone, and ran toward the field. It was hard going in that mud and my heart was pounding and my lungs were on fire. I must have gone a quarter of a mile before I saw Daddy, standing between cotton rows with his sack tied up on his shoulder.

When I reached him, I was winded and gasping, barely able to talk. All I could say was, "They . . . they . . . they got . . ."

Daddy grabbed me and shook me. "What is it, boy? What is it?"

I still couldn't speak.

"Don't you see he's out of breath," Mother shouted. There was panic on both their faces.

Finally, I blurted it out: "They got Junior. Two white men took Junior."

They dropped their cotton sacks and ran toward the house. I was right behind them, exhausted but still running, running on fear and adrenaline. The wet earth pulled at my feet like a magnet and time seem to slow down, as though I were plodding and heaving through a blurred nightmare, thinking, Those men killed my uncle and now they got my brother.

When we reached the house, Junior was sitting in the doorway with Catherine, holding the baby in his arms.

"They're stuck down there," he told Daddy, pointing toward the car, which was bogged into the mud a hundred yards or so down the road. Junior told Daddy he jumped out and ran when the car stopped.

We couldn't see anybody in the car or around it, but Daddy went into the house to get his gun. He may have been too rough on us, whipped us too much, but he didn't allow anybody else to mess with his children. The fear I had seen in him earlier became a rage. I don't think I have ever seen him so angry.

If those men were still down by the car, there might well be a killing.

Mother begged and pleaded with him. "He's here now," she said. "He's safe. We got him back. Don't go down there."

She had no illusions about what would happen if he found those men. It would be as bad for Daddy as for them. I was beginning to learn that also. Later on, when I started school, we stood and faced the flag every morning and recited the pledge of allegiance. I loved doing that. I thought those were beautiful words—*liberty and justice for all*—but I could see they weren't true.

Liberty and justice for black people was still a long way off. A black man who killed a white man, no matter what the circumstances, could expect just about anything but justice.

Mother pleaded with him not to go. He was a proud and stubborn man, but he, too, was aware that nothing but trouble was down that road. For a long time he just stood there in the yard, fuming and burning, but Mother convinced him to let the law handle it.

Besides, the two men were probably far away but they had left their car behind, so the sheriff would be able to find them easily enough—if he wanted to. Daddy went to see him.

Mike Omar was a popular sheriff and probably a good one, because he held that job for many years and when he retired the town of Lambert named a street after him. But he didn't seem to think that two white men snatching a black child out of his yard and driving away with him was much of a crime, or not one serious enough to justify putting somebody in jail.

"You just settle down, Mack," he told Daddy. "I'll look into it. They probably were just having a little fun and didn't mean no harm."

Somehow I don't think he would have seen the humor in it if two black men had snatched a white child from its home. That was the most traumatic experience of my life and the sheriff of Quitman County didn't think it was any big deal.

From the car's registration, it was not difficult for the sheriff to identify the two men, but he never told Daddy who they were—just that they were from "over around Clarksdale." Some time later Daddy learned that one of them was a banker.

Nobody was ever arrested, but Sheriff Omar probably felt he had to do something, if only because of Daddy's reputation: He protected what was his and was not timid with anyone who violated his property or his personal code. The sheriff went to Clarksdale to do us—and anyone over there who thought kidnapping a child was funny—a favor. He spread the word around: Don't mess with Mack Pride.

It was good advice for the folks around Clarksdale, but it was all the justice we got. A small footnote to that story is that many years later Daddy stopped farming and moved into Lambert, to a house on Mike Omar Drive.

Daddy was born in the Delta in 1907 and grew up there when life for most black people was only a little better than it had been in the time of slavery. The whites owned the land and the blacks worked it. The system of tenant farming had a way of ensuring that the sharecropper rarely got ahead or even out of debt.

You borrowed money to make a crop and when it was harvested the landowner got his share of the crop and the money you had borrowed, with interest. There was little, if anything, left, and so you had to borrow from the landowner to start all over the next spring. I remember a year when Mother and Daddy fought the heat and the cold and the wet all season to bring in a crop and didn't have enough money left over to buy shoes for all the kids—and there were only four of us then. It was a continuous cycle and nearly an impossible one to break.

"Well, they're sharpening the pencils about now," Mother used to say at harvest time.

Finding a better job or a better deal wasn't always a practical option. You had to get permission from the landowner to leave his farm and go to work for someone else—a rule that was enforced with threats and intimidation—and unless another family was waiting to take your place, the landowner wasn't inclined to let you go.

It was common for families to pack up and move under cover of darkness in order to be gone when the boss man showed up in the morning.

Even in that environment, Daddy maintained his measure of dignity. Like everyone else, he had to abide by the rules of segregation, but just from the way he carried himself, he demanded that he be respected as a man. He was—he didn't accept all the treatment that blacks were supposed to accept. He wouldn't let people treat him like dirt. He conveyed that in his manner. His attitude was, "I don't mind not drinking from your water fountain, but what's mine is mine. My house is mine and my kids are mine and they are not to be abused."

One year our family hired out to help harvest cotton for a big landowner. Daddy went to him and said, "You don't talk to my kids. Whatever you want them to do, you tell me and I'll tell them." A lot of black kids were abused by the landowners they worked for and he wasn't going to have that.

Though strong-willed and uncompromising, he was not confrontational. He had keen instincts and would not hesitate to walk away when they alerted him to potential danger. He seemed to know the battles he could win, the ones he couldn't, and the ones that were not worth fighting.

He took a job in a neighboring county once, but came back to Sledge in a day or two. "That foreman was bad," he told Mother. "I knew there would be trouble if I stayed there."

Where his property and family were involved, though, the line was drawn. We always had some kind of firearm in the house, usually a pistol, and Daddy didn't mind letting it speak for him.

One particular argument that the pistol won handily stands out in my mind.

We used to tie our cow to a stake in the ground and let her graze in a circle around it. When she had eaten all the grass in range, she would pull against the chain, trying to reach fresh food. If we didn't move the stake often enough, she could pull it out of the ground and wander off.

We left her in one place too long one day and she pulled the stake loose and strayed onto a neighbor's property, where she feasted on oats for a good part of the afternoon. When Daddy went to get her, the neighbors told him he couldn't have her until he paid for what she had eaten.

He stormed into the house and got his gun, a .38 on a .45 frame.

"Where you going?" Mother asked him.

"I'm going to get my cow."

We sat there looking at each other and saying nothing, half expecting to hear gunshots down the road. There were none. A few minutes later Daddy came back, leading the cow.

Nobody got killed. Mack Pride may not have been capable of killing someone. I'm just glad I never found out.

As much as it has sometimes pained me to acknowledge it, I am like my father in many ways. His genes, after all, are my genes and my sensibilities were molded growing up in his house. For better or worse, I did not become a stern, disciplinarian father, but he influenced me in other ways.

There is probably a bully or two in every elementary school and ours was no exception. In the first or second grade, I came home with a bruise on my face. Another kid had hit me and knocked me down.

"Did you hit him back?" Daddy asked.

"No," I said, almost in tears.

"Boy, next time somebody hits you and you don't hit back, I'm going to knock you down myself," he said.

By example as much as by words, he taught me that it may not be possible to eliminate the injustice and indignity around you, but you can at least set limits on what you will tolerate.

Sledge was like a hundred other small Delta towns in those days. "Downtown" was one block of storefronts separated from the railroad tracks by a partially paved street. There was a grocery store, a barber shop, a hardware and farm supply store, a general merchandise store, a café, and a gas station. Across the street, snuggled up to the tracks, was the cotton gin and grain elevator.

The code of segregation was held inviolate and conforming

to it required careful study of nuances that seem silly today. We woke up one morning and discovered a white man lying in the haystack near our house. We couldn't tell if he was asleep, sick, dead, or what, but we didn't dare try to find out. Daddy walked to the home of a white farmer who lived around the bayou from us and brought him to check on the guy.

It turned out that he was just a drifter who had found that haystack and gone to sleep there, but if we had approached him and he had been dead, it could have been trouble for the Pride household. Such was the high, wide wall between the races.

We used to go to the courthouse in Marks, Mississippi, to get commodities and items that were rationed during the war. I can remember being there one day with my mother and father and needing desperately to go to the restroom. But there were no facilities for colored people. Unable to wait any longer, I lay on my side on the grass, had my brothers gather around to shield me from the view of the crowd that was milling around the courthouse lawn, and peed as inconspicuously as possible. But the ground sloped just enough that the urine ran back onto my pants. I had to wear wet, soiled clothes until we got back home.

In school we were reminded every day of the racial separation and the inequities that went with it. From my classroom I could look out and see the school for the white kids. It was a newer, larger building with a gymnasium where they could play when the weather was bad. Our school had no such facility and when it rained, we took recess at our desks.

The white kids had school buses to pick them up in the morning and deliver them home each afternoon. The black kids walked. I can still remember how the white kids would yell at us and call us names as their buses passed us on those dusty roads.

At end of World War II, when the Russians were taking

over Eastern Europe, a group of Latvian refugees made it to the United States and, for reasons I understood too well, they were placed in Sledge. At first they were put in available farmhouses and given work in the fields, where most of the workers were black.

Some of the young black men started going to their houses, talking to the girls and trying to date them. As soon as that started happening, you never saw so many houses go up so fast as they did in downtown Sledge. The Latvians weren't Americans but they were white and the townsfolk wanted to get them away from the blacks as quickly as possible.

I watched that happen with no small measure of resentment. Black Americans had been here for generations, living in shacks and attending inferior schools. Now a group of white foreigners who barely spoke our language was getting new houses and attending the schools I should have been attending.

I had nothing against the Latvians. They were good people. Many of them were craftsmen and with help from the town they built a factory where they made desks and chairs and other things from wood. They hired blacks to work for them. My brother and I worked there awhile and learned to speak their language a little.

They were happy to be out from behind the Iron Curtain, to be in a land of freedom and opportunity. I didn't begrudge them a thing. I only wished for the same freedom and opportunity they had found in America.

I had very few friends or acquaintances of the other race and I believe we were all the poorer for it. But for the rules of segregation, I could have known Harold Dorman when I was growing up.

Dorman was a little older than I and worked at the store where we bought groceries every Saturday. I saw him often and we exchanged nods or hellos but never really talked.

Many years after leaving Sledge, I met Harold Dorman again. He was writing songs for my producer, Jack Clement, and I recorded four of them: "Mountain of Love," "Mississippi Cotton Pickin' Delta Town," "Pretty House for Sale," and "Lie to Me."

I said to him, "Damn, Harold, I had no idea you wrote songs."

He said, "I didn't know you sang, either."

Harold is deceased now and I've always regretted that we never had the chance to be friends back in Sledge. But rules were rules, and you were never allowed to forget who was *them* and who was *us*.

When I was about twelve or thirteen years old, I was hanging around town on a Saturday afternoon and ran into three white boys I had met casually. They were baseball players, a couple of years older than I. They invited me to sit in the car with them and talk. It wasn't supposed to be done, but I had never had much aversion to testing the rules. I got into the car.

For a while, we were just four kids killing a lazy day and making small talk, mostly about baseball. That was a few years after Jackie Robinson had been signed by the Brooklyn Dodgers, making him the first black player in the major leagues. To say that he was my idol would be an understatement. As far as I was concerned, Jackie Robinson had rewritten the future.

I mentioned the previous day's Dodger game and how Robinson had stolen two bases.

"Damn," one of the other boys said, "that nigger can run."

I'm not sure what I felt. Anger. Hurt. Disgust. A pleasant conversation about something we all loved had turned ugly, even if the kid who said it had not meant it to be. I could have punched him—I certainly wasn't afraid to—but it would have accomplished nothing. He still would have thought of Jackie Robinson as a nigger. Nothing would have knocked that out of his head and I saw no reason to try.

I opened the door and got out.

'Where ya goin', Charley?" one of them asked.

"I don't want to listen to this kind of talk," I said.

My daddy's instincts were becoming my own. Protect yourself and what's yours but don't fight the battle if there is nothing to be won.

A few years later, I got a job in the gas station in Sledge. Everyone else who worked there was white and they treated me well enough. But one day I pumped gas for a customer, took his money, and went inside to give it to the owner, Otis Jenkins, who handled the cash register.

"Otis. . ." I said.

Before I could finish, the customer snapped his head around and corrected me: "Mister Otis."

I nodded and waited for him to make change, saying nothing. When I finished work that day I went home, still a little wounded by the experience. I never returned to that job.

Several days later, I saw the station owner and he said, "Why haven't you been back to work?"

"I don't work for you anymore," I told him, and went on my way.

I could have grown up to be as militant and hostile as anyone, and there was a brief period when I felt that I would. It wasn't brought on by any one thing, but an accumulation of incidents that were too minor, I guess, to have affixed themselves to my memory.

But I recall thinking, sometime in my early teens, that I would join the army or the air force and become the best fighter pilot in the world. I would fly over Sledge and the farmlands around it and strafe everything in sight. Then I would think, What if my mother's down there while I'm doing all this strafing?

Whenever I felt that way I would remember something Mother said to me once: "Don't go around with a chip on your shoulder. There's good people here. There's good people everywhere. You've got a lot you're going to have to do and you can't do it carrying a load of resentment with you."

Those words still follow me around. There *was* a lot I wanted to do and the time I spent thinking about how I was better than somebody else or worrying about somebody else's attitude was time I could put to better use.

CHAPTER FOUR

The World by Radio

As far back as I can remember, the radio held a special fascination for me. Many times I sat and listened to it and stared at it in wonder and curiosity. *How did all those people get inside there? Where do they go when I turn it off? If I can hear them, why can't they hear me?*

As I grew older, of course, I solved those mysteries, but that old Philco still fascinated me. More than any other medium, radio embraces the imagination, and I had plenty to hug. I allowed myself to be drawn inside that box and absorbed into the music and drama and sports shows that occupied our evenings. I rode with the Lone Ranger and fought with The Phantom and laughed with Amos and Andy, not knowing at the time that they were not black comedians but two Jewish boys named Freeman Gosden and Charles Correll.

Usually the whole family listened together, after the chores were done and dinner was over. But there was one night when I was at home alone, in bed, and *Inner Sanctum* came on. The narrator was Everett Sloane. He had a dramatic voice and the sound effects on *Inner Sanctum* were very convincing. That night the show was about two guys going into a cemetery to dig up a body.

Daddy had left a coal oil lamp on in the house and it started to burn low, casting long shadows that leaped and danced around the room. From the radio I could hear somber voices and coarse breathing, footsteps in the graveyard, and the *thump . . . thump . . . thump . . .* of a heart beating.

I wanted to get up and turn off the radio but was too scared. I imagined noises outside the house. There were animals out there, and pitch darkness and Lord knows what else. I preferred the safe warmth of the bed. I lay for the rest of the show huddled under the covers in the flickering glow of that old coal oil lamp.

Probably everyone who grew up in the 1940s has those vivid memories of radio and how a few words and sound effects drew elaborate pictures in the imagination.

During World War II, I was captivated by the daily reports we received about a guy named Hitler, who was invading one country or another and committing all kinds of atrocities. Arriving at the house from the field each afternoon, we turned on the radio for news reports from correspondents such as Gabriel Heatter, Winston Burdett, Cedric Foster, Richard C. Hottelet. They were the big boys, the Brokaws and Rathers of their day.

My brother and I talked about the war a lot. We didn't understand it all, just that Hitler had some idea about a master race—something called the Aryan race—and it didn't take a brilliant scholar to figure out that he had no good plans for us if he won.

There was a shortage of almost everything and we spent a lot of our spare time picking up scrap metal and selling it for ten or fifteen cents a pound. It gave us a little extra money but we did it mostly because we thought we were helping the war effort, helping to defeat Hitler.

My fondest attachment was to the weekly drama and comedy shows. The characters and their antics and their lines became embedded in my mind, and even now, nearly fifty years later, I can still quote verbatim from many of those programs.

In Sacramento for a show, I met Dennis Day and Don Ameche and spent an hour with them talking trivia about those old radio programs. It was as enjoyable an hour as I have ever spent.

One of my childhood favorites was a serial called *Mr. District* Attorney. Each episode began with the announcer saying, "Mr. District Attorney ... champion of the people ... defender of truth ... guardian of our fundamental rights to life, liberty, and the pursuit of happiness.... Jay Jostyn in the title role, Lin Doyle as Harrington, and Vicki Voli Jostyn as Miss Miller."

Then Jostyn came on with his opening:

"As it shall be my duty as district attorney not only to prosecute to the limit of the law all persons accused of crimes perpetrated within this county but to defend with equal vigor the rights and privileges of all its citizens."

It was a show about good versus bad, right versus wrong, and, of course, decency always prevailed over evil-the kind of world you wanted to believe in. Pictures of the characters formed in my mind. Mr. DA was rugged and fearless; Harrington was tough; Miss Miller was gorgeous and intelligent.

Many years later, I had an opportunity to meet one of those characters face to face, but I blew it.

Three of my band members lived in San Antonio and we went down there every year to rehearse before starting our season's tour. One day I picked up this little book that told what was going on in the city. Who's playing there? Marvin Kaplan and Vicki Voli.

That's Miss Miller, I thought. I got on the phone and dialed the theater. I was so excited I didn't notice the dates of her performances.

"She's in Austin now," a guy at the theater told me. "She'll be here next week."

We were leaving for Corpus Christi the next day and would be in Austin the following night. As soon as we got there, I spent the first thirty minutes trying to find her. It took some serious cajoling, but the folks at the theater gave me the number at her hotel. It was almost time for me to go on and I was nervous for two reasons. President Lyndon Johnson and Lady Bird were attending my show and I was about to talk with Miss Miller. I wasn't sure which was more important to me.

When she answered the phone, I said, "Miss Voli, I'm Charley Pride and I'm a country singer. I've got a show here tonight and noticed that you and Marvin Kaplan were in town. I wanted to talk to you."

"Yes," she said, probably wondering if this was some kind of kook on the line.

"Do you remember a show called *Mr. District Attorney?*" I asked.

There was a pause, and she said, "Of course. It was the number one show for ten years."

"I'm a big fan of yours." I was as excited as a kid at Disneyland. "I remember Jay Jostyn and Lin Doyle."

"Lin Doyle just died in a car crash a week ago," she said. "In Colorado."

"I used to listen to you every week," I told her, and then recited the preamble to the show. I recounted a scene from one episode: Harrington and the chief go to a deserted little cabin to look for some crooks. Doyle played Harrington, the protector of the chief, Jostyn. He says, "Wait a minute, Chief, I've got to look in here." He opens the door and, *bam ... pow ... whack . . .* , he knocks out all the crooks.

I was ranting on and she said, "What did you say your name was?"

"Charley Pride."

She was silent for a minute. "You're an entertainer, too? Oh, my goodness. You're probably a big entertainer and I should know who you are."

Wanting badly to meet her, I decided to forsake modesty and try to impress her as much as possible.

"Yes, ma'am. I've sold out tonight and President Johnson is going to be at my show."

We talked for another minute or two and agreed that later in the evening, after our shows, we would try to get together. We never did, and it was my fault.

Darrell Royal, the University of Texas football coach, was throwing a party that night and invited me to come by after my show. I had planned to stay there a few minutes and then call Vicki Voli. It turned out that Willie Nelson and the Gatlin Brothers and a bunch of other singers and songwriters were at Royal's party and we got to drinking and picking and jamming and having so much fun that I didn't realize how much time had passed.

By the time I left Darrell's, it was much too late to call Vicki Voli and I left town the next day without meeting her. I've kicked myself many times for missing that opportunity.

It was from that old Philco radio that I also learned to love country music, and I guess I'm indebted to my father for that. He controlled the knobs and every week he set the dial to WSM in Nashville for The Grand Ole Opry.

I had been exposed to other music-blues and gospel, mostly-but Roy Acuff, Ernest Tubb, and Hank Williams came into our house just as regularly as Miss Miller and her crew. It was natural that my taste in music would lean in their direction. I sang along with those guys, memorized their songs, and country music just grew inside me.

I never consciously tried to mimic their voices, to sing like them, but because I had a knack for imitating sounds and dialects, I had trouble convincing my brothers and sisters of that. I once won a 4-H Club award for imitating animals, any animal you could name—ducks, chickens, turkeys, geese, cows, hogs, roosters, just about anything. I also could imitate accents—British, Australian, Irish, Scottish. So when I sat around the house singing country music, some of my family thought it was a contrived voice, just another of my imitations.

"Charley," my sister Bessie asked me once, "how come you want to sing white folks' music?"

Truthfully, I had never really thought about it. What came from my throat was my voice, no one else's. No one had ever told me that whites were supposed to sing one kind of music and blacks another—I sang what I liked in the only voice I had.

The first live country music performances I can remember were on the streets of Sledge, outside Sander's Grocery Store on Saturday afternoons when I was about five years old. To draw customers to his store, Mr. Sanders used to hire Eddie Hill and his band to come down from Memphis and play from the back of a flatbed truck. I'd watch them hook up the microphones and tune their instruments and wanted desperately to get up there and sing with them.

After I began singing professionally, I met Eddie and told him that.

"You should have asked," he said. "We probably would have let you." Probably not. Music transcends a lot of things, but not the segregation of Mississippi in the 1940s.

My first guitar was a mail-order purchase from the Sears, Roebuck catalog when I was fourteen. It was an inexpensive Silvertone, but I spent most of a year saving for it. I learned a few chords and discovered that by using my index finger like a capo and playing open bar chords, I could get a lot of mileage from those few. Jimmie Rodgers, who had several big hits, including "Honeycomb," back in the 1950s and 1960s, played guitar that way.

But the guitar had to be tuned differently for bar chords—
to a lower pitch—and I learned to do that by ear. I would sit
by the radio and wait for the last chord of a song and tune
the guitar to it. I've often wished that I could have taken
lessons and become a better musician, but that method has
served me pretty well.

That first guitar did not last long enough for me to become
accomplished on it. I left it outside one night, a night that
we happened to have a generous rain. The glue that held the
guitar together came loose and it would never stay tuned
after that. The more I tightened the strings, the more it
buckled and bent.

Finally I put it in a small attic space under the tin roof of
our porch and the heat up there worked a more severe hardship on it.

Stepping onto the porch one afternoon, Mother was star-
tled by strange sounds coming from that attic space.

Boing . . .

She stopped and listened. I was in the yard nearby.

Boing . . . *boing* . . .

"Charley," Mother said with a puzzled look, "there's some
rats or something up there messing with that box of yours."

I climbed up, looked into the storage space, and found the
Silvertone bent double from the heat and humidity. The neck
had broken completely off. I threw everything away but the
neck, which I kept for a long time, thinking that I would be
able to find some musical use for it.

Losing that guitar didn't force me to stop tinkering with
musical instruments. I played the comb, which is done by
folding paper around a comb and humming against it. The
vibration produces a sound and the tone varies according to
the size of the comb and the type of paper.

I even rigged something akin to a crude one-string steel
guitar. What you do is tack two nails into the wall three feet
apart, string bailing wire between them, and then use a

hammer—I used a brick—to bend the nails away from each other so the wire tightens. You can use a glass jar or Coke bottle to run up and down the wire while you pluck it with your finger or a piece of metal.

If anyone had told me then that music would ever be anything but a diversion to me, I would have laughed at them. Singing, like the radio, was just another form of amusement. My brothers and sisters all sang, too, and they all have good voices. We used to sing together a lot but not one of us, as far as I can recall, thought of singing as a way to make a living.

As far as I was concerned, my future was in baseball. Once I saw what Jackie Robinson did, that was my goal. Before he reached the major leagues, there were no real role models for kids like us. There were good players in the Negro leagues—players who could hold their own against any big leagues—but the pay was low and the possibilities limited.

Robinson changed all that. For kids like me and my brothers, baseball suddenly was something worth working at.

C H A P T E R   F I V E

The Field of Dreams

Mack Jr. was a hell of a baseball player. At the age of fourteen he was catching on a men's team that traveled from county to county as part of an informal sandlot league. I admired him and wanted to play like him.

Hardly anybody thought I had much of a chance. They told me I was too skinny and awkward, but I didn't let that discourage me. In fact, it probably made me more determined. It was as though I had been dared to do it. I wanted to show them I could play as well as my brother.

Baseball got into my blood early and I worked harder at it than I ever had at anything. I was aware that the odds are against every kid who thinks about making it in sports, but I began to think of it as my way out. I was determined to do whatever I had to do, learn whatever I had to learn in order to play.

I used to bug Junior and Ed to practice with me before school, after school, and on weekends. If we didn't have a catcher, we used a haystack or the henhouse for a backstop.

We didn't have school teams or youth leagues. If we wanted to play, we had to play with men and we had to play at their level—and that included the rough stuff. Cups and other protective gear were almost unheard of.

Eventually Junior's team let me play if a regular player was hurt or didn't show up. In a lot of ways it was a ragtag league—we sometimes used cow chips for bases and the balls got a little misshapen from overuse—but there was some pretty good baseball played in those pastures. A lot of the players shared my ambition of playing professional baseball someday.

Teams came from little towns like Crenshaw, Birdie, Sledge, Wynona—all over the Delta. Many a day I walked seven miles to a ball game, pitched nine innings, and walked back home.

Although the teams were not well equipped, Junior and I at least had a few baseballs and gloves that were given to us by our uncle, Lee Andrew Stewart. We used to sneak down the road on Saturday nights and hide our gloves in the bushes so Daddy wouldn't see us leaving the house with them on Sunday mornings. He believed in honoring the holy sabbath. Playing baseball on Sunday was a sin to be punished with a good thrashing.

We came home from school one Monday and Daddy was waiting for us in the yard with a belt in his hand. He had heard about our ball game the day before. He beat the living stuffing out of us, and afterwards Mother walked over to him and said, "Mack, I think those boys are going to play baseball and you ought to stop whipping them for it."

Believing that life would be easier elsewhere, I dropped out of school at fifteen and went to live with my uncle, Robert Pride, my father's oldest brother, in Clarksdale. For a while life was easier. I hung around the pool hall a lot—enough to become a pretty good player—and when it was time for school to be out, I would run down to Myrtle Hall School and check out the girls. I wasn't drinking or getting into trouble, just idling and drifting.

Before long, my uncle cracked down and I discovered that he could be about as hard as Daddy. He told me when to be in at night, ordered me to stay away from pool rooms, and gave me an ultimatum: Enroll in school or find a job. In short, he became a grouch.

Without much enthusiasm, I got a job hopping cars at Deacon's Drive-In. One night I got a seventy-five-cent tip, and that looked like a fortune to me. It didn't take long, though, to learn that big tippers were few and far between and there wasn't much future in hopping cars. I went back home, got back in school, and plotted my next move.

Next time, I promised myself, I would go father than Clarksdale.

Early in the spring I went to Memphis to offer myself to the Memphis Red Sox of the Negro American League. Homer "Goose" Curry, the manager, gave me a quick tryout but he already had a strong pitching staff, one that included Marshall Bridges, who would later play in the majors for the Cincinnati Reds and the New York Yankees.

While I was hanging around town, I met a guy named Jim Ford, who was putting together an all-Negro team to go up north and play in the Iowa State League. I signed on with him, although I was a little hesitant about hitting the road again. Mother was about to give birth and had not been feeling well. I told her I would send her an address when I got to Des Moines and she promised to write when the baby was born.

Things started off badly in Iowa and got worse. If I wasn't worrying about Mother, I was worrying about how to survive. Ford had arranged for us to stay in a rooming house in Des Moines but we had no salaries. Our only income would be from our percentage of the gate. For the first couple of weeks, it rained nearly every night and we were unable to play, which meant we didn't get paid. The little money I took with me vanished in a few days and I began to think I might starve before we made any money.

I got so hungry that I pulled up weeds, washed them off, and ate the bottoms of them.

Meanwhile, I hadn't received any word from home. Every day I asked the woman who ran the boardinghouse, "Did I get a letter?" and each time the answer was the same.

I never had any proof, but I always suspected that she was opening our mail and throwing it away. She could see that we were destitute and probably thought we were writing home for money. If she opened a letter and found no money in it, she couldn't very well bring it to us and say, "Here's your mail." Mother would have written to me, I was convinced, and some of the other guys also were not getting mail they expected.

Leaner and hungrier, we left Des Moines and went to Wall Lake, which is Andy Williams's hometown. There, too, rain caused games to be canceled nearly every night and we still were not making any money. Things were pretty bleak until a businessman named August Fisher came to our rescue. He ran the National Oats Company in Wall Lake and people around there called him the Popcorn King because that was one of his company's major products. He subsidized us until we could get in some playing time.

The Popcorn King was about the only good thing that happened to me in Iowa.

Once we were able to play, we didn't win many games, so Ford went back down to Memphis and raided the Red Sox, enticing some of the best players, including Brantley and Marshall, to switch teams. I don't know how he did it. The Red Sox paid one hundred dollars a month and two dollars a day meal money. You didn't get rich playing in Memphis, but you didn't have to eat weeds, either.

To make room for them on the roster, he cut me and a few others from the team and sent us home. It was a long unhappy ride. Not only was I going home unemployed once again, but the homecoming would be gloomy for another reason.

Before leaving Iowa I received a letter from Mother. She had given birth to twin boys. They were stillborn and would be buried long before I could get back.

It occurred to me that Jim Ford had done me one huge favor by pirating talent from the Red Sox and shipping me back from Iowa. The Sox would be looking for pitchers, I reasoned, and after a few days in Sledge, I headed back to Memphis to have another talk with "Goose" Curry. He did not offer me a contract, but he gave me a uniform and put me on the roster. I became the youngest member of the Memphis Red Sox, a bona fide professional baseball player with a regular paycheck, a home stadium, and hopes bigger than a thunderhead.

Walking onto the grass at Martin Stadium that first time was almost like a religious experience. Players whose names will never be forgotten had walked on that same grass, stood at that same plate, raced around those same base paths. Hank Aaron. Ernie Banks. Willie Mays. Jackie Robinson. Anybody who ever played in the Negro American League would have played in Martin Stadium at one time or another.

It was a nice stadium, rivaling many of the minor league parks and accommodating crowds just as large. I remember standing on the field that first time, watching the other players warming up, the people coming in and taking their seats; hearing the voice on the public address system reciting the lineups; smelling the grass and dust and heavy night air, and thinking, This is what you were born to do, Charley.

This time I wasn't going to be sent home.

Playing for the Red Sox was both an adventure and an

ordeal. We were given small living quarters at Martin Stadium, and while the pay was enough to get by on, it didn't leave much for partying.

But I was pitching and playing the outfield and, except for the financial strain, having the time of my life. I was on my own—something I had wanted for a long time—paying my own way and showing my stuff now and then to a major league scout. As they say in the Delta, I was walking in high cotton.

I had brushes with cops and robbers, my only ones, while playing for that team.

The first happened before a game in Jackson. Our catcher discovered that $120 was missing from his bag and reported it stolen to the police. They naturally assumed that one of his teammates had taken it. One by one we were searched, our bags were inspected, and we were interrogated.

Finding nothing, they released us from custody and sent us on our way. One thing about the incident always puzzled me: Why didn't the police search the bus driver or the team manager, who were as black as the rest of us?

The second happened in Memphis. We had just finished a game and I was on my way to get something to eat. About two blocks from the motel where we stayed, I turned the corner and saw three guys walking toward me.

The tall one jumped off the curb and circled into the street. The other two walked up to me, and one said, "Hey, buddy, you got a match?" I sensed he didn't really want a match and I braced myself just as one of them hit me on the jaw. The other one caught me in the chest and the tall one grabbed at me but missed when I spun away.

I ran back toward the motel with them chasing me. Two of my baseball buddies heard the commotion and saw us coming.

"They tried to rob me," I yelled.

"I've got a pistol," one of my friends shouted.

When the muggers heard that, they turned down another street and disappeared into the night.

Nothing ever came of that, but two or three years later, during a period when I was not playing baseball, I learned who one of the muggers was. I was working in a hardwood flooring company in Memphis and told a co-worker about the attempted robbery. He didn't say anything, but later that week he said, "Remember when you were telling me about that robbery?"

"Uh-huh."

"One of those guys was my brother," he said. "I ain't bragging. We never wanted him to do those things." I never really understood why he told me, except that he must have felt bad about what his brother had done.

On road trips I often stood in the aisle of the bus and sang country songs, all those old Hank Williams and Roy Acuff tunes I learned listening to *The Grand Ole Opry*. The team was not in unanimous agreement about my talent.

"Knock off that noise," was a fairly common comment. But a few gave me encouragement.

"You sing pretty good," one of the other players said to me one day. "What are you doing playing baseball for a hundred dollars a month and two dollars a day meal money? You could do better singing."

"I want to go to the major leagues," I told him. "Years from now, when they ask who hit the most home runs, I don't want the answer to be Babe Ruth, I want it to be Charley Pride. When they ask who was the last player to hit four hundred, I don't want the answer to be Ted Williams, I want it to be Charley Pride."

It may have sounded cocky, but my confidence was that hard. There's nothing wrong with dreaming and wanting to be the best. At some point my family even began to believe I wasn't wasting my time. Mother became a serious baseball fan. She learned to figure batting averages and things like that. At the end of my first year with the Sox, I took her to Chicago for the Negro League's East–West All-Star Game. I didn't get to play, but it was a big outing for her and for me.

In the off seasons I went back to Sledge and tried to finish high school.

The principal was sympathetic and made every effort to accommodate me; he even let me play on the school's basketball team. But each year it became more difficult. Being two or three years older than the other kids in my class made me feel out of place. And having been away from Sledge for months at a time, traveling all over the country, the Mississippi Delta was becoming a smaller and smaller part of my life. I managed to finish the eleventh grade.

I also spent a lot of time on baseball. After joining the Red Sox and playing in a league of tough pitching, I discovered that I had difficulty hitting the curveball right-handed, so I decided to switch-hit. In the mornings, before school or work, I would take Ed outside and let him throw while I batted from both sides of the plate. We used the henhouse as a backstop and nearly tore it down getting me ready to switch-hit.

Having a ball thrown at your head is also part of the game, so I asked Ed to throw a beanball at me every now and then. It paid off. I could dodge beanballs and hit from either side of the plate as well as anyone.

Mother had drilled into me the importance of getting a high school diploma, but as my baseball career seemed to find its footing, it was hard to focus on anything else. I was determined, in fact, to do better than the Memphis Red Sox.

William "Dizzy" Dismukes was a scout for the New York Yankees, the first black man to hold that position. He was also the secretary of the Kansas City Monarchs of the Negro American League and he knew the players in that league pretty well. After my first year with the Sox, Goose Curry encouraged Dizzy to take a look at me.

I received a letter from him about the time spring training was getting under way. He offered me a three-hundred-dollar bonus to sign with the Yankees' farm team in Boise, Idaho, and told me to report, if I was interested, to Rio Vista, California, where the team was holding spring workouts.

Because I was a minor, Mother and Daddy had to sign for me. I don't think Daddy was really in favor of it. It meant I would have to drop out of school again and go to a Class C team in a place that seemed as far away as another planet.

But the offer was persuasive—three hundred dollars for signing a piece of paper. You could pick cotton all season and not make that much money. Mother and Daddy signed the contract. Before leaving for California, I bought a forty-dollar ring and a suit, sent the rest of the money to Daddy, and boarded a train for the three-day ride to California.

Spring training went pretty well. I had a strong pitching arm but a tendency to overwork it, throwing too hard before I was ready. But when we broke camp I was in the rotation and feeling good. Everything was going fine until we got to Lodi, California. I pulled a muscle in my shoulder and had to come out of the game.

I stayed with the team until we broke camp and returned to Boise. The manager told me he was sending me down to Class D. "You're going to Fond du Lac, Wisconsin, until you get back in shape." He gave me my choice of going by bus, train, or plane.

"I want to fly," I said. It was something I had never done.

We took off from Boise just before sundown in an old DC-6 and had to stop in Salt Lake City for refueling. It was after sundown when we left there. As the plane rose over the mountains, the air became turbulent and the plane bounced and swayed uncomfortably. From the window I could see the lights below—nothing between us and them but angry wind.

We're going to fall, I thought. Across the aisle was a guy calmly reading a newspaper and I wondered how he could be so calm when we were about to fall.

The stewardess could tell I was scared. She walked up and said, "Would you like a pillow?" What she was really saying was, Would you like for me to keep you from shitting your pants?

"Yes . . . yes I would," I said.

Looking around at the other passengers, I could see that none of them was getting ready to mess their pants. I leaned back, told myself that if they could be calm, so could I. It was easier said than done, but when we landed in Chicago, I deplaned feeling like a veteran air traveler.

I took a bus to Fond du Lac and stayed with the team for a week. Again I tried to push the arm too soon and it stayed sore the whole time. The manager gave me a bus ticket back to Memphis.

CHAPTER SIX

Without Mama Here

Goose Curry put me back on the Red Sox squad, but it was the beginning of an unpleasant period—two or three years of bouncing around from one team to another, wondering where I was going to land, and losing my mother.

Goose Curry left to coach a new team, the Louisville Clippers, being formed in the Negro American League. He took me and a guy named Jesse Mitchell with him. We took spring training with them in Biloxi, Mississippi, but our stay was short, thanks to the feeble economy of that league. The Clippers needed a bus to travel in and the only way they could raise money was by selling players. I don't know how much they got, but Goose sold Jesse Mitchell and me to Soo Bridgeford, who owned the Birmingham Black Barons, for enough to buy a bus.

Jesse and I may have the distinction of being the only players in history to be traded for a used motor vehicle.

Birmingham was another dead end. Soo Bridgeford sold the team at the end of that season and we were all cut loose.

The next year, I scoured the country for a place to play, eventually finding my way to El Paso. After a few weeks with the Kings, I was sent to Nogales, a border town in Sonora, Mexico. I was unaccustomed to Mexican and Tex-Mex food and it seemed that the whole time I was on the border my mouth bore wounds inflicted by hot peppers. I had fun playing down there—we drew good crowds and many of the local restaurants had team pictures and newspaper stories about us tacked on the walls—but I was not unhappy for the season to be over.

I went to Colorado to stay with my sister Catherine.

Sometime in late January I had a premonition that something was wrong back home. I was working odd jobs in Colorado, trying to save enough money to buy a car, but something told me I had to get home. I believe in things like intuition and mental telepathy, believe that it's possible to sense when someone you're close to is ill or in danger. The feeling I had was so strong that it frightened me. With the little money I had saved toward a car, I bought a bus ticket to Sledge.

While I was gone, Mother and Daddy had had some kind of row and she left him and went to stay with his nephew in Lambert. She got sick while she was there and wasn't feeling very well when I went to see her. I told her I would be back the next day. I think I will always feel guilty because I didn't go back. I was hanging out with some buddies and goofing off when she got worse and had to be taken to the hospital.

Daddy and I brought her back home, but she was in a lot of pain. The doctor kept her heavily sedated with morphine. Every time the drug wore off, he would come to the house and shoot her up again.

On his third or fourth visit, I asked the doctor, "What is wrong with my mother?"

"I don't rightly know," he said.

That went on for nearly a week. Daddy and I stayed with her the whole time, feeding her and washing her and trying to ease her pain. Under the morphine she slept a lot. Without it she suffered. One afternoon she was hurting real bad and Daddy went to get the doctor.

By the time he got back, she was dead.

Daddy walked in the house and I was on my knees by the bed, crying and screaming. He grabbed me by the shoulders and threw me away from the bed. He stood there, looking down at her, struggling not to show emotion. I think it would have been easier for him to bite a fence post in half than to let his feelings out.

My insides were torn up. There is that second when you think, She's gone—no more Mother, and you realize what you have lost. She was the one soothing thing in my life. She always had the right answers, said the right things to make me feel the way I wanted to feel. "Mama, you so pretty," I used to tell her when I was young. "You shouldn't be scrubbing clothes and doin' all those things." In her forty-seven years, that was all she knew—taking care of kids, cooking and cleaning, bringing in crops, just getting by year to year—and then she died and I couldn't understand why.

We requested an autopsy to find out what she died from. The doctors said it was acute meningitis with septicemia and discoid lupus, but I've never believed that. I've always believed that she was allergic to morphine and that was what killed her. I'll never be sure. The doctors' ruling was made official on the death certificate, and that was it.

Her funeral was held on a spring day when the skies poured blinding rain onto the Delta. The last rites were said in a small white church beside a dirt road a few miles south of Sledge and she was buried in a cemetery near Crenshaw. I've never been back to her grave and I'm not planning on going back. I don't think it is possible to love anyone more than I loved my mother and even after all these years—more than thirty years now—I don't think I could bear the hurt of standing on the ground where she lies.

* * *

My ties to Sledge had been fragile enough, but Mother's death seemed to cut the cord altogether and I was anxious to leave. Another baseball season was getting ready to start so I made another pilgrimage to Martin Stadium. I was older and stronger and the years of knocking around had not wounded my confidence. They may have given me a measure of grit.

I managed to rejoin the Sox, and going into the 1956 season I was in better form than ever. Moving up to the big leagues sometime that year was not out of the question. A few major league scouts, including ones from the Brooklyn Dodgers and the St. Louis Cardinals, showed some interest in me and I began the season playing well enough to keep them on the hook. My pitching arm had never been stronger, switch-hitting was paying off with a batting average well over .300, and I had good speed in the outfield.

The quota system loosely employed by the major league teams was a hefty obstacle. After Jackie Robinson made it in 1947, the integration of baseball evolved slowly. It took a few years before every team had a black player and a few years passed before a team had more than one. By 1956, two or three was still pretty much the limit. But it was an opportunity, if a small one.

Everything was on track for me that year until we got to Sikeston, Missouri, for a game with the Birmingham Black Barons.

Before that game, I was hitting .367, had ten home runs and seven wins on the mound, all of them close—3–2, 2–1, in that range, close and low-scoring. At Martin Stadium, the night before we left for Missouri, I had a home run. A scout from the St. Louis Cardinals, I was told, would be in Sikeston the next day to watch me pitch.

In each of the first two innings, I struck out the side and held the Barons scoreless.

The third inning was a disaster.

The first batter grounded out and the second hit a soft pop to right field. But our usual right fielder wasn't playing that position. In his place was a catcher—wearing a catcher's mitt. A catcher's mitt was designed for a very specific purpose and in the entire history of baseball it is unlikely that anybody ever tried playing the outfield wearing one. It would be just as easy to scoop up grounders or shag flies with a brick in your hand.

The ball bounced off his mitt and the runner advanced to third base.

I stood on the mound staring at right field and fuming. I shouldn't have gotten angry but I did, and it showed on the next pitch, a curveball. Instead of stretching and putting my body into it, I stepped on the rubber, stood straight up, and nonchalantly brought my arm over my shoulder and flipped the wrist down. Something snapped in my elbow and pain shot through the whole arm.

I bent the arm a couple of times trying to shake off the ache, got the ball back, and threw a fastball. The agony nearly sent me to my knees. Goose Curry, who was also back with the Red Sox, came to the mound, signaling for a new pitcher. I didn't argue with him. It was over.

The Cardinal scout who was there that night found out that I had cracked a bone in my elbow and I never saw him again.

Teams in our league didn't have trainers in those days. We had small rosters, which meant you had to play every day. Even pitchers got no days off. You threw every four days and played another position in between. If you got hurt, you were cut from the team, with no pay, and had to go nurse your wounds on your own.

My oldest brother, Jonas, lived in St. Louis, so I went there to rest my arm and hope that it would recover enough for a comeback. Jonas helped me get a job doing handyman work for some people around their house. I washed windows and cleaned up around the place, all the while trying to give my arm as much rest as possible.

One of the most depressing days of my life was going to see the Red Sox when they came to town. Watching my old team leave the field, board the bus, and drive away without me, I was overcome by an awful sense of desertion and desolation.

I decided to move on, too.

Rather than going home, I headed north to Chicago, to stay with my cousin, Mary Lee Neither. She put me up for a few weeks and helped me get my arm back in shape by rubbing it with salve and alcohol.

It began to feel better and I tried throwing again. Afraid to try a curveball and pretty certain that my fastball had lost some of its zip, I reasoned that my best chance of getting back in the game was to develop a knuckleball, a pitch that didn't have to be thrown hard to be effective.

Most of the time nobody knows where a knuckleball will go—not the pitcher, not the catcher, and especially not the batter. "There are only two ways to catch a knuckleball," some catcher is alleged to have said, "and neither of them works." Bob Uecker, the catcher who later became an actor, had a good line about it. "The best way to catch a knuckleball is to follow it until it stops rolling and pick it up," he said.

The pitch is easy enough on the arm that some good knuckleballers—guys like Phil Niekro and Charlie Hough—have played into their mid and late forties.

So, believing it was my only passport back into the game, I worked on that pitch and worked on it with a passion. If I couldn't find somebody to catch for me, I'd throw at a wall or fence. Slowly, as the arm got stronger and the pain went away, I thought of returning to Memphis to see if I could win back my old job.

* * *

Goose Curry was leery when I walked into Martin Stadium that summer. Only three months or so had passed since I injured my arm and he was convinced that it needed more time to mend.

"It feels fine," I argued, "and I've developed a pretty good knuckleball."

He watched me throw a few times and finally gave in, reinstating me on the team. There was still a lot of season left and it turned out to be one of my best years in baseball. I won fourteen games and was bound for the All-Star team.

Along the way I met the woman I was going to marry.

C H A P T E R S E V E N

Kiss an Angel Good Morning

Marriage wasn't exactly on my agenda that summer. Like a lot of young athletes, I sometimes had more girlfriends than I could juggle at one time.

My bride-to-be probably didn't have marriage on her mind, either, and even if she did, I would have been the least likely candidate. I spent half my time chasing her and the other half trying to avoid her. She was unlike the other girls I had dated and was the first one who troubled me in ways I didn't understand. I wanted to be with her but was frightened of my feelings for her.

We met in Memphis in a place called the Gay Hawk, a restaurant and hangout for ballplayers and fans just down the street from Martin Stadium.

I had gone there with a date, and as we were leaving I saw some of my buddies from the team sitting at a table with three girls I had never met.

My date kept walking, but the lure of three attractive females caused me to pause at their table. I was going out with two or three other girls at the time, but when you are nineteen years old, you can never have too many. One of the guys introduced to me to the three girls: Katherine Baldwin,

Pauletta Cohran, and Pauletta's sister Rozene. My attention went immediately to Rozene, who was sitting at the end of the table.

"Hey, I like your hair," I said. It wasn't just a line. She had very pretty hair.

She didn't answer, just gave me one of those who-do-you-think-you-are looks. I wasn't used to that and wasn't about to give up.

"Call me tomorrow at Martin Stadium and I'll take you to the movies," I said.

Again she didn't respond, which left me feeling as though I had slammed into the outfield wall with an empty glove. My date was already outside, so I hurried to catch up with her.

Before noon the next day, I was in my room and heard one of the players outside yell, "Charley, you got a phone call."

I scrambled down to the pay phone and said, "Hello."

"Do you know who this is?" a female voice asked.

It didn't sound like any of the girls I had been going out with and I didn't want to start reciting a list of names. "Uh . . . no," I said.

"Didn't you tell a girl last night that you liked her hair and for her to call you and you would like to take her to the movies?"

Damn, I thought, the old charm wins again. "What time do you want me to pick you up?"

"I'm not the girl," the voice said.

"Well, who are you?"

"I'm Katherine Baldwin."

"Why didn't Rozene call?"

"She's not going to call you. If you want to see her, you'll have to do the calling," she said.

Oh, boy. The hard-to-get type. When you're a hotshot with the Memphis Red Sox, girls call you. This one didn't know the rules. "All right," I said. "Where does she work?"

"She's a cosmetologist in Binghampton," a section of Memphis.

The team was leaving for Omaha at three o'clock that afternoon. There was plenty of time. I caught a bus to Binghampton. When I arrived the beauty parlor wasn't busy, so I sat down and made small talk with Rozene, kidding her about not wanting to call me, things like that. All the while, Mrs. Taylor, who owned the shop, was sitting nearby with her antennas on, listening to our conversation and sizing me up. I didn't mind. I was more concerned with impressing Rozene.

After I left, Mrs. Taylor gave Rozene her assessment of me. "I'll tell you one thing," she said. "He sure can talk."

I took a bus back downtown and, on impulse, went to a record store and picked out a 45 rpm record, "It Only Hurts For a Little While," by the Ames Brothers.

There was a drugstore across the street from the stadium and I knew the clerks there pretty well. I took the record in and asked if I could leave it for someone to pick up in a day or two.

When the team arrived in Omaha the next night, I was broke except for the day's two-dollar meal allowance. I bought a hamburger and a Coke and put the rest of the money in a pay phone.

"There's something for you at the drugstore across from the stadium," I told Rozene.

"What is it?" she said in a tone that suggested that she was still uncertain of me.

"Just go in and ask for the record Charley Pride left there."

My budget didn't allow for another phone call to see if she picked it up, but I was sure she would and I spent the rest of the trip confident that my little gesture had won her over. How could she refuse to go out with such a clever, thoughtful guy? I was right. Back in Memphis after several days on the road, I called her and we made plans to go to the movies.

After practice on the day of our date, I lay down to take a short nap. Even for young men, it takes a couple of days to recover from long road trips. Our bus was not built for luxury and any sleep we got on board was fitful and unsatisfying. I figured on a two-hour nap, getting up at six o'clock and being at Rozene's by seven.

I slept until nearly nine.

Groggy and kicking myself all the way, I stumbled to the pay phone and dialed her number.

"I was awfully tired," I told her.

"I understand." Her voice was as frosty as a nickel root beer—about what I had expected.

"Can I come over for a little while?"

"It's kind of late. Mrs. Ada doesn't like late visitors."

She lived in a house with an elderly woman who rented bedrooms to single girls—the kind of arrangement appreciated by the parents of young women moving into Memphis to be on their own for the first time. The landlady was a companion, protector, counselor, and surrogate mother.

"I won't stay long. We'll just talk."

"Some other time."

"All right. I'll call you."

We had our first date a few days later and my behavior took a sharp turn toward the weird.

Rozene came from a background that was as alien to me as a camel in a cornfield. She had finished high school, attended college and cosmetology school, and had an air of maturity and self-assurance. She came from a home where love and affection were openly expressed. She and her sisters—Pauletta, Hortense, and Irma—were part of a family in ways that my brothers and sisters and I were not. They were allowed to take part in family discussions and speak their minds without fear of being punished if they disagreed with their father.

Ebby Cohran was a craftsman—a carpenter—and a land-owner. He was well read and had a lively curiosity about the world. On weekends and vacations he took his daughters on trips and explored things that farm kids usually only learned about from books—not necessarily grand adventures, but small things that, nonetheless, expanded their experience and exposure to life beyond the farm. He found interest and education in something as simple as spending an afternoon in Batesville watching the trains come and go.

He played with his daughters, had water fights and pillow fights with them, hugged and praised them. He seldom spanked them, seldom raised his voice, and in return they adored him and were eager to please him. If they needed discipline, he usually could make them see their error by saying nothing more than "I'm disappointed in you."

Their infrequent spankings were not in the same league as the whippings I had endured. He would tap them lightly with a small switch and the girls would scream and pretend they were in pain. When he walked out of the room they giggled.

But he did not overly pamper them. As they grew up, the four had to do their share of the work—bringing in the crops, tending the animals, and maintaining the household. At one time, they lived in a house on a paved road that was well traveled, especially by their classmates going to and from school or town. The girls were embarrassed to be seen outside doing work that normally was done by boys.

Their father had no fear of making boys out of his daughters. He wanted them to be educated and self-reliant, but he also wanted them to understand the honor of labor and contributing to the family's welfare.

If they were humiliated by doing men's work, they had no hesitancy about sharing his passion for what was then the mostly male domain of professional sports, especially baseball. Like him, they devoured the sports pages of the Memphis *Commercial Appeal*, which was delivered to their house each day. They knew the teams, the rankings, the players, the starting lineups, utility players, pinch hitters—everyone in both leagues—and their statistics.

During baseball season, they rushed home from school to read the sports pages so they would be prepared for the inevitable discussion when their father arrived. He playfully tested their knowledge with little quizzes about the previous day's sports news.

There were meaningful things in life besides farming, he felt, and one of them was the World Series. The Series is played during the harvest season, yet Mr. Ebby always brought his daughters in from the field at game time, turned on the radio, and settled back for the duration. The crops could wait.

At first Rozene and her sisters took an interest in baseball to please their father, but in time their affection for the game was genuine. After leaving home, they continued to follow the major leagues and became regulars at Martin Stadium for the Red Sox home games.

Many of the young women who hung around the stadium did so just to meet ballplayers and be a part of the social life of the season. But Rozene could talk baseball with the savviest of the players or coaches.

How often does a guy who lives and breathes baseball meet a woman who loves the game and understands it as well as he? She was smart, beautiful, independent, and could explain the infield fly rule. What else could a guy want?

We dated several times but were not going steady. Once in a while I went out with one of the other girls, but more and more I found myself thinking about Rozene—especially when the team was traveling. Many times, when we got back into town, I ran to the telephone, started to dial her number, and stood there trying earnestly to talk myself out of it. This is getting too serious, I thought.

Sometimes the conflict was like a storm inside me. There was one night when the urge to see her was overwhelming, but I was determined not to give in to it. I paced around my room, walked by the pay phone a few times, and finally headed for a picture show, alone, just to keep myself occupied.

My mind wasn't on the movie. I sat there and stared at the screen and left the theater without the vaguest idea what I had seen. Walking the streets, I wrestled with my emotions, argued with myself, tried to rationalize my behavior, and finally gritted my teeth and thought, All right. I'll do it.

It was a short bus ride to her house.

"Well, son," the landlady said, "she just left to go home . . . down to her mother's in Mississippi."

That made me angry with myself. The team was leaving town the next day and I wouldn't see her for a week or more. I brooded about it the whole trip. But when I got back and was with her a few times, the fear returned, and again I looked for reasons to avoid her.

That went on all summer and into the fall, and I was making little progress toward resolving my ambiguous feelings.

One afternoon at the end of the season, we had finished practicing for an upcoming game against the Willie Mays All-Stars, a team of black major leaguers that toured around playing black teams at the end of their regular season. We were in the locker room and our catcher, Charlie Jennings, was kidding me about my girlfriends.

"Why don't you give me one of those phone numbers?" he asked.

An idea that seemed brilliant at the time occurred to me. Grinning to myself, I gave him Rozene's number. Why, I can't explain. It would prove I wasn't really hung up on her. It would give me a chance to go out with one of my other girlfriends. It would test her devotion to me. Whatever it was, it made sense at the time.

Besides, there was no real harm in it. Charlie Jennings was a big, rough guy. She'll never go out with him, I thought.

Damned if she didn't go out with him—on the night of the All-Star game. To make it worse, I made a date with one of the other girls and she stood me up.

That night I pitched and played outfield. We lost to the All-Stars, as we usually did, but the postgame was the rough part.

We all drew handsome paychecks. The Willie Mays All-Stars and the Negro League All-Stars split the gate 70–30. Because there were only fifteen of us on the squad, my cut of the 30 percent came to ten or twelve dollars—half a week's pay for one night's work.

I blew almost the whole wad trying to keep an eye on Rozene and Charlie.

After the game, I took a cab to a club where I thought they might be, a place with live music and dancing—the kind of place that served Falstaff beer in quart bottles, the kind of place where you have to pay to get a table. I paid for my table but didn't drink. For maybe twenty minutes I sat there, scanning the crowd, looking for Rozene's head. Even in that mob I would have recognized her hair.

Nothing. I left and took another cab to a place called Davidson's. My night's earnings were disappearing quickly, but it was worth it. I spotted Rozene first. She was wearing a red suspender-type dress over a white blouse, and old Charlie Jennings was right beside her, grinning like a possum in a cabbage patch.

I slipped outside and waited for them to leave. *We* took her home, Charlie and I—the two of them in Charlie's car and me in a cab right behind. I followed them all the way to her house and waited there until he left. If Charlie managed as much as a kiss, it was a quick one, because I had my eye on them every minute and I didn't see anything.

For a few weeks, I didn't see Rozene again. My knuckleball had worked well enough to earn me a spot on the Negro American League All-Star Team and a chance to tour around the South playing exhibition games against the Willie Mays All-Stars.

Some of my fondest baseball memories are of those post-season games. It was a chance for us to play against and measure ourselves against a few of our heroes. Facing guys like Elston Howard, Monte Irvin, Gene Baker, Willie Mays, Hank Aaron, Lew Burdette, and Warren Spahn also helped our confidence. Many of us discovered that we had the ability to play at their level if given an opportunity.

They usually won, but we didn't lay down for them, and some of the games were close.

When I first began making those exhibition tours, the major leagues had teams made up of black players and white players, and locations for the games had to be selected carefully. Some states—Mississippi and Louisiana are two that I remember—and some towns would not allow blacks and whites to play together.

One year, I had a chance to hit against Warren Spahn, who was well on his way to becoming a legend in the game. It was an experience I'll never forget. The game was in Muskogee, Oklahoma, his home state. As I walked to the on-deck circle, I watched him pitch to the batter ahead of me and tried to pick up his timing. I was about to find out that it would take more than a hit to beat this future Hall of Famer. I drove a single through the infield, took a lead off first base, and watched him stretch for his next pitch. Timing is important in base running. You have to be sure the pitcher has committed to the plate before you commit to the base path. "Come on, you can hit him," I yelled to the next batter.

I was sure Spahn was going home and . . . *swoosh* . . . he went to first and caught me leaning the wrong way. It was so clean it was comical. I went back to the dugout.

A few innings later, I went to the plate again, determined to get another hit and make it pay off. I nailed one into the outfield gap and reached second standing up. Okay, Spahn, we're even, I thought. He made a couple of moves to the plate, and just when I though he had forgotten about me . . . *swoosh* . . . he spun and picked me off again.

Nobody likes to lose, but there is something about baseball, about watching the great players work, that makes being had by them almost an honor.

But this year I didn't want to be had anymore. I took my knuckleball against the Willie Mays All-Stars, a team of black major leaguers who had won thirty-three postseason games the previous year. They started off this tour whipping us at every stop, too.

There was nothing I wanted more than to beat them. It almost happened in Albany, Georgia. I was pitching a close game, one I thought I would win. My knuckleball was giving them fits, and between innings a player named Al Smith came over to me and said, "I'll give you five dollars to throw me a fastball."

"You must be out of your mind," I said. I wanted that game badly and was close to having it. Close, but . . . Going into the ninth inning, the score was 1–0. One or two bad pitches and it was over. They beat me 2–1 and I cried like a baby.

Mays and Hank Aaron were the big bats for the major leaguers that year. They won sixteen straight and it was beginning to look like this year would be another clean sweep.

Four or five days after my outing in Albany, we were in

Victoria, Texas, and I was pitching in relief. Ollie Brantley, who was still playing in the Iowa State League, went five innings and I pitched the last four. Mays had injured his shoulder and had to sit out that game, but still we had to throw against hitters such as Aaron, Al Smith, and Gene Baker.

This is how the Associated Press reported that game on October 30, 1956:

After 16 consecutive reversals, the Negro Minor League All-Stars caught up with the Major Leagues here Tuesday night by winning a 4–2 baseball game.

Home runs by first baseman Bob Boyd and Lonnie Harris supplied the margin of difference in the contest that pleased a crowd, which numbered 940 cash customers.

All of the profits will be turned over to the Little League Baseball fund.

The Minor Leaguers hopped away to a three-run lead in the first inning on a pass, single, sacrifice fly, and the circuit clout by Boyd, who managed the Minor Leaguers. Boyd plays for Baltimore and in 1955 was a star with Houston.

Ollie Brantley, a tall right hander of the Waterloo, Iowa, team in the Three-I league, retired nine straight Major Leaguers with a smoking fast ball. He gave up a pair of hits and two runs in the fourth, two more base hits in the fifth and then retired.

Charley Pride of the Memphis Red Sox, mixed up offerings well the last four innings of shutout ball.

A scout for the Dodgers began circling around and I imagined that before spring training time I would be bound for Brooklyn.

CHAPTER EIGHT

Greetings from Uncle Sam

November brought greetings from the Selective Service System with instructions to report to Fort Chaffee, Arkansas, for basic training with the U.S. Army. It was the second blow that year to my baseball aspirations.

Cracking my arm seemed like a minor setback, considering how I closed out the season. Coming back from a couple of years in the army would not be so easy. But the draft notice was a boon to my love life and may also have been the prologue to my professional singing career.

Forced to be away from Rozene for a few weeks helped me decided that my feelings for her were not so frightful after all. Every evening after drills, I raced across the parade ground to the telephone and fed the coin slot, a practice that depleted my meager funds long before the first army paycheck was due. Before reporting to Chaffee, I had given everything I had earned on the All-Star tour to my father, except for one dollar, which I took to camp with me.

Singing in the barracks at night was something I had been doing since I arrived for basic training. It was just a way to pass time while shining boots or polishing brass. One of my buddies got the idea to pass a hat and collect for the entertainment. It was mainly a lark but some of the guys tossed in a penny or nickel and I ended up with enough for a phone call. Singing and passing the hat became a ritual, and anytime we collected enough for a phone call I considered the concert a success.

One night I called and the landlady answered.

"She isn't here," she said.

My first thought was, Oh? Who's she with? I felt testy all of a sudden and that bothered me.

Sitting alone in the barracks later, I told myself, *If you're going to be acting like this all the time, you might as well be married. You won't have to worry about who she's with or if she's going out.* A couple of days later I asked her to marry me.

A month into basic training we were given passes to spend Christmas at home. I took a bus to Memphis, saw Rozene, and headed south to Sledge. She went to her parents' home in Oxford, Mississippi.

"I'm going to get married," I told my dad and my brothers and sisters.

"No you're not," Daddy said. "You got no business getting married."

For once, my brothers and sisters took his side, agreeing with his reasoning that the marriage would fail, what with me being so far away from a lonely, bored wife. They had heard stories of soldiers—absentee husbands—and two-timing wives. I wasn't swayed. They didn't know Rozene, and if they did, I told them, they would have had no such thoughts about her. The argument went on for a couple of days. On December 28, Daddy's birthday, it came to a head.

"You get married and go in the army and these girls start going out with everybody and doing anything they want to do . . . ," he said, trying once again to dissuade me.

"I want to go over and see her, anyway," I said. "You going to take me over there?"

"No, I'm not going to take you."

"Well, I'm going to walk."

When he saw that I meant to go, he gave in. "Okay, I'll take you." We got in his pickup and drove to Oxford.

Rozene's parents didn't object to the marriage. They had raised their daughters to think for themselves and trusted them to make their own decisions.

Rozene, Hortense, and I drove up to Hernando, a small town just below the Tennessee state line that was a popular venue for weddings. State laws in Mississippi made it easier to get married there than in Tennessee, where a blood test and waiting period were required. Therefore, the justices of the peace in Hernando were visited by a stream of young couples from the North, as well as from northern Mississippi.

Rozene had a new dress and I was in full army uniform. With Hortense as our only witness, we were married in a short civil ceremony. There was not much of a honeymoon. I had only five dollars in my pocket and, besides, I had to be back at Fort Chaffee in a couple of days.

Basic training wasn't nearly as bad as I expected. One of our sergeants, a guy named McKay, was a hard-looking character with deep-set, icy blue eyes and a voice guaranteed to get your attention. But he also had such a droll manner that I sometimes felt like I was taking part in a comedy skit instead of combat school.

We first met him when we got to the field for bayonet training. He strutted to a platform at the front of the formation and said, "Good morning, men."

"Good morning, sergeant," we said in unison.

"Goddammit, I don't want you to say it. I want you to growl and sound off."

"Good morning, sergeant," we growled in unison.

"I'm Sergeant McKay of the bayonet weapons committee and I'm going to give you your first three hours of bayonet training this morning. We're going to do it by the numbers. When I'm through with you, you're going to be able to execute all three maneuvers at one time. When my demonstrator comes out here, I want you to watch him closely. When he puts that bayonet on that weapon, he's going to tap it on the bottom to make sure it is securely attached. *Demonstrator, post!*"

The demonstrator ran to the front, attached the bayonet, and tapped it on the bottom. Then another guy ran out and the demonstrator began jabbing at him with the bayonet— left, right, into the ground—missing him by inches. We all looked at each other. I was thinking, Who the hell am I going to let jab at me like that?

Now it was our turn. The sergeant was on the platform and we were in formation in front of him. We had to hold our bayonet in one hand, our M1 rifle in the other, and our arms extended to the sides. Those rifles weigh about fourteen pounds and my arms were burning.

"You might wonder why I haven't said, 'Arms down.' There's a trooper in the back who's got his on the ground. He probably thinks I can't see him. Until he gets his up, you're going to have to hold them right there."

About two hundred voices yelled, "Get it up back there."

Soon McKay said, "Arms down." Mine felt like lead.

McKay instructed us to attach bayonets and emphasized why it had to be done with care.

"This ten inches of cold steel is made for one purpose and one purpose only, and that is to kill," he said. "If you don't make sure it is securely fastened to the weapon, I'll tell you what will happen. While you are executing your maneuvers, it is going to fly off and about three inches is going to go up your buddy's ass. That will piss him off. He's going to turn around and give you the whole ten."

We paired off and went through the drill—thrust, recover, hold. High four, twirl, thrust. Long thrust, hold. The bayonets would pass within a few inches of our necks and faces.

After an eternity, give or take a few minutes, he blew his whistle. "Okay, men, I want to see who wants a break," he said.

"Yeah," all two hundred of us replied.

He put us through the routine again before calling a break.

"Now I want to see who's tired," he said.

Most hands went up.

"That's what I thought. Ninety-five percent of you. What are you going to do when you get out there and face that ol' enemy? Say, 'Wait a minute, I'm going to take a smoke break and then I kill your bad ass?' He ain't going to wait for you to rest.

"Get in close," he said, "so close you'll be in your buddy's ass pocket. When I say, *'Ready seats,'* I want to see you all sit at once. *Ready seats!"*

We slouched to the ground.

"Get up, you didn't all sit at once. When I say, *'Ready seats,'* I want to see helmets spinning in midair. *Ready seats."*

We dropped like pool balls hitting a pocket.

"Take ten, expect five, and get three," he said.

I was mesmerized by the guy. He had probably gone through that routine hundreds of times, but he could still do it in a way that kept your interest and made you almost enjoy it. I think he taught me something besides how to use a bayonet, and it was this: If you have a job, a certain thing to do, and you let it become a chore, it will become a chore. You might as well accept the challenge and make the job as much fun as possible.

The only sour experience I remember from basic training was the week we spent on bivouac. It was hard duty—getting through infiltration and obstacle courses, crawling in the mud with live bullets flying a few feet above, sleeping in cold tents, sharing our chow with every insect in Arkansas.

The officers and NCOs arranged a little contest. The unit that could get through bivouac with the fewest trainees getting sick would be the first to leave the bivouac area and get extra time off.

We had one kid who came down with a bad sore throat, but we wouldn't let him report to the infirmary. We offered to rub his throat, do anything, to keep our record clean. "Just a few more days, man," we pleaded. "Gargle with salt water." We knew three other units had sent at least two guys to sick bay and we had a good chance of winning.

He toughed it out, but for reasons I never understood, the prize went to another unit, one that had sent the most— six—to sick bay. They left bivouac early and went on furlough while we scrubbed pots and pans. They walked right past us, laughing at us on their way out. We all felt dumb, making our sick buddy stay on the job and getting KP as our reward. It was as though we were being punished for trying to be the best. Times like that make you understand why nobody ever said life is fair.

From our wedding day until early in March, Rozene and I didn't see each other. Late in February, having completed basic training, I was sent to quartermaster school in Fort Carson, just outside Colorado Springs. We talked by phone, wrote letters, and waited to see what kind of living arrangement would be possible.

We couldn't afford our own apartment off base so we eventually made arrangements to share an apartment in Denver with my sister and her husband. They both worked, and with Rozene there they could have a live-in baby-sitter. It would be a long commute for me—seventy miles each way—but worth it to be able to be with my wife. She came to Colorado in March. Our half of the apartment rent was forty dollars a month, which was manageable on the one hundred and forty dollars a month we were getting from the army.

Meanwhile, my tenure as a quartermaster truck-driving

trainee got off to a rocky start. I had only been at Fort Carson a couple of days when I was accused of shooting dice in the barracks. I had rolled the bones a few times in my day and found it an enjoyable pastime, but that day I was innocent. I walked into the barracks and there was one guy standing by his locker. On the floor was a pair of dice. I bent over, picked them up and started to ask who they belonged to, but before I could do anything, Sergeant Carter walked in, saw what was in my hand, and took down my name.

Carter was black, but it seemed like he was harder on the black soldiers than the white ones.

At roll call the next morning, my name was called, along with those of four other guys, and we were told to report to the company commander.

"PFC Pride reporting as ordered," I said, as crisply as possible.

"At ease, Pride. I hear you've been gambling." He was a little skinny guy named Bray, from Virginia—a lieutenant bucking for captain.

"No sir."

"Sergeant Carter caught you with the dice."

"I did pick some dice up off the floor," I said, explaining what had occurred.

"Well, since you just got into this company and this is your first time . . ."

He's going to let me go, I thought. He's going to give the new kid a break.

". . . I'm only going to give you an Article Fifteen. You're confined to the base for fourteen days with two hours extra duty each day."

Every night for two weeks, right after dinner, I reported to the duty officer for my list of chores. I buffed floors, scrubbed kitchens, fed furnaces, did every dirty job that needed to be done and still had to shine my shoes and brass for the next morning's inspection.

But worse than that, I was a marked man. Anytime a pair of dice turned up, Ol' Charley was a prime suspect.

A few weeks later, we moved to new barracks and some of us were shooting craps on a blanket in the latrine. I had already left the game and was getting cleaned up. Sergeant Bersett, who was white, walked in and everybody else got busy shaving or showering, but they left the evidence on the floor—the blanket with a dollar bill and the dice on it.

I was all the way across the room and there were twenty or thirty people in the latrine, but the sergeant took down the names of a few known offenders.

"Corporal Blue. PFC Pervis. PFC Penroy. PFC Pride," the platoon sergeant called out the next morning. "Report to the company commander."

When I got to company headquarters, Sergeant Bersett was in Lieutenant Bray's office. I paused outside the door and eavesdropped on their conversation.

"Sergeant, you said you saw a blanket and some money and some dice. You should have taken the dice, or some kind of evidence." Lieutenant Bray was a lawyer, and from the way he was talking I realized he had nothing on us. He was going to try to bluff a confession from one of us.

"Well, Private Pride," Lieutenant Bray said, "I got you gambling again."

"Sir, I wasn't gambling the first time you gave me fourteen days," I said. I didn't deny I had been gambling the second time, I just didn't admit it.

"The sergeant said he came in and saw a blanket, a dollar, and some dice on the floor. What was going on in there?"

"I was shaving."

"What did you see?"

"I saw other people shaving, others were showering, some were shitting."

His face tensed with anger. We were confined to the base

and for the next five days he called us in regularly, trying to get someone to plead guilty and incriminate the others.

Corporal Blue grew edgier as the time passed. "Man, I think I'm going to have to give in," he said at one point. "I got two stripes and I don't want to lose them."

"I got one and I don't want to lose it, either," I told him. "I got a baby coming, too. Just stick together. We didn't see nothin'. We didn't hear nothin'."

Eventually, Lieutenant Bray dropped his inquisition, but I never felt like I got away with anything. I had paid for gambling I didn't do, so I figured he owed me one.

There was another sergeant who took a quick dislike to me but my problems with him were resolved in an eerie way.

At the garage where we worked on our trucks, there was an oil-change pit that got a lot of use and the grease and gunk had to be scraped out daily. My name kept turning up on the pit-cleaning detail more than it should have.

One morning when I drew that duty for the third day in a row, I was in the pit scraping grease and not in a very good mood. The sergeant stood over me, giving me the usual hard time.

"Let me tell you something," I said, unable to restrain myself, "you're the kind of sergeant that the enemy didn't do away with during the war. You're the kind who was done away with by your own men. What you are doing to me is not right. It's not fair."

A strange glaze crossed over his eyes. I hadn't said what I did to be threatening. I was just angry and frustrated. But his eyes had a faraway look, as if he were having a flashback, remembering something he had seen or something that had happened to him.

"I don't care about no court martial—" I started to say, but broke off in mid-sentence. He seemed far away in thought, no longer hearing my voice. He turned and walked away and I never saw him again. I learned later he had requested a transfer out of the company.

That spring, after quartermaster duty, our company assembled in formation to receive our permanent assignments. Each soldier's name was called, followed by the location of his next duty station. Germany. Korea. The Persian Gulf. The company commander got through the P's and my name wasn't called.

The brass had gone through the personnel records and learned that I had played professional baseball before I was drafted. That was enough to rate me a permanent assignment to Special Services at Fort Carson and it was there that I began to see potential in the military. Special Services was for soldiers with particular talents other than soldiering that the post commander wanted to exploit for one reason or another.

Fort Carson had a baseball team and it wasn't just some weekend recreation squad. The competition among the various army posts was serious enough that players were given special considerations, such as getting out of regular duties for practices and games.

Once on the team, the drudgery of military duty was pretty much behind me. Our special situation was resented by some of the other soldiers, especially the NCOs who thought baseball was a distraction from more essential activities. They called us "jocks" in a sneering tone and accused us of having a soft ride.

That year Fort Carson went to Fort Knox, Kentucky, for a tournament to decide the All-Army Sports Championship. We won four straight games, beating Fort Knox for the championship. One of the players on the Fort Knox team was Bill White, who is now president of the National League.

*　*　*

Our first son, Kraig, was born while we were in Colorado, and I felt pressure to start planning our lives after the military. I got word before the end of 1957 that I would not have to serve my full two years. There was no war on and the army was scaling back. Some officers who had received battlefield commissions were busted back to NCOs.

Many of us were given tests to determine whether Uncle Sam would keep us. I flunked and was given one hundred dollars in mustering-out pay and sent back to civilian life.

After fourteen months of military service, I had a wife, a child, half an apartment, no car, and no job.

CHAPTER NINE

North to Montana

My plan turned out to be more complicated than I imagined. Legally, I was still under contract to the Red Sox, but I didn't want to go back to Memphis. Rozene and I liked Colorado and we had a young child, so staying put would simplify things for us. Bob Housin, who was running the Denver Bears, had indicated he could use me, but not if he had to buy my contract from the Red Sox.

"I'm going to try to get this release," I told Rozene, "but I'm going to have to find a job in the meantime. We gotta have a car."

She pulled out a big wad of money and my eyes kind of popped open. "Where did you get this?" I asked.

"I've been saving it," she said. From the time we arrived in Colorado, she had been baby-sitting my sister's kids and my brother-in-law's sister's kids, fixing hair for her friends, and putting the money aside.

"From now on," I said, "you're handling all the money."

I wrote to the Red Sox owner, Dr. W. S. Martin, and explained my situation, which was much different from the one I had been in in Mississippi. I had a son now, I told him, and a chance to play with the Bears for more money than the Red Sox would pay me. Could we please work something out? I wanted a new contract with more money or a release.

I got no reply, which didn't really surprise me. After the major leagues were integrated and began skimming off the top *colored* talent, the Negro American League went into decline. The owners learned to play contract hardball. To keep their best players—the ones who drew the crowds— they signed them to long-term contracts and refused to sell them except at outrageous prices. The Sox had one pitcher who was being seriously wooed by a major league team but couldn't go because Martin demanded $15,000 for his contract. That was more than a lot of veteran major league players were making.

Curt Flood had not yet challenged this system with his free-agency lawsuit and therefore the players had little leverage in dealing with the owners, who literally could own you for life. If you wanted to play ball, you went along with that form of legal slavery.

Time was getting short. My discharge came through in February. The baseball season would start on the first of April and positions would already be filled. I wrote to Martin again, this time sending the letter by certified mail so he could not deny having received it. All I got back was a note acknowledging receipt of my letter—nothing about my contract.

I wrote to Happy Chandler, the commissioner of baseball. He replied with a letter certifying that since I had not received a response from the Red Sox owner before April 1, I was free to sign with anyone I chose.

It was too late. The Bears had their quota of *colored* players. They tried to help me find a job in Bellingham, Washington; Saskatoon, Saskatchewan—*everywhere*—but there were no more slots for colored players.

So I was a free agent, free of the Red Sox, and had no place to go but back to the Red Sox. With the money Rozene had saved and what I had been earning on my job loading shingles, we bought a 1951 Chevrolet and drove to Memphis. I would have to persuade W. S. Martin to take me back.

We arrived in Memphis just in time for his funeral.

As befitted a man of his wealth and importance, Martin's last rites were elaborate and well attended. When the prayers and eulogies were done, I walked outside the chapel while the pallbearers brought the casket out and approached the hearse that would carry it to the cemetery.

Smoke suddenly began pouring from under the hood of the vehicle. The engine was on fire. The pallbearers retreated with Martin's body.

"Gee," I muttered, to no one in particular. "Can't even get him buried."

It was just an offhand comment and no disrespect was intended, but Martin's brother, J. B., who was also a wealthy and powerful businessman, happened to be standing next to me. He spun around and looked like he would attack. "I ought to kill you . . ." he said.

Way to go, Charley, I thought. Tomorrow or the next day you get to sit down with this guy and negotiate a new contract. J. B. Martin was in no mood then to accept my sincere apologies, but I offered them anyway and hoped that by the time we met again he would be in a more agreeable mood.

Fortunately, he was. My record with the team had been good enough to give me a little bargaining power and Martin even accepted one condition that I was firm about: If a better offer came along, I would be free to negotiate for myself and could buy out my contract with the Red Sox. It could be an expensive proposition if he set a high price, but it kept me from being indentured to him.

We rented an apartment and Rozene went back to work

at Mrs. Taylor's Beauty Shop. Later she took a job in an office that was shared by two doctors. It was mostly cleaning work, but it turned out to be a great opportunity for her. She became friends with a woman who worked there as a lab technician. In her spare time she showed Rozene how the lab equipment worked and taught her how to take and read X rays. In time she became a proficient lab technician.

That season with the Red Sox went pretty well—well enough to get me into the East–West All-Star Game and good enough, I thought, to demand more money the next year. One hundred a month was not enough for a man with a wife and child, but J. B. Martin guarded his bankbook like a bulldog.

Unable to wrangle a raise out of him, I elected to set out the next season, even though doing so would probably mean I would never play for the Red Sox again. I spent most of the year working for Nickey Brothers Lumber Company in Binghampton.

Once in a while I read the *Sporting News*.

Pride Will
Try Out
With Jacks

Charley Pride, 22-year-old right handed pitcher and outfielder, who hails from Memphis, Tenn., arrived in Missoula late Friday evening for a tryout with the Missoula Timberjacks, [General Manager Nick] Mariana reported.

"Pride made the long trip from Memphis at his own expense and if he makes the club will be reimbursed," Mariana stated. "I just couldn't turn this boy down or discourage him from coming all the way out here because he was so sincere in his correspondence. I felt

the least we could do was give him a chance to make the club. We like players with gumption and I hope he makes good."

Pride starred with the Memphis Red Sox of the Negro American League as a pitcher and also as a hitter. He is a switch hitter and was outstanding in the league.

That's the way the *Missoula Sentinel* announced my arrival in Montana in the spring of 1960. I don't think I had ever heard of Missoula until I saw an advertisement in the *Sporting News* a few months earlier. The Timberjacks of the Pioneer League were looking for ballplayers. Write Nick Mariana, general manager, the ad said. So I did and he wrote back: "Get in as good a shape as you can," he said. "If we sign you, we will reimburse you."

The Timberjacks and the other Pioneer League teams were not major league farm clubs, but they had loose working agreements with the majors. The Timberjacks got financial support from the Cincinnati Reds, and in return the Reds had first shot at any Timberjack players they wanted.

We were dead broke and Rozene was probably already fed up with my baseball schemes. She never said anything to discourage me, but from the day she learned I had cracked my arm she had had doubts about my future in the game. She had been around baseball enough to understand that an injury like that was usually fatal to a pitching career. Still, she didn't try to hold me back. We had that kind of relationship from the beginning. Neither one tried to dominate the other or make decisions for the other.

It had to be a test of her patience and good nature, though, when I told her I was going to hock the furniture to pay for a trip to Montana. I mortgaged the whole houseful for four hundred dollars, gave her half, bought a train ticket with the rest, and hit the road.

Missoula is up in the Bitterroot Range of the Rocky Mountains, one of the most beautiful places I had ever seen. Montana was a far cry from the South. It had the kind of free, frontier spirit that made anything seem possible and I fell in love with the state immediately.

"I think this is a place where we can make something for ourselves," I wrote to Rozene.

The Timberjacks took off on a road trip to Billings, Pocatello, and Idaho Falls a few days after I joined them. I got two hits in three at bats on that trip but when we got back to Missoula, Rocky Tedesco, the manager, took me aside and said, "We like the way you run . . . the way you hit. You got two for three . . . drove in two runs. That's .750 all day, Charley. But I'm going to have to let you go."

That should been the end of baseball for me, but something in my head or my heart wouldn't let me hang it up, wouldn't let me believe that I could not make it to the major leagues.

"What do I do now?" I asked myself. I was twenty-three years old, out of money, out of prospects, and seventeen hundred miles from my wife and son and mortgaged furniture.

Nick Mariana told me about the Montana State League, which was made up of amateur teams sponsored by the various smelting companies in places like Helena, Anaconda, Butte, and Billings.

"If you want to work in a smelter," Nick said, "I can probably place you on one of those teams."

My options were not exactly abundant. I could make nearly one hundred dollars a week *and* keep playing ball. "Thanks," I told Nick. "I'd like that."

He called someone he knew in Helena and I had a job with the American Smelting & Refining Co. and a position on the company baseball team, the East Helena Smelterites.

"What are we going to do with the furniture?" Rozene asked when I called to tell her to come to Helena. "It's mortgaged."

"Put it in storage," I said. "We'll worry about it later."

* * *

We did begin to make something for ourselves in Montana. With what she had learned from her co-worker and doctor employers in Memphis, Rozene was able to get a job as a technician in one of the largest clinics in Helena. She was hired by the doctor who gave me the medical examination for my job at the smelter— Dr. Amos Little, who had been a physician for the Olympic ski team.

In that first spring and summer I worked days at the smelter and played baseball at night. We had a comfortable lifestyle, better than we had ever had, and we made a lot of friends.

There were very few black people in Montana but we never felt out of place, although at times I found myself trying to explain to people there what the South was like. Montana wasn't just geographically far removed from the South, but the thinking was pretty isolated, too. When the sit-ins and boycotts and protest marches began in the South, guys I worked with would ask things like, "What's going on with y'all down there?"

There it was again, the same thing I had grown up with in the segregated South, the same racial division in everyone's mind. Us and them. Y'all and us. There was no physical segregation in Helena, but the mental partitions were un-avoidable. I won a five-dollar bet, which I never collected, from a guy who was further out of touch than most. We were talking about the Montgomery bus boycotts and how a black woman named Rosa Parks had refused to give up her seat to a white man and move to the back of the bus.

"How would you like to pay the same amount of money as the next person and be told you could only sit in certain seats?" I asked him. "Have you ever had that experience? Well, a woman got tired of being told to move. Somebody had to do it and she just happened to be the one."

He didn't seem to be getting it.

"I've got a son," I said, "and he may be president someday . . ."

"Charley," he interrupted, "I've met your son and he's a fine boy, but he won't ever be able to be president."

"Why not?"

"Well, first you have to be a natural-born citizen . . . an American."

"That's correct."

"And . . . uh . . . you have to be at least thirty-five."

"Correct."

"And you have to be white."

"Wrong," I said.

"No, you have to be white." He wasn't speaking in anger or hostility. That simply was what he believed. He had been told that being white was a prerequisite to being president and it was embedded in his mind.

Having a fondness for gambling, I proposed a wager. "Any amount you want. Your whole paycheck, if you want," I said. We settled on five dollars. He asked me to give him a few days to find the proof.

Three or four days later, I asked him about it.

"I need more time," he said. Another week passed, and then a month and I asked him again. He admitted he had been unable to find proof, but said, "Well, I think you are wrong."

He still owes me five dollars, and he probably still thinks I was wrong.

Coal came into the smelter on railcars. It was dumped into a grinder and crushed and carried into a large bin that fed into the furnace. My first job was emptying the coal into the crusher. Black dust covered everything—you had to wear goggles to keep it out of your eyes, and you went home at night with the stuff caked on your clothes and skin.

We were getting slag from other smelters that had already removed copper or nickel or other elements from the ore and we extracted zinc from what was left. The furnaces had to heat the slag pots up to 2,400 degrees Farenheit. Someone had to work at the mouth of the furnace, using sharp steel bars to stir the chunks of coal and keep them moving.

It was not unheard of for workers to slip and fall into the fire. That happened to Oscar Jones, a construction contractor who went to work in the smelter when his business got slow. I didn't see it happen but was told that Oscar was jabbing and poking around the mouth of the furnace and, pulled off balance by the weight of the steel bar, tumbled right into the fire.

After everything of value had been squeezed from the slag and the pot skimmed, it was moved by rail and dumped on a hill a short distance from the main building. Those were big pots, twelve or fifteen feet in diameter, and heavy. At the dump site one night, someone had apparently tried to pour the slag out too fast and it sloshed, which caused the wheels of the carrier to lift up and come back down off track.

We were summoned to get it back on the rails.

The temperature, with the wind-chill factor, was 74 below and we probably all would have frozen, but the heat from the pot kept our faces and hands warm while we worked it back onto the track. Afterward, the sixty- or seventy-yard walk back to the building was brutal. The wind blew directly into our faces, and when we reached the shed, I touched my nose and thought it was going to break off of my face.

Respect for nature was one of the first things I learned in Montana.

For the most part, though, I didn't mind the smelting job. In fact, I was grateful for it. I had done dirty, dangerous work before for a lot less money. Rozene and I not only paid off the four-hundred-dollar loan against the furniture two months early, but we were able to save a little, too.

During baseball season, the players' work schedules were kept flexible to accommodate games and practices. Those amateur teams were important to the companies that sponsored them. We drew big crowds and got the kind of local press coverage that professional teams got in their cities. While I played for them, the East Helena Smelterites won the Montana State League championship four times.

Maybe if I had bombed in that league, I would have put aside my baseball fantasies then and there. But in my first season, I hit .444 and carefully clipped all the newspaper articles for the portfolio I would present to the major leagues. I had this one from the *Helena Independent Record*:

EAST HELENA BEATS SOUTH SIDE TO COP CHAMPIONSHIP

The East Helena Smelterites brought the Copper League Championship home to Smelterite Park Monday night when they beat the South Side 4–2 in a game in which the script was straight out of Hollywood.

All the action in the game took place in the sixth inning and by the time the game was over the huge crowd had more than their money's worth.

After a scoreless pitching duel of five full innings between East Helena's Ken Leland and South Side's Ray McLaughlin the tension had mounted to the breaking point.

Then in the top of the sixth, a fireworks display opened up that would make the eruption of Vesuvius look like an everyday occurrence.

The South Side started things with two gone when Dan Sullivan slashed an outfield single. John Dunstan, one of the top hitters in the loop, then smashed a Leland offering over the right field barrier and the Mining City crew enjoyed a 2–0 lead.

But the heroics were just beginning.

Earl Fred led off the bottom of the sixth for East Helena with a walk and Charley Pride, a man with an inborn feeling of the dramatic, pasted McLaughlin's second pitch over the center field wall. The horsehide was still going up when it went out of sight. This tied the game.

Then Dick Muffick got aboard with a single and after Bud Sautter had popped out another flannel clothed hero arrived on the scene in the person of young Neal Dougherty. Dougherty closed the door on McLaughlin when he smashed a home run over the center field fence to give East Helena its final total.

And this one from the *Daily Missoulian*:

EAST HELENA ENDS DROUGHT

Charley Pride drove in three runs with four singles and a home run in firing the East Helena Smelterites to an 11–3 triumph, their first in the young 1961 Montana State League season, over the league-leading Missoula Highlanders in Campbell Park Sunday night.

Pride slapped his circuit clout over the right field fence with no one on base in the fifth inning. But doing more damage for East Helena were Pride's line-shot singles just over the infielders' heads. In addition to driving in three runs, he also scored three times.

The clippings piled up fast that season and my hopes grew with them.

CHAPTER TEN

Singing for Tips

Smelterite Park in East Helena was not in a class with minor league parks, but it was decent—the infield was well tended and the outfield was level—and had a few amenities, including one that turned out to be important to me: a public address system.

Before games, I used to sing the national anthem over the PA and, if time permitted, tacked on a country tune or two. I received no extra pay for the entertainment, so my amateur status was unquestioned. But it was a good way to advertise that I could carry a tune. After games, the team usually went to a bar in East Helena to celebrate and unwind with a beer and a bull session. A lot of those joints had small bandstands or an area set aside for live entertainment. If there was an idle guitar around, my teammates would encourage me to pick and sing a little. Before long they were passing a hat among the patrons and it wasn't unusual to collect several dollars in tips.

One night I got a call from a guy who identified himself as a union secretary.

"I understand you've been singing in bars," he said.

"That's right," I said.

"Are you a member of the union?"

"Yes, I'm a member of the AFL-CIO," I said.

"No, I mean the musicians union."

Musicians Union? I had never heard of such an organization.

"No, why?" I said.

"You have to join if you're going to sing professionally," he said.

My first thought was that somebody was trying to keep the *colored* guy in his place, scare him with some phony union talk.

"How much does it cost?" I asked him.

"The initiation fee is forty dollars and the annual dues are twenty," he said.

"Forty dollars? I don't have forty dollars. I don't think I'll join," I told him.

"Then you can't sing," he insisted.

Later, I checked around and confirmed that there actually was a musicians union. Because I was only singing for tips, it didn't make sense to join, not at those dues, but I couldn't defy a union either. I continued to sing in bars after ball games but we stopped passing the hat. I was an unpaid amateur again and therefore outside the union's jurisdiction.

I was working the 3:00-to-11:00 P.M. shift at the smelter when my foreman told me that the owner of a place called the White Mill Bar in Helena had heard about me from my landlady and wanted to talk to me about a singing job.

"He asked me if I would let you off on Thursday night so he could give you a tryout," the foreman said. "I told him I would."

The next day I called the White Mill and made the arrangements. I didn't even have a guitar, microphone, or amplifier. I rented everything I needed from a music store.

On Thursday night I walked into the White Mill about

seven o'clock and the place was already crowded. As was usually the case with Montana's saloons, the White Mill was noisy, boisterous, blue collar, all white, and country to the core.

I could feel the stares and hear the noise level shift when I walked across the room, set up my equipment in a corner, and began tuning the guitar. But I felt then, and still do, that the undertone was one of curiosity about how or what I might sing rather than about my color. It was unlikely that anyone there had ever heard a black person sing country music and they probably figured they were in for a night of rhythm and blues.

"I'm a Hank Williams fan," I said, when the guitar was tuned and ready, "and I'd like to do one of his songs for you. Hope you enjoy it."

That brought polite applause, but when I finished, the crowd really warmed up. They weren't just polite, they were downright enthusiastic. In a lot of saloons the music—even live music—is just a backdrop to the talking and arguing and pool shooting that's going on. Singing at the White Mill Bar turned out to be more like performing in a concert. People turned their chairs toward my corner. Several came over with requests, and when I sang them, they actually paid attention.

I performed there free a few times and things sort of snowballed after that. The owner of the Main Tavern downtown called.

"I'll give you twenty dollars a night to sing at my place two nights a week," he said.

Twenty dollars was as much money as I made on a full shift at the smelter. I decided to join the musicians union after all. I also bought a guitar, amplifier, and microphone.

Word about the black country singer in Helena spread around fairly quickly and Johnny Walker, who owned the Corner Bar in Anaconda, bid the price of my services up to forty dollars a night. Anaconda was eighty miles from Helena but it only cost five dollars for gas to make the round trip. I took the job and kept it for two and a half years.

When I worked the day shift, I would leave the smelter at three, shower, eat dinner, and head south through the mountains in my old 1954 Ford. I'd play until 2:00 A.M., make the eighty-mile drive back to Helena, sleep two hours, and punch in at the smelter again.

I think I put on a good one-man show and the crowds always accepted me. I never heard a racial slur whispered, and if anyone ever walked out when I walked in, I was unaware of it. But those audiences may have been more mindful than I of the novelty of a black country singer. Everyone seemed to take for granted that country music was a Caucasian business.

It always had been and I wasn't particularly concerned about it. I wanted to play ball.

Major league baseball wasn't going to come to me, so I would have to go to it. During the off-season, I put together newspaper clippings from my Red Sox and Smelterite exploits and mailed them, with a letter of introduction, to several major league teams. The response I got from the Chicago Cubs was fairly typical:

Dear Charley,
This is in reply to your recent letter and, having checked with our scout, Buck O'Neil, who scouts all of the colored ball players, we would not be interested in your services. With the player talent that we presently have, we do not feel that you could make any of our clubs. Therefore, it would be senseless to send you a contract and pay your expenses to spring training.
Under the circumstances, even if you had the money

Pride at age 11

Pride with sons Kraig and Dion,
Easter 1965

Pride *(left)* with Ernie Banks, 1955

Charley and Rozene with their first
son, Kraig, age one

ERNEST C. WITHERS

First appearance on Grand Ole
Opry, introduced by Ernest Tubb,
1967

WALDEN S. FABRY

Charley and Rozene, Montana, 1968

J. E. HARVEY

Pride performing for servicemen at NCO club in Germany on one of his many USO tours

First complete traveling band in 1969: *(left to right)* Preston Buchanan, Tommy Williams, Charley, Gene O'Neal, Rudy Gray

BILL BEACH

Pride performing at Geneva Ballroom, Waco, Texas, 1969

Performing in 1970. At left is
Gene O'Neal, first musician
Pride ever hired. At right is
Tommy Williams, member
of the original band.

With John Wayne, who flew to
Vegas to see Pride's show at the
Hilton International

Charley and first
manager, Jack
Johnson, 1971

In Manchester, England, during
one of his early tours of Europe

J. E. HARVEY

Charley and Rozene celebrate first
gold album with a kiss.

Performing at Guantanamo Bay,
Cuba, during Bob Hope's
Christmas tour in 1972

Performing at Panther Hall in
Fort Worth

Appearing on *Hee Haw* with *(left to right, front row)* Tom T. Hall, Loretta Lynn, and George Lindsey

Receiving CMA award in 1973 from Dolly Parton and Porter Wagoner

BILL GOODMAN

At celebrity golf tournament with Bob Hope and Houston Oilers' football coach Bum Phillips

Receiving first New Zealand gold record from Morrie
Smith, head of RCA in New Zealand

With golfer Lee Trevino at celebrity tournament

After one of many concerts at
Houston's Astrodome. Pride was the
first artist to sell one million tickets
at the arena.

With Roy Acuff, backstage at the
Grand Ole Opry

With Earl Campbell of Houston Oiler
football fame

Reacting to missed putt at golf tournment,
Tucson, 1983. Playing partners, Craig
Stadler and Joe Garagiola look on.

yourself, we would not recommend you going to that expense after checking our reports.

Wishing you success, I am,

> *Sincerely yours,*
> *Gene Lawing*

Keeping those clipping had not been a complete waste of time. That year was the beginning of a period of expansion in major league baseball and that meant more jobs, especially for black players, because the quota system was loosening a little.

The National League was founded in 1876 and the American League in 1901. Each had eight teams at the beginning and remained at that level until 1961. The American League expanded first, adding the Los Angeles Angels and the Washington Senators, which later became the Texas Rangers.

Gene Autry, who owned the Angels, had made a lot of money as a singing cowboy actor and he invested it wisely in hotel chains, music publishing, and a chain of radio and television stations. One of his radio stations in southern California, KMPC, had tried to get the contract to broadcast the Los Angeles Dodger games and failed. So Autry teamed up with a guy named Bob Reynolds and went after and won the Los Angeles franchise in the American League expansion.

Since the new teams did not have established lineups, they were more receptive to free agents.

I sent my portfolio to Fred Haney, the general manager of the Angels, and got a reply from Bill Rigney, the manager. The Angels would begin spring training in Palm Springs, California, on March 1, and if I could be there, I would have a tryout.

No small risk was involved. Because I did not have enough accumulated vacation time, I would have to take a leave of absence from my job, and the Angels would not pay my travel expenses. The trip would make a big dent in our savings.

Rozene was as tolerant as usual. She wasn't confident that I would make the team, but she didn't tell me that. As usual, she accepted my decision, not wanting me to feel later that she had held me back or stood between me and something so important to me.

I caught a flight to Palm Springs. The *Los Angeles Examiner* noted my arrival at the end of a story announcing the Angels' first practice game:

> *The Angels signed another free agent, Charley Pride, a pitcher-outfielder who played for Memphis in the Negro American League. . . . Pride, 23, is a switch hitter.*

The *Los Angeles Times* also gave me passing mention:

> *Free agent Charley Pride, a pitcher-outfielder who played with the Memphis Red Sox of the Negro American League, suited up for a trial. . . .*

It was a short trial. My pitching arm was sore a lot during that camp, probably from trying too hard to impress Marv Grissom, the pitching coach. At the end of two weeks, Grissom took me aside and said, "Charley, you just don't have a major league pitching arm. We're going to have to let you go."

"I just tried too hard too early. Give me some more time," I said.

"Sorry, Charley."

I went looking for Gene Autry at his hotel. I found him sitting on the veranda eating a hamburger.

"Mr. Autry, don't let them cut me," I pleaded. "Just let me stay and I'll pay my own expenses."

He said, "I don't run the team, young man. Bill Rigney is the manager."

"But . . ."

"He has to make those decisions."

"But . . . somebody had to help you when you left Oklahoma and were riding Champion."

He explained again that it was not his decision to make. I left camp that same day.

Back in Montana, Ray T. Rocene, a sports columnist for The *Daily Missoulian*, wrote on March 17, 1961:

> *A Missoula Timberjack discard spent two weeks in the camp of the Los Angeles Angels of the American League ere he was dropped last Sunday. Yes, it was Charley Pride, who talked himself into a Jack job last spring. A happy, cheerful, pleasant Southern chap, a singer and musician as well, Pride lacked the skills to play in the Pioneer League and lasted quick.*
>
> *Mariana placed him with the East Helena Smelterites and there he was a hero of a team amassing an amazing independent record along with two other ex-Timberjacks. How acute the situation for ball players is now amply indicated by Pride making a considerable stay with Bill Rigney's Angels. Pride might do better if he found out just what he could do best in baseball, not trying all spots.*

I was such a "happy, cheerful, pleasant Southern chap" that I didn't let the sarcasm of that column—"lacked the skills . . . lasted quick . . . acute . . . situation"—discourage me. I was a happy, cheerful, pleasant Southern optimist. The next year, the National League would add two teams, and one way or another Charley Pride was going to talk himself into camp.

For the rest of that year, I settled back into my routine. I kept my job with the Anaconda Company in Helena, rejoined the Smelterites, and made the drive down to the Corner Bar two nights a week. Financially, we were doing well. With Rozene's job and my two, our income was getting close to

$10,000 a year. She became pregnant with our second child and we moved into a larger apartment.

Early in 1962, I was preparing for a run at one of the new National League teams when spring training opened. The choice was between the Houston Astros and the New York Mets and I chose the Mets. George Weiss, a well-respected baseball executive, had gone over from the New York Yankees as general manager and had brought Casey Stengel out of retirement to run the team. Anybody would have coveted a chance to play for Casey Stengel. If I could not get invited to the Mets camp, I would show up anyway.

Once again, fate scowled at me. At the smelter one night that winter, a slag truck ran over my ankle and broke it. While I hobbled back to work two or three weeks later, it not only prevented me from going to the Mets camp, but knocked me out of a big chunk of the Smelterite season.

It did not deter me from keeping my singing dates in Anaconda, though. Johnny Walker even used it for promotional purposes. He ran ads in the Anaconda newspaper that said, "CHARLEY PRIDE . . . *And His Broken Leg Will Be At The CORNER BAR . . . Saturday night . . . Come on Down And Watch The Fights.*" That was a reference to televised boxing, not the customers.

Rozene gave birth to our second son, Dion, that year, and more and more we began to think of Montana as our home. We were happy there. We talked about buying a house and looked at a few in our spare time. Within a few months, my ankle had healed well enough for me to rejoin the smelter team and we won the Copper League Championship for the third straight year.

We might have settled in Montana permanently had it not been for Tiny Stokes, a local disc jockey, and his friendship with a country singer named Webb Pierce, who was coming to Helena to do a show with Red Sovine. I was acquainted with Tiny as a result of my saloon singing but never imagined that he would be the one to start me on my way to Nashville.

CHAPTER ELEVEN

Singing for Foley and Sovine

The two celebrities coming to Helena were major draws, but my schedule was so full that I had not made plans to attend their show.

Tiny Stokes changed my mind.

"I've got it all set up for you to audition for Webb," Tiny told me over the telephone.

"Who?" I said, not sure I heard him correctly.

"Webb Pierce."

That's what I thought he had said. Audition for Webb Pierce!—one of the biggest stars in the business. Red Sovine, the patron saint of gear jammers, the man who had made truck-driving songs a mainstay of country music, would also be there. I could not have asked for a more important audience.

For a few days I was as restless as a bird dog in a duck blind. On the day of the show I called the hotel and the auditorium several times, trying to find out if Sovine and Pierce had arrived.

That afternoon something occurred to me. When singers came into town for a show, they usually went down to the radio station and spent some time on the air, talking with the local DJ and promoting the show.

I got in my old purple and white Dodge and drove to the station.

Sure enough, when I walked into the studio, they were just coming from behind the microphone. Only Webb Pierce wasn't there. Red Foley had taken his place, but that was just as good. Red Foley had been on top in country music throughout the 1940s and 1950s, and some of his songs had become classics. He was something of a patriarch, an elder statesman, if not a godfather, of the business. Tiny introduced me to him first.

"Red," he said, "this is Charley Pride. He's a country music singer."

I extended my hand and said, "Hello, Mr. Foley."

He looked at me warily and asked, "Is this something pertaining to civil rights?"

Before I could answer, Tiny spoke up. "No, no. This guy is for real," he said. "I want you to hear him. It's got nothing to do with civil rights. He sings locally here."

Foley said, "I see," shook my hand, and walked away.

"Tell you what," Tiny said. "Come to the show and I'll get them to listen to you during intermission. I'll give you a signal to come backstage."

That evening I put on a pair of casual trousers and a jacket, drove to the theater, and, like everyone else, paid my dollar and a half admission.

Tiny was the emcee. He came out holding a piece of paper. He said he had received a telegram informing him that Webb Pierce was unable to appear because of a back injury and that Red Foley would perform in his place.

I must have sat there an hour or more, holding my jacket, watching the show and waiting for the signal. What if doesn't come? What if there is no signal, I kept thinking. Foley had not seemed exactly overjoyed at our introduction. Well, I wasn't going to get dressed up and lay out a buck and a half for nothing. I got up and invited myself backstage.

I hung around waiting for the intermission. When it finally arrived, I introduced myself to the musicians and got each one to sign my program.

Then I picked up a guitar and started strumming it— *ching . . . ching . . . ching.* It sounded strange because it wasn't tuned for the way I play a guitar. Everyone was looking at one another, no doubt wondering who this character was. When I had it tuned for open bar chords, it sounded much better.

"Can I sing now?" I asked.

Nobody said anything so I sang "Heartaches by the Number," a song that had been a hit for Ray Price, and a Hank Williams standard, "Lovesick Blues."

The producer heard me and came a little closer. Foley and Sovine also were attentive.

When I finished, Foley looked at Sovine and said, "Man, that's different."

Sovine smiled at me and said, "I don't believe it. You ought to go to Nashville. I don't care what color you are."

The producer apparently liked my singing, too. "Would you like to be on the second half of the show?" he said.

"Just ask," I said.

"I just did," he said.

Near the end of the show, I was brought on stage. I don't recall how many people were in the auditorium that night, but it was easily the largest crowd I had ever appeared before. And it was the first time I had performed with a full band backing me up.

I was not at all nervous about singing to that audience. Many of those in the crowd had heard me sing around Helena and, besides, audiences had never intimidated me. As soon as I began singing in bars, I became hooked on crowds and the kind of energy you derive from performing and being applauded for your work. There is no rush that compares to it.

But going on that stage was a big moment for me—a small-time saloon singer, a *colored* one at that—appearing in concert with Red Sovine and Red Foley. The importance of it—whether it would broaden my singing career or increase my fees in local bars or whether it mattered at all—wasn't clear to me, but I felt that buying a ticket to that show was the best dollar and a half I ever spent.

The promoter told me I could sing two songs. I did "Heartaches by the Number" and "Lovesick Blues" again.

Afterward, Red Sovine and I talked some more. He was more congenial toward me than Foley was and I had an immediate fondness for him.

"You should go to Nashville," he told me again. "Go to Cedarwood Publishing and tell them I sent you. They're a big outfit. They do my bookings, Webb Pierce's, and lot of others'."

He gave me his phone number and told me to call him if I needed help. I thanked him and asked him to sign my program.

Red Foley and Red Sovine died long ago, but they both still fill a special place in my memories—Sovine in particular. Whenever I think of him or hear one of his songs, I smile a little and say to myself, "Mr. Gitty-Up Go." His son Roger and I have been friends a long time.

I took home the program they signed and put it in a drawer or on a shelf and, in time, lost track of it. We moved from that house a few years later and somehow the program was left behind.

Several years ago, I was filming a commercial in Minnesota and decided to hop over to Montana for a visit. The woman who had bought our house had found that program and kept it for years. She looked me up while I was in Helena and returned it to me.

It is one of my prized mementos.

C H A P T E R   T W E L V E

Flunked by the Ol' Perfesser

Being rejected by the Angels had affected me more than I wanted to admit. I had seen good players that spring and I was confident that I could play at their level. What am I doing here? I often thought when the smelter ached in my bones. I believe I'm good enough. In the months after returning from California, I often felt overwhelmed by frustration and futility. The prospect of working the rest of my life over a caldron of molten ore became very real.

My daily routine—a full shift on my day job and a long night of singing in saloons for the few extra dollars it took to stay even, getting home a lot of mornings just as Rozene was going to work—had become fatiguing. Each day that passed, I felt more inadequate and more inferior. Normally I kept those emotions inside, but one morning they spilled out.

I came home from the night shift and soot and dirt were caked on my face and hands and clothes. There was nothing unusual about that, but it had never really bothered me. For some reason that morning the grime felt like a terrible disease.

Rozene fixed breakfast and sat down to talk before she had to leave. I looked at my clothes and at her and started to cry.

Tears streamed down my face so suddenly that it surprised me. Nothing in particular brought it on. It just burst out of me like something that had been caged too long.

"I'm better than this," I said, pounding a fist on the table. "I'm better than this. One of these days I'm going to show you. You're going to have a nice home and you won't have to work. You're going to drive down the street and people are going to say, 'There goes Mrs. Pride.' "

It must have sounded like overwrought babbling to her, just as it did to me, but she said nothing except to console and try to cheer me up. After she was gone, I showered and went to bed but had trouble sleeping. My mind was preoccupied with what I was going to do next.

A few weeks later, Rozene saw me getting old newspaper clippings together and didn't have to ask, but she did.

"What are you going to do, Pride?"

"We've got a little money saved," I said. "I'm going to give it one more shot."

Another year would soon fall off the calendar and the sense of urgency I had been feeling grew more powerful. The clock was ticking faster. I could wait another year and get back the step the broken ankle had cost me, but I was running out of time. Having passed my mid-twenties, I was sliding into the twilight time for professional athletes. In those days, if you weren't established in the major leagues by the time you were twenty-five you could forget it.

There were fewer teams then and, therefore, fewer positions. Every year a new crop of young players came along to challenge the old guys. They played better, or as well, and worked cheaper. I was in danger of becoming an old guy trying to challenge the young ones. There wasn't a year to spare, although I would have liked to have had more time.

The ankle bone had healed but still bothered me. It wasn't painful, just stiff, and I couldn't run at full speed, but I was going anyway. I could still throw and I could still hit and there was one team in the majors that could use both talents.

In 1962, the year after the Los Angeles Angels were formed in an American League expansion, the National League also enlarged, granting franchises to Houston (Astros) and New York (Mets). Except for the broken ankle, I would have knocked on the Mets' door that spring, but after watching that team through its first season I was even more encouraged.

It was not the Mets you and I know today. Before the decade was over, the Mets would be known as the miracle team of its time, but in that first season they lost 120 games and finished 60½ out of first place, one of the worst showings in major league history. That team was managed by Casey Stengel, who had run the Yankees for twelve years and accomplished things that may never be equaled. The Yankees won the World Series seven times during his tenure, five of them consecutively, and won the American League pennant 10 times.

But with the Mets poor Casey, the Ol' Perfesser, as he was called, was saddled with a hodgepodge of veterans trying to squeeze one more year out of the game and rookies still trying to learn the signs. Sportswriters had a field day with them.

Jimmy Breslin, the New York columnist, wrote:

They lost an awful lot of games by one run, which is the mark of a bad team. They lost innumerable games by 14 runs. This is the mark of a terrible team. They lost at home and they lost away. They lost at night and they lost in the daytime. And they lost with maneuvers that shake the imagination.

Richie Ashburn, an outfielder who had had an admirable career with the Cubs and the Phillies before joining the Mets

in 1962, admitted he was stumped by his team's performance. "I don't know what's going on but I've never seen it
before," he said.

Casey himself was amazed. "They've shown me ways to
lose I never knew existed," he said.

Something else caused me to rate my chances there as
pretty good. Unable to find a roster it could win with, or even
live with, Stengel's team had more turnover than a maternity
ward. "The Mets is a very good thing," a pitcher named Billy
Loes said. "They give everybody a job, just like the WPA."
The locker room, it was said, had more transients than a
train station.

They had one guy, a catcher named Harry Chiti, who became famous as the man who was traded for himself. The
Mets got Chiti from Cleveland for a player to be named later.
They were not pleased with him and when it came time to
pay the debt to Cleveland, the Mets sent Chiti back to the
Indians. Don Zimmer also played on that team. According to
one story that made the rounds, Zimmer went to the plate
thirty-four straight times without a hit, and when he finally
got a single, the Mets traded him—something about wanting
to deal him while he was hot.

That they were bad didn't bother me; in fact, it seemed to
weigh in my favor. When you're looking for a place to start,
the best place to look is the ground floor.

Surely I could get a shot with the worst team in the country.

This time, instead of just sending old newspaper clippings
as I had done with the Angels, I wanted a more impressive
calling card. I mailed the clippings to George Weiss, the
general manager, telling him I would be in Clearwater, Florida, for spring training camp. Then I ordered six Louisville
Slugger bats, the W 166 Brooks Robinson model, with my

name engraved on them. I shipped the bats so they would arrive at the camp a few days ahead of me.

I made arrangements at the smelter to use some vacation days, packed one small suitcase, and bought a one-way plane ticket to Florida. It was all we could afford, but I didn't care much about the return trip anyway. If I didn't come back as a member of the Mets, I could hitchhike or, provided there was enough money left, take a bus. Before leaving, I sent a telegram to Stengel and Weiss informing them when I would arrive. There wasn't much more I could do, short of hiring a band to escort me into town.

My flight was supposed to leave Great Falls early in the morning and with connections in Chicago and Atlanta I would be in Florida by mid afternoon, in plenty of time to meet Stengel and learn my way around. Instead the flights were delayed and I arrived in Tampa well past midnight, and since I had neglected to obtain the name of the team's hotel, I had no idea where to go from there. I took a cab across the bay to Clearwater, which is on the Gulf coast, and with help from the driver managed to locate the hotel. By then it was 4:00 A.M.

The place was as quiet and deserted as a condemned silo, except for a tired-looking desk clerk reading a newspaper. I approached the counter and announced, in the most confident voice I could muster, "I'm here to join the Mets."

He looked at me suspiciously. "Are you with the team?"

"Well, sort of." I didn't want to lie, but I didn't want to be bounced out, either.

"Well, we don't have any rooms."

"Is anybody sleeping single?" I asked.

The registration book was open on the counter and he scanned through it sort of perfunctorily, as though he intended to go through the motions and then show me the door. I also studied the names. One stood out. Sammy Drake.

Sammy was a second baseman who had played for the Chicago Cubs a couple of years earlier. I had met him in 1961, while I was in the Angels' training camp. We had talked a couple of times and played against each other in an exhibition game, but we were not exactly buddies.

"That's my buddy," I said, pointing to Sammy's name. "I can bunk with him."

Reluctantly, the clerk took me up to Sammy's room and I knocked on the door. No answer. I knocked again. The door opened and there was Sammy in his underwear, half asleep and rubbing his eyes. He squinted at me for a second. I didn't know if he would punch me or have me arrested or simply toss me off the premises.

"Charley!" he said. "Damn. Come on in."

Satisfied, the desk clerk went back to his newspaper. I told Sammy I was going to try out for the team.

"Yeah, I know. Everybody's heard your name. Those bats showed up and everybody was saying, 'Who is this Charley Pride?' You only got five bats now, you know."

"What do you mean?"

"Well, somebody opened the package and a pitcher, name of Jack Fisher, took batting practice with one of them. Broke it right in half."

I laughed. I didn't care that much for the bats anyway, and losing one was a small price to pay for having my name known by every member of the team. We talked for a while and Sammy went back to bed. I stretched out on the floor to grab a few hours of sleep. Tomorrow I would meet the legendary Casey Stengel, probably the most beloved character in baseball. No doubt he was just as anxious to meet the guy whose name was on the Louisville Slugger Brooks Robinson W 166s.

He came down the hall like a man with a purpose, his step quick and his head lowered as if deep in thought. This was a man who had begun playing baseball twenty-five years or more before I was born and was revered by players and fans as much for his comic genius as his baseball talents. No one knew the game better or how to enjoy it more. He once walked onto the field during a game, tipped his hat, and two birds flew out from beneath it.

The press loved him for his antics but also for the colorful way he spoke. It was a kind of doublespeak. What he said wasn't always what it sounded like he said. Words and meanings were bent at funny angles. The writers called it Stengelese.

While he was managing the Yankees, he announced one year that he would quit if the season went badly. It did but Casey stayed on.

"You said you had made up your mind to quit," a sportswriter reminded him.

"I made up my mind, but I made it up both ways," Casey said.

Another bit of Stengelese poured forth at the end of that disastrous 1962 season. He assembled his players and gave them a pep talk. "Now, fellers, don't feel too bad about this. It has been a team effort all the way. Not one or two of you could have done it by yourselves."

There he was, striding down the hall toward me, less imposing than his legend, but still larger than life. My mouth felt dry and butterflies the size of wild turkeys fluttered around in my stomach.

"Mr. Stengel," I said, starting to extend my hand, "I'm Charley Pride and . . ."

He snorted and muttered something I didn't understand.

". . . and I'm here to . . ."

"We'll be going to the ballpark in a few minutes," he growled, brushing past me.

It wasn't the happiest possible beginning to my spring training. It'll get better, I thought.

It got worse.

127

When I got to the lobby, there was a ruckus at the desk. Someone quite agitated was speaking in a loud voice to the clerk I had met earlier that morning. I wandered over to eavesdrop.

"You just let anybody come in off the street . . ." the voice was saying. It belonged to a guy who, I was told later, was the Mets' secretary, and there was no doubt who he was referring to. Sammy Drake had told some of the other players about me conning my way into the hotel and the word got back to the team brass. Now the night clerk was taking the rap for it.

"Sir, it wasn't his fault," I interrupted.

"You be quiet." He turned to glare at me.

"I just wanted to explain . . ."

"If I want you to explain, I'll let you know. I'll talk to you later."

Most of the team had gathered in the lobby and they watched the show with amusement. I heard one of them say, "The guy that sent the bats down has arrived."

Walking toward the front door, I felt everyone's eyes on me. So what? I didn't want to be anonymous in this camp and I was anything but that. I took a seat in the back and put on dark glasses so I could watch the others without them being able to tell who I was looking at. I wanted to see their expressions and how they looked at me and at each other. Maybe their faces would tell me something about the reception I would receive at the practice field. Maybe I could pick up a whisper or two.

No such luck. That was the quietest bus I had ever ridden. A few furtive glances were cast my way but nothing revealing and hardly a word was spoken all the way to the park. It was as though they were holding their breaths and waiting to see what goofy stunt I would pull next. Or maybe they thought they were about to witness my execution.

They were. I never got a chance to step onto the field.

Casey Stengel, George Weiss, and a guy named Johnson, the Mets' minor league director, were standing by the third base fence when we arrived. I started to approach them and realized, again, that I was the topic of discussion.

"We ain't running no damn tryout camp down here," I heard Casey say.

George Weiss had been with the Yankees for many years before he signed on with the Mets. He recruited Stengel, who had been fired by the Yankees and was one year into retirement when the Mets were born. Weiss had a reputation for being hard to get along with, hard-nosed if not downright tyrannical. But he seemed neutral in this discussion.

Johnson tried to speak up for me.

"Well, he sent his clippings . . ." he said.

"I'm not going to look at him," Casey interjected.

". . . and spent his money to get down here."

"Tell him to go out in one of those cow pastures and somebody else can look at him," Casey said.

The discussion went on like that for a few minutes and finally I heard Casey say, "Take him downtown and put him on a bus to anywhere he wants to go."

My heart sank. They were hell-bent against giving me a tryout and there was nothing I could do about it. This was the bunch that had lost 120 games and they wouldn't even look at a guy who had doubled off Warren Spahn and struck out Ernie Banks. I was hurt, angry, humiliated, and devastated. I gathered up my five bats and started back to the bus. The three men were still talking when I walked past them.

"One of these days you're going to hear from me," I said.

Nobody responded. At the hotel I got my things from Sammy Drake's room and someone who worked for the Mets drove me to the bus station.

Before buying a ticket, I looked through my wallet for the

piece of paper on which I had written the address Red Sovine had given me. Cedarwood Publishing.

I called Rozene. "I'm taking the bus home," I said. "But don't expect me too soon. I'm stopping off in Nashville."

CHAPTER THIRTEEN

"Sing One in Your Natural Voice"

The Nashville bus station, it has been said, is the place where the best and worst faces of country music are pressed back to back. On one side are the arrivals, where eager young men and women from the farms and forests and small towns of the South alight with bright eyes, strutting gaits, and guitars across their backs. On the other side are the departures, where the dejected who took on the town and lost sit holding the trophies of disappointment—tickets for the trip home.

At the station that afternoon I probably stood somewhere in between—not particularly expectant but not entirely defeated, either. Clearwater was still a bad taste in my mouth but I arrived in Nashville with more curiosity than hope. I didn't even have a guitar. That made the walk to Cedarwood Publishing a little easier.

Finding the place wasn't difficult. Most of the recording studios and publishing companies were clustered in an area known as Music Row, and it seemed as though everybody there knew everybody else and where their offices were located.

Two men were standing in the reception area when I walked into Cedarwood, tired and rumpled from travel. They looked at me with a decided absence of enthusiasm. This was, after all, the South, and it was 1963 and racial tensions were prevalent. When a black man showed up at a business office, no one could be sure if he was there to sweep up or sit in.

"Can we help you?" one of the men said. It was Bill Denny, the owner of Cedarwood.

I said, "Well . . . uh . . . uh . . . uh . . ."

Denny started to speak, but I managed to find a few words.

"Well . . . Mr. Sovine told me to come here."

"Red Sovine sent you here?"

"Yeah . . . see, I met him up in Montana. I'm a country singer."

They said "Oh" at the same time and looked at each other.

"I sing up in Montana and Mr. Sovine was doing a show up there . . ." I stopped in mid-sentence. Walking across the back of the room was someone I recognized, a big fellow in a blue mohair-looking suit and black hair slicked back from his face. He went into an office.

"Is that Webb Pierce?" I said.

"Yeah," Denny said.

"Can I meet him?" The answer wasn't what I expected. Pierce was a big stick in Nashville, surely too big to have strangers just off the bus walking through his door and taking up his time.

"Sure, go ahead," Denny said. It was almost as if they had been expecting me.

Pierce had taken his coat off and was behind a desk, leaning back in a large swivel chair. I walked straight toward him, extended my hand, and introduced myself.

"I'm from Montana," I said. "You were supposed to have been on a show up there last year, in Helena."

"Oh, yes," he said, "Red Foley filled in for me that day. I had to take care of some business at my radio station in Georgia."

"But . . ." I cut off what I was going to say. I nearly blurted out, "But a telegram was sent saying you had back trouble." Walking in uninvited and unannounced and challenging the veracity of one of the industry's most prominent figures was not the best way to launch a career in country music. But it would not have been out of character for me.

Saying things best left unsaid is a tendency that has caused me discomfort on more than a few occasions. A memorable example was a chance meeting with Ralph Edwards, who was the host of a popular television show, *This Is Your Life*. We were on an airplane and I was excited about meeting him. Without much forethought, I said exactly what I was thinking. "I watch your show all the time," I told him. "You look older in person."

He was not flattered.

Fortunately, looking down at Webb Pierce, I caught myself. What I blurted out, though, could have caused him to wince just as hard. For reasons I would discover later, it did not.

"I want to make a tape. I'm a country singer," I said.

"Oh." I had heard that before.

"There's this DJ up in Montana and . . . well, he had set it up for me to sing for you up there."

He grabbed that line like it had a fish on the end of it. "Son, I do my own singing," he said.

"I mean audition for you."

He smiled, stood up slowly, walked to the door, and summoned one of the men I had talked to earlier. "Get this boy a guitar and take him downstairs," he said. Just like that. It all seemed a little too easy.

He pointed to a door and told me to go wait. "Someone will be with you in a minute," he said.

The downstairs room was a place where a lot of songwriters worked. It was an austere place, with chairs, lockers, tape recorders, and a few guitars. Mel Tillis used to spend a lot of time in that room. I didn't know who he was then, since he had not yet made it big as a singer, but he was one of the most prolific songwriters in Nashville. Bobby Bare was the first to record one of his songs—"Detroit City"—in 1960, and within a few years singers were lining up to bid for his songs. Mel Tillis would become very important to me.

I picked up a guitar, strummed it once, and began tuning it down for bar chords.

Jack Johnson came in, introduced himself, and we shook hands. He was wearing thick glasses that had slipped down the bridge of his nose. He pushed them up and looked me over.

"You Obrey's boy?" he asked.

"Who is Obrey?"

He realized I had no idea who he was talking about.

Unknown to me when I walked into Cedarwood Publishing was that Jack Johnson had been looking for a black country singer. It wasn't an easy assignment. For one thing, there just weren't many black country singers. For another, the segregation that existed in those days made it tough for someone like Johnson to locate and scout black artists. He wasn't likely to hang around black clubs waiting for a hillbilly singer to show up. He had talked to a rock singer named Obrey Wilson and told him, "If you ever run across a colored guy who sings real country music, send him to me."

He thought I was the one.

"Obrey Wilson didn't send you?" Jack asked.

I shook my head.

"Well, they tell me you sing country music," he said. "So sing some country music for me."

While I finished tuning the guitar, he turned on a tape recorder. I sang "Heartaches by the Number" and Johnson looked pleased enough, but he seemed a little skeptical.

"Okay, sing another one," he said. I don't remember what

I sang the second time, but it was probably a Hank Williams number.

When I finished, Johnson said, "Pretty good. Pretty good. Now sing one in your natural voice."

"What do you mean?" I said. "This is my natural voice."

He shrugged. "Sing another one."

I did, put the guitar aside, and we talked. He wanted to know where I was from and how I happened to wander into Cedarwood Publishing. I told him about Tiny Stokes, the DJ, and Red Sovine's and Red Foley's show, and about the saloon singing I had been doing in Montana.

"How do they take you up there?"

"About the way you're taking me now when they first see me," I said.

Why, I wondered, was he so concerned about how the folks in Montana "took" me? Either he liked my singing or he didn't. Did he need a Gallup poll of Helena to help him decide?

Maybe I was a little naive. Since leaving home, baseball had been my obsession. I had pursued it with a single-mindedness that left me with little capacity for anything else— except family, and at times I'm sure even that part of my life suffered from my infatuation with the diamond.

There was no physical segregation in Montana—there weren't enough of *us* to justify separate schools and neighborhoods and restaurants—but we were aware of the civil rights movement and what was going on in the South. More than once I found myself explaining to my neighbors and co-workers what the freedom rides and protest marches were all about. Segregation and inequality were all too familiar— Mississippi and the major leagues had taught me plenty— but in Montana those things were not a part of our daily lives. Living there—working, singing, playing ball—I had come to believe that some things transcended the worst of human nature and that music was one of them.

135

There had been no resistance to me as a country singer in Montana, but now I was back in the South, a different world, and had only a vague idea of the mean work that had been cut out for Jack Johnson—to find a black singer and make him acceptable to country music.

"I think," he said, "I can do something for you." He paused for a second and then added, "But we might have to change your name—to something like George Washington W. Jones III . . . something like that."

He may have been joking, but he didn't laugh. He may have been trying to test me, to see how badly I wanted to be a country singer, how much I was willing to bend and compromise.

"Hold it," I said. "There ain't gonna be no name changing. My name is Charley Frank Pride. It's been good enough since I've been in this world and I don't see any reason to change it."

"We'll talk about it later," he said, abruptly changing the subject. "Where are you staying?"

"Nowhere, yet."

"How long are you going to be in town?"

"I'm in no hurry to leave. I'm on vacation. Since I'm here I intend to meet everybody in Nashville that I can."

"Fella," he said, "you've met everybody here you need to meet. I'm going to be your manager. You go on home and I'll send a contract for you to sign. I'll start trying to find you a record label."

That was it. One day Casey Stengel hands me my hat and the next some guy at a Nashville publishing company is going to manage my singing career. Singing as a full-time job was not something I had given a lot of thought to and I had no clear notion of the money to be made in it. Having a record or two on the streets, I imagined, could add a nice supplement to my smelter salary.

"Come on," Johnson said. "I'll give you a ride."

He took me straight to the bus station and got me out of town so fast I thought I was getting the bum's rush. Later, I found out different. Jack was no dummy. He saw potential in me but he was certain it was not going to be easy to persuade that town to accept me. Some groundwork had to be laid.

And he may have wanted me out of town to minimize the chance that I would be tempted by another offer from another manager. If that was his motive, he has my gratitude for it. Down the road, Jack Johnson and I would make a hell of a team. But in all the years we worked together, I never asked him if he had been serious about changing my name to George Washington W. Jones III. There was already a guy in Nashville doing pretty well with a shorter version of that name.

Jack wasted no time sending the contract. It was waiting at home when I got back to Montana. I looked at it and groaned. The legal gibberish made it almost indecipherable. "Party of the first part . . . party of the second part . . . second party agrees for first party. . . ." The thing had more parties than an army furlough and there I was, with an eleventh-grade education, trying to figure it out.

One part that was clear was the clause that said Jack Johnson would get 25 percent of everything I made.

Twenty-five percent! About halfway through it, I wanted to talk to somebody who understood those things. I grabbed the phone and called Red Sovine in Nashville.

"I met you in Montana," I reminded him. "You told me to go to Cedarwood Publishing."

"I remember," he said.

"Well, I got this manager's contract here and it's got a lot of stuff in it I don't understand. See, I don't think you need a manager to—"

"Wait a minute," he said. "You are going to need a manager."

137

"I'd kind of like to manage myself." I was still thinking I could cut a record, make a quick five or ten thousand dollars, and go home, not splitting with anyone. "This guy wants twenty-five percent."

He said, "I know that seems like a lot, but let me ask you something—how much are you making now?"

"About sixty-five hundred a year."

"Well, what do you think about seventy-five thousand or a hundred thousand next year? Doesn't seventy-five percent of a hundred thousand sound pretty good?"

"Uh-huh. Uh-huh." It sounded good—maybe too good to be true.

"Take that contract to a lawyer and let him explain it to you," he said. "But don't forget. Seventy-five percent of a lot is better than a hundred percent of nothing."

For the next few days I showed the contract to anybody who would look at it. Nobody discouraged me from accepting it but I think I had already made up my mind after talking to Red Sovine. Why would he steer me wrong? If it had not been for him, I would not have gone to Nashville, would not have knocked on the door at Cedarwood Publishing, and would not have this decision to make.

After a week, I signed and mailed the contract back to Jack Johnson. I expected to be in Nashville within a month or two making records. I was wrong. Bill Denny and the folks at Cedarwood may have thought it was time for a black singer in country music but the record companies felt otherwise.

Jack Johnson was going to have to earn his 25 percent the hard way.

CHAPTER FOURTEEN

Signing with RCA

From time to time, I called Jack Johnson to check on his progress toward the recording contract.

"Be patient," he would say without laying out all the details. "I'm working on it. It's just going to take a little time."

"How much time?" The months were turning into years and I was growing impatient. He had no answer.

"Why don't you think about moving to Nashville so you can be closer to the people we're trying to deal?" he said, offering to help me get a job there. Workers in the city's sanitation department made seventy-five dollars a week and garbage collectors were always in demand.

"Well, I have a good job up here . . ."

"How much are you making?"

"Between us Rozene and I are making about eleven thousand dollars a year."

He thought for a second and said, "Maybe you'd better stay there. You're making more money than I am, more than a whole bunch of people."

By the summer of 1965, we had three children. Our daughter, Angela, had just been born and our families had not seen her. We planned to spend our vacation that year in

Mississippi, but I also was going to use the trip to try to make something happen in Nashville. Before leaving Montana, I called my manager. It had been two years since I had walked into Cedarwood, and I was beginning to think that Jack Johnson wasn't seriously trying to help me.

"I'm coming through Nashville," I told him. "I'd like to get moving with this thing."

"Okay . . ." He was hesitant.

"It's been two years now, Jack," I said, pushing him just a little.

"Well, come on by," he said.

In the meantime, Johnson got in touch with a producer named Jack Clement and they came up with seven songs. "When you've learned these," Johnson told me when I got to Nashville, "make a tape of them and mail it to us."

He also warned me that there was a wide gap between a demonstration tape and a recording contract. He had taken the tape recording I had made at Cedarwood in 1963 all over town and was meeting a fair amount of resistance from the record labels.

What had been happening, Jack told me, was that he would play my songs for recording company executives, they would respond favorably, sometimes enthusiastically, but when he showed them my picture, the reaction was usually the same: "Well . . . uh . . . who are we going to sell these records to? Ah . . . are the DJs going to play them? We'll have to think about it."

A low buzz of gossip began making the rounds in Nashville, he said: "Did you hear that Jack Johnson is going around trying to get a jig into country music?"

"Don't worry," he said. "We'll keep plugging away."

I took the songs and drove to Rozene's parents' house in Oxford, Mississippi, where I holed up in the bedroom to rehearse them. Rozene's sisters have since told me they didn't quite know what to make of the whole thing. Like me, they had grown up listening to *The Grand Ole Opry* but they were not devoted country music fans, didn't know what was good and what wasn't. Frankly, I think they didn't believe I would make it. But I sat in that room with the door closed and sang those seven songs hour after hour.

After two or three days, I was confident enough to call Jack Johnson and tell him I had them down pat. He had reservations.

"You haven't spent much time on them," Jack said.

"I can sing them, Jack." I said. "What else do I need to do?"

I also informed him that I was not going to mail a tape. I would return to Nashville and record them there, in his and Jack Clement's presence.

"Okay," he said.

"I'll be there tomorrow."

I drove back to Nashville by myself and met them in Clement's office. Accompanied by Clement on a guitar, I sang each of the songs.

Clement looked at Johnson and said, "Jack, I think he's ready."

He told me he had reserved a studio at RCA for two o'clock on August 16 to do some recordings of his own. "Do you think you could record two songs in three hours?"

"I can do it in one," I said.

"Can you be back here on the sixteenth?" he said. "RCA. Studio B."

That would be a Wednesday, two days later.

"I'll be here," I said.

Back in Mississippi, I got in another day of rehearsing. Wednesday morning, I got up early and drove to Nashville.

After meeting the studio technicians, becoming familiar with the equipment, and going through the material with the musicians a couple of times, I recorded "Snakes Crawl at Night." Mel Tillis, who wrote the song, happened to be walking through the studio and, from the story I heard later, was a little astonished to hear his words being sung by a black singer.

There was a small office building behind RCA where some agents and talent managers and others worked. Mel, I was told, went running back there, burst through the door wide-eyed and stuttering, and said, "T-T-T-There's a c-c-c-colored guy in there s-s-s-singing my song and he s-s-s-sounds just like Stonewall Jackson."

I also recorded another of Mel's songs, "Atlantic Coastal Line," as well as "Just Between You and Me," which Jack Clement had written. It was a short session, easier than I had imagined it would be. Jack Johnson gave me a copy of the recordings and I left town.

Rozene, the kids, and I stayed in Mississippi a few more days and returned to Montana.

For the next few weeks, Rozene and I played those songs over and over on a reel-to-reel tape recorder, but only for ourselves. We didn't play them for anyone else because there was always the possibility that nothing would come of it and we didn't want anyone to think we had been deluded by foolish fantasies.

But we were hopeful and anxious. Instead of an amateurish demo tape made on a desktop recorder with no instrumental backup, Jack Johnson now had the dubs of a real studio session to shop around and he had help from Jack Clement.

Clement took the tapes to Chet Atkins, probably the best guitar player who ever lived. In tandem with his music career, Chet was also a rising executive with RCA and played a large role in shaping the sound of country music. He had gone from recording artist to producer to manager, and in 1965 he was in line to become an RCA division vice president. He had a shrewd business sense and a keen eye for talent. It was Chet Atkins who brought to RCA people such as Floyd Cramer, Connie Smith, Don Gibson, Waylon Jennings, and

Bobby Bare. He had personally supervised the recordings of Elvis Presley, Eddy Arnold, Perry Como, Jerry Reed, Al Hirt, and several others.

Those successes gave him a lot of influence with the suits at RCA. Chet took my tapes to Monterey, California, and played them for the executives out there. He was confident they would like what they heard.

They did.

"Wait a minute now," Chet said. "I need to tell you that he's colored."

Almost in unison, those in the room said, "What's that?"

Some eyebrows were raised and a few feet shuffled, but Chet lobbied hard for RCA to take a chance on me. Before the meeting was over, the others were sold. Their strategy was cautious. They would put out a record and let it speak for itself. Nothing would be said about my race, at least not in the beginning.

On September 28 I got a call from Jack Johnson.

"RCA is going to sign you," he said.

"Is that good?" I honestly wasn't very familiar with RCA. It was just another label. No one had told me it was the biggest record company in the world.

"Is it good?" Johnson laughed. "It's the best there is."

It is hard to describe the way I felt. On the one hand, I still had my routine—working days in the smelter and making the 160-mile round-trip to Anaconda two nights a week. On the other, I had that restless sensation of standing at the threshold of a great adventure, the same feeling that came with stepping up to bat against Warren Spahn or boarding an airplane for the first time to fly out of the Rocky Mountains.

The RCA contracts arrived in November or early December and Jack Clement became my producer. He told me my first single—"Snakes Crawl at Night" with "Atlantic Coastal Line" on the flip side—would be released just after Christmas.

"What about 'Just Between You and Me'? I kind of like that song," I said.

"No, no," he said. "Not yet. I don't want people to think I'm using you to promote my own songs."

No doubt he honestly felt that way, but later I realized that in all likelihood there was more involved in the decision. Jack and RCA probably didn't want me singing love songs— not just yet. People pay attention to lyrics and the race matter was delicate. For a long time considerable care would be exercised in selecting my songs. "Snakes" didn't set off any alarms because it was just about a guy who shot his cheating wife and there was a certain racial neutrality to it. A love song was different. A white guy might say, "Wait a minute, who's he singing this to? He's singing to our women."

There was one particular song where that issue came up early in my career. "Green, Green Grass of Home" was one of my favorites but I couldn't use it in my show. There's a line that goes, "Down the road I look, and there runs Mary/ hair of gold and lips like cherries. . . ." A black man singing about a blond girlfriend was potential trouble.

Even after I was established I had to be selective. Red Lane brought me a song he had written called "Blackjack County Chain." It was about a sheriff in Georgia who was killed by a black convict on a chain gang. As much as I liked Red and admired his songwriting, I looked at that one and said, "Red, you're out of your mind. Somebody else will have to do that one." Willie Nelson recorded it.

So my first single was a cheatin' song instead of a love song, but I have no complaints. It was a good song and it set everything in motion.

Jack Johnson sent a few copies to me and the first thing I did was drive over to Great Falls and leave one with KNON Radio, which was the closest genuine country music station. It was on a weekend and I didn't have time to stay. I just slipped the record through the window and said, "Would you please play this Charley Pride record?"

Word had gotten around Montana that I had signed with RCA and had a single coming out, so I wasn't exactly a stranger to the radio people. Al Donahue at KNON Radio was the first owner to play my record. He and I became good friends and he gave me a lot of advice on how to handle the entertainment business. We still stay in touch.

Al had a stroke a few years ago and it caused partial paralysis and speech impairment. It hurts to see such an active guy—he was involved in just about everything that went on in Great Falls—sidelined by something like that.

Al liked me, but he really loved Rozene. I didn't dare argue or disagree with her in his presence. He'd give me a hard look and say, "Dammit, you leave her alone."

Burt Kane was my supervisor at the smelter and I could not have asked for a more understanding and accommodating boss. After "Snakes" came out and was doing pretty well, I had to make other trips to Nashville for recording sessions. There were other singles to do and we had started work on an album.

But I still needed the smelter job to pay the bills and cover the cost of traveling back and forth to Tennessee. Burt always gave me a leave of absence when it was necessary and he always welcomed me back.

After my co-workers in Helena began hearing my songs on the radio, they often came up to me and said, "You ought to tell them where to shove that job."

Burning bridges was not something I was ever inclined to do anyway, and I wasn't going to tell anybody to shove anything. I had nothing against the smelter. Until I went to work there, I had never made more than ten or twelve dollars a day. But with me skimming slag during the day and singing at night and Rozene working as a technician in a medical laboratory, we had a pretty solid middle-class income and that was a big step up from where I had been.

Each time I took a leave of absence, I was not completely convinced that I wouldn't be back. I had learned something of the music business but not enough to give me a clear idea where all of this was heading. I had a manager, a recording contract, and a couple of songs getting reasonable air play, but I still had not received a cent in royalties. The smelter job was the only source of income I could bank on.

As time passed, though, the absences became longer. I was getting more offers to sing in clubs. I could draw bigger crowds and command a bigger paycheck. I had landed a five-night-a-week job at The Ranch in Great Falls and for a while continued to work days and make the 180-mile drive from Helena and back each night. It soon became too much. Sometime in the summer of 1966, I went to Burt Kane again to ask to be off work. He and I both had a feeling, I think, that it would be my last leave of absence.

"You quit right, Charley," he told me, although I didn't actually quit. "If you don't like the singing business, you can always come back here—up until you're forty-five years old."

"Thanks, Burt. I appreciate that."

That wasn't just an idle expression of gratitude. It was reassuring to have steady work waiting. I was aware that the entertainment business is pretty fickle and that one or two moderately successful singles don't guarantee a long career.

While playing in Great Falls, I put together my first band and got initiated into the fine art of labor relations. I was getting one hundred and fifty dollars a night and each band member got union scale, which was twenty dollars apiece. That was a pretty good night for a band at that time, but some of them drank quite a bit and didn't watch their pennies very closely.

They began asking me to take a smaller cut and give them more. There were not too many good musicians up there to choose from and they used that against me, threatening to walk out if their demands were not met.

When we began working together, I had told each of them that if my recording career took off, I would be happy to take them along with me, the way Buck Owens had with Don Rich and some other musicians. It was a good band and the offer was sincere, but they weren't impressed. No one ever said it, but I could read their thinking. They didn't believe I was going anywhere, didn't believe the country music business was actually going to let me in. They just wanted a bigger piece of the nightly pie and to hell with the future.

I finally realized I couldn't depend on people with that attitude and I was fed up with their threats to walk out.

"If you guys are going to use this kind of tactic, then you can go. I don't need you," I told them.

In truth, I did need them. I might have become a minor celebrity but had been enriched not at all by it. Royalty checks were a long way off and a long time coming. Without a band I would be back tapping slag. There was a little turnover, but I managed to keep a group together, even if it meant giving in to them once in a while.

One of the guys had borrowed some money and was behind in his payments. He told me that if his creditors garnisheed his wages, he was going to quit. So I paid off the loan—grudgingly.

Rozene and I still lived as frugally as we had before, determined to pick our way slowly across this new terrain, taking nothing for granted, spending nothing until it was in the bank.

My second single, "Before I Met You," had been out for a

short time when another singer came by to visit me. He had just released a record on some small label and I guess he wanted to talk about our newfound success. He looked my old Dodge over and said, "Man, you got your record out, but you ain't got your Cadillac yet."

No, I didn't have a Cadillac and I had no plans to buy one. I'd heard stories about singers who cut one record and ran out and hired a band they couldn't afford and bought a bus and couldn't pay for it. The biggest financial gamble I had ever taken was hocking the furniture for four hundred dollars to pay for our move to Montana. If I was going to go into debt again, it would be for something more practical and durable than a Cadillac.

It wasn't until "Just Between You and Me" was released and started climbing up the charts that I began to sense a permanence about what I was doing. That song was big enough that it promised a friendly financial reward, but more important, it got me into the major leagues. A few months after it was released, I was driving to Detroit to play with Merle Haggard and Buck Owens and Red Foley.

I remember what I had written to Rozene when I first arrived in Montana. "I think we can make something for ourselves here." In my wildest dreams I hadn't imagined this.

PART
2

CHAPTER FIFTEEN

Confronting Race

If I believed the Detroit concert had settled the question of whether I would be accepted in country music, I was wrong. Winning the approval of audiences was one thing. Getting a break from club owners and promoters was another.

There was a place in Chicago called the Club Rivoli, owned by an Italian guy named Sammy See, who had built it into one of those prestigious stops that could be a generous boost to the career of someone still trying to get a toehold in the singing business. Playing there meant you were on your way.

Jack Johnson spent a lot of time trying to book me there but Sammy was a hard sell. At that point in the civil rights movement, major cities—and not just those in the South—were edgy about protests and sit-ins and the possibility of violence. Nobody wanted to be a part of something that might touch off a disturbance.

After spending an hour on the phone with Sammy and not getting anywhere, Jack said, "Look, why don't you at least talk to Charley."

"Fine," Sammy said. "I'll do that."

My approach to him was something less than aggressive.

I had no interest in being party to a racial incident and told him so.

"My manager says you're not sure you want to get involved at this early stage of my career," I said.

"Well, yes, something like that," he said.

"I can understand how you could feel that way," I said. "I'm not even off the ground yet. I don't want anything to happen to hurt my career at this point either. If you think it's the wrong time, I understand."

He apparently was not expecting me to be so agreeable.

"Tell you what," he said. "I'm going to book you. You didn't call up here making demands or creating some big rigmarole, so I'm going to book you."

"I'm jubilant," I said, meaning it sincerely.

Earlier he had mentioned to Jack Johnson the possibility of bringing me in quietly during someone else's show and springing me on the audience unannounced. Now he was prepared to do better than that, but just a little better.

"I'm going to book you for Friday and Saturday night, but I'm not going to advertise you," he said.

"How do you expect to bring anybody in?" I asked. The club seated about eight hundred, and with no advertising I could find myself singing to empty chairs.

"I send out a thousand or two fliers to my regular customers telling them who's appearing here each weekend. I'll handle it like that," he said.

Jack and I agreed it was worth the gamble. If nobody showed, we hadn't lost much. If eight hundred showed and half walked out, it would be just another setback we'd have to overcome later. If I went over big, other doors should start to open.

On Friday night we had maybe eighty people. Sammy paced the bar like an expectant father. Finally, the announcer brought me on and you could feel the shock in the room. After a couple of songs, the crowd, if it could be called that, loosened up and we had a good time.

The next night we had eight hundred people, including two of the biggest promoters in the country: Smoky Smith from Des Moines and Lucky Moeller from Nashville. They were watching the audience reaction. From the stage I could see them sitting there with their heads together, comparing notes.

After the show, I went over to meet them. They were very cordial, but I didn't get a booking out of either one of them.

Six months or so passed and I was at a club called the Black Poodle in Printer's Alley in Nashville. Dottie West was performing that night and Lucky Moeller was in the crowd. Dottie called me up to the stage and asked me to sing. Afterward I got word that Lucky wanted me to come to his table.

"The crowd really liked you," he said.

"I believe so," I said.

"They could book you and fill this place," he said.

"Yeah, I believe so," I said.

He nodded, but said nothing.

I said, "Here's what I think, Mr. Moeller. You are just like a lot of the other promoters. You are skeptical. You are waiting for someone else to book me and see how I come out and then you'll come in out of the rain."

He grinned and said, "Now, Charley."

I wasn't berating him. It was a calm conversation and I felt I was just stating facts that were obvious and he didn't bother to deny them.

Faron Young talked to him sometime after that and Lucky recounted our conversation. "He was right," he told Faron. "I saw him up in Club Rivoli but I didn't want to take a chance on him yet."

As far as I'm aware, Lucky Moeller never did book a show for me. He had an agency and some of his people might have been involved in some shows or tours I did, but I have no knowledge of that.

Smoky Smith from Des Moines was a different story. He later booked a lot of shows for me and we even rode together, which was an experience—him puffing on that big cigar and talking me to death. I reminded him about the Club Rivoli and the trouble we had persuading Sammy See.

"Well, he's got a couple hundred thousand in that place," Smoky said. "That's a lot of money to risk on bringing in someone like you."

Those early years amounted to a series of tests. Okay, we passed Dallas. Would they accept me in Atlanta? We played Atlanta—no problem. How about Houston? We played Houston—no problem. Okay, what about Charlotte? Chicago? New Orleans? It went on and on, and each time I passed the test—sometimes in ways that surprised me.

I did a show in Texarkana, which straddles the Texas-Arkansas line. I had been told that it was not the most enlightened place in America.

Just as I was getting ready to go on, a guy walked up to me and told me his name, which I have long since forgotten. But I'll never forget the rest of what he said: "I'm the Grand Wizard of the Ku Klux Klan here."

Before I could even swallow hard, his arm shot out and he said, "I just want to shake hands with a man."

That's all he said. I shook his hand and stood there, a little confounded, while he walked back to his table. He just as easily could have said, "I'm here with the tar and feathers." But he sat down, stayed for the whole show, and seemed to enjoy it. I think that was because I kept a close eye on him all the time I was singing.

After finishing my first show in Atlanta, someone come to the stage and told me one of the patrons wanted me to come to his table.

"Charley," the guy said in a pronounced Southern accent, "that was a good show. I'm from 'way down in Georgia and, I'll be darned, I ain't never heard a nigger sound like you in all my life. You put on a hell of a show."

Should I have been offended or flattered? There wasn't a trace of malice in his voice. He was as sincere and affable as anyone could be. "Nigger" was just a natural part of his vernacular, I suppose, and its use implied nothing. I was coming to realize that many people, particularly Southerners, weren't aware that there was any other way to refer to a person of African descent.

I didn't set out to be a crusader for racial harmony or change anybody's heart or mind, but I learned early that you can accomplish more with tolerance than with indignation. What my mother had told me—"you've got a lot you're going to have to do and you can't do it carrying a load of resentment with you"—had never made clearer sense than during that period of my life.

In one way or another, the color issue was always there, hanging around with the unpleasant odor of an old wet dog lying on the doorstep. I had to find ways to deal with it.

And the problems were not just with white audiences.

On my first USO tour in Germany, I was mildly heckled by black soldiers because I sang country music. Those USO tours are fast paced—sometimes you play at two clubs a day at two different military installations—and the demands were more intense because of the situation I kept running into at those shows. It was as though someone had built a fence down the middle of the room—an imaginary fence, of course. All the black soldiers were on one side, all the whites on the other. Of course, that's the way most of them had lived back home, with an imaginary barrier separating them.

One night I got a few catcalls from the black side of the room. It wasn't vicious. In fact, those involved probably found it amusing. I had sung a few country songs and there was some snickering and someone yelled out, "When you gonna do one for us brothers?"

It was time to clear the air. I stopped the show and said, "It looks like we're going to have a question-and-answer session. What was the question?"

"When are you gonna sing one for us brothers," the guy yelled.

"I'm singing for my brothers on this side of the room and for my brothers on this side," I said. "I told you in the beginning. I'm not James Brown. I'm not Sam Cooke. I'm Charley Pride, country singer. I'm just me and that's what you get."

There was some laughter and foot shuffling but things settled down and we finished the show. It would have served no purpose to pretend to be someone I wasn't and perform two shows—one for each side of the room. That would only have fortified the air of separation that already existed in that place.

It was on that same tour that I experienced one of the most poignant moments of those years of confronting the race issue, of trying to find my place in the white world of country music.

We performed an outdoor show at an army post. Afterward, I sat at a table in front of the stage, signing autographs and talking to the soldiers. I noticed one young man who seemed to be hanging back, as though waiting for the others to leave before he would approach me.

When everyone else had gone, he came over to talk privately. He told me he was from Alabama. "I came out here to see you make a fool of yourself, but you didn't," he said. "You did Hank Williams and Ray Price songs about as good as they do them, maybe even better."

I wasn't sure where this was leading, but I didn't have to wait long to find out. He had something to say and it spilled out of him like air from a punctured balloon.

He was having second thoughts, he said, about the things

he had been taught by his parents and the segregated environment back home, things he had always believed unquestioningly. But in the army, he had befriended black soldiers and apparently watching my show had intensified his doubts.

"My parents taught me that black people were under me . . . inferior . . . or something," he stammered. Tears formed in his eyes.

"It's not just you," I said. "That's been going on for a long time in a lot of places."

"What am I going to say to my parents? You have to believe what your parents tell you," he said.

"You're supposed to love your parents."

"I don't think I really believe what I was taught anymore. I just wanted to tell you that."

"Well, you have to make your own decisions," I told him.

We shook hands and he left. I've often wished I had not forgotten his name. It would be interesting to learn where life has taken him.

This is as good a time as any to set the record straight about the bomb scare in Augusta, Maine. It has been reported from time to time that I was the target of a bomb threat by racist elements up there and I have never been convinced of that.

We arrived in Augusta to do a show at seven-thirty. At the theater, I was waiting in a little room backstage. Usually someone alerted me about ten minutes before I was to go on. Seven-thirty passed. Seven-forty passed. I was getting restless but had heard from no one. I could hear noises in the theater, feet stomping and shuffling. About seven-forty-five, someone came to the door.

"Charley, let me tell you what's wrong. We got a call and . . . everybody's in the manager's office."

I walked down to that office, where several people were

huddling, trying to decide whether to proceed with the show. They told me that an anonymous call had been received warning that a bomb would go off in the theater at nine o'clock. There was general agreement that the call was a hoax, but nobody could be certain. Still, the majority wanted to proceed as though nothing had happened.

"Let me tell you what we're going to do," I said. "I'm going to go out and tell them what the situation is and let them decide what kind of chance they want to take."

I walked straight from the manager's office to the stage. The audience sensed something was not right, partly from the way I was dressed. I was wearing a leather jacket on over my stage clothes. Too, the band wasn't in place and there was no introduction.

Scattered applause rippled across the room but I waved my hand to ask for silence.

"Ladies and gentlemen, I've got to announce something. We received a call, a bomb threat for nine o'clock."

Immediately people started getting out of their seats.

"I personally don't believe anything is going to happen," I said, "but I was supposed to start the show at seven-thirty. Let's all take our time and clear the building. At exactly one minute past nine, I will come back on this stage and give you the same show you were going to see at seven-thirty."

The police searched the building and found nothing. Just after nine, people returned to the theater. We lost only about three hundred out of seven thousand, which I thought was pretty good. The show went off without incident.

I have always been convinced that the threat had nothing to do with me, except that I happened to be appearing there that night. For several weeks before I arrived Augusta had been the scene of a nasty protest over increased electricity rates. Some people were so angry that they had been knocking out power stations, transformers, and generators that belonged to the local utility company.

A full theater, no matter who was performing, was a convenient venue for furthering the protest. It got reported in a few places as a possible racial incident, but I never believed it was.

I had a booking agent back then who sometimes portrayed things a certain way, maybe for publicity reasons.

There was another time when it was reported that a gunshot was fired as I was leaving a theater in Minneapolis. I never had any proof that it was a gunshot—it may have been a car backfiring—but the police came to the theater and cleared the parking lot before allowing me to leave.

I tried not to let such things concern me, but episodes like those in Augusta and Minneapolis, and whatever rumors grew from them, may have had a detrimental effect—not on me but on those I depended on for work. They were precisely the kinds of incidents club owners and promoters feared most.

Meeting Nashville

"Let me tell you something," Jack Johnson said on one of my visits to Nashville. "There are a few guys you're going to have to get by before you're accepted in this town. We've got them pegged out. One of them is Faron Young."

"Okay, what do you figure I have to do?" I said.

"We'll look him up and get right to it, get it out of the way," he said.

"What's he like?" I had heard "Hello Walls," "Live Fast, Love Hard, and Die Young," "Wine Me Up," and a lot of other Faron Young songs. I was aware that he was a major figure in the country music establishment and had started out in 1953 on the *Louisiana Hayride*, which was broadcast from his hometown of Shreveport. He was involved in other things besides singing. He was part owner of an automobile race-track, Sulfur Dell, in Nashville and was connected with a monthly newspaper called the *Music City News*. And I think he had been in a few movies.

"There's no telling what he's going to say," Jack Johnson said with a smile, explaining Faron's reputation for being something of a redneck, outspoken, and just a shade on the profane side. "He might just walk up and call you anything. Just be prepared."

"Fine. I'm glad you told me."

I had come to Nashville to cut my first album, *Country Charley Pride,* on the heels of a disastrous package tour of Montana with Carl Belew, Johnny Paycheck, Karen Kelly, and Johnny Darrell. We didn't draw flies. We were all newcomers and not well known. At every stop each of us was looking at the others, wondering, Who's the big star here who isn't drawing? Because I was from Montana, a favorite son, the others probably had counted on me to pull up the slack, but it didn't happen. Each night, the question was, Who's going to close? Who's the star of this show? None of us was the star. That's why the tour flopped and I headed to Nashville in hopes of hooking up with more established performers for a more successful tour.

My career had reached the point where the issue of who would or wouldn't work with me had to be addressed. That's why Jack Johnson figured it was time to confront the big boys and settle it.

Faron Young was one of the big boys, and Jack and I had been told that he had said he wouldn't work with me, that he wouldn't jeopardize his career that way. "Goddammit, I make two hundred thousand dollars a year going on the road," he was supposed to have said. "I'm not going to risk that by going on the road with some goddamn jig."

Being from Louisiana, Faron had been brought up a separatist, but that wasn't uncommon and it didn't scare me. At that time we had all grown up in a segregated society and I understood long ago what it was like to face people with that attitude. I had plenty of training for my encounter with Mr. Young.

We went by his office and he wasn't there. We looked all over town for him and made a swing by a club he frequented. He was there. When we walked in Faron didn't see or hear us. He was sitting in a chair with his back to the door. He had a bandana around his head, a microphone in his hand, and was bent over a tape recorder, talking a mile a minute.

Not inclined toward shyness anyway, and especially not at a time like this, I walked right up behind him and said, "Hi, Faron."

He stiffened, hunched up his shoulders, and cut his eyes toward me. He seemed to be thinking of what he was going to say and I braced for the worst.

"Hello, Charley," he said, standing up facing me. "You sing a good song."

"Thank you, Faron," I said. "You do, too."

We all sat down and talked for a while and the conversation was relaxed and pleasant. There was a guitar nearby and Faron picked it up and started singing. After a couple of songs, I joined in with him. That went on for ten or fifteen minutes before Faron looked over at Jack with a big grin on his face.

"Goddamn, here I am singing with a jig and I don't even mind it," he said. "Who'd have ever thought it?"

I guess he expected me to throw a punch or something.

"Aw, I was waiting for something worse than that," I said.

"You were?"

"Yeah. Guess what I was going to say if you had said something really bad."

"What?"

"I was going to say, 'You little pucker-mouth banty rooster son of a peckerwood!'"

He blinked. "You were going to say that to me?"

"Just like that."

"I'll be damned."

Within a few weeks we were on tour together. He was one of my best supporters in the early days and that helped break some ground for me. When someone who is considered a diehard redneck stands beside a black man and says, "Hey,

I like this guy," it disarms people who might have been reluctant to associate with him.

Young invited me to parties at his house, took me for rides in one of his old antique cars, and introduced me to a lot of people in the industry. By and large, Faron seemed more curious about than resentful of me.

"Charley," he said once, "I've told you that I grew up in Shreveport. Well, I haven't had a chance to talk to many of *y'all*. Since we got a chance, there's something I been wanting to ask you. Is it that extra bone in your heel that makes *y'all* outjump *us*?"

"What . . . ?"

"That extra bone . . ."

"What extra bone?"

Happy to dispel another racial myth, I told him it was my understanding that he and I had the same number of bones and if *we* jumped higher than *you*, it may be because *we* worked harder at it.

He just may have been putting me on with that question. Faron was like that. He said and did things just to shock people. He liked to be talked about by other artists and was always willing to give them material for their tales. Jack Johnson was absolutely correct: Faron Young was as unpredictable as a knuckleball.

Leaving a club in Nashville, we walked past a guy playing a pinball machine. Faron stopped, looked him over, and said, "Who are you?"

The guy looked around, as though he wasn't sure Faron was talking to him.

Faron said, "With that snozzle, you look like one of those guys Hitler was after."

My impulse was to get out of there so I wouldn't have to watch Faron get his hat blocked. When Faron came outside, I said, "Man, what are you doing? That guy might have put your lights out!"

He laughed and said, "Well, he did look like one of them."

While we were touring together, we arrived in San Antonio and checked into a motel where the rooms opened out onto a private courtyard with a swimming pool. We were in his room that afternoon, talking and killing time, and Faron stood up, pushed open the sliding glass doors, and said, "I gotta take me a leak."

He walked straight toward the pool, unzipping his fly. There was no doubt in my mind that he was going to pee in the pool where anyone, including the motel manager, could see him.

"No, Faron, don't do it, man." I jumped up and started after him. It was hard enough for me to get into a motel in those days. The last thing I needed was to be involved with someone arrested for public indecency.

As he got to the edge of the pool, with me in pursuit, pleading, he turned and laughed. "You thought I was going to do it, didn't you?" he said.

"Why wouldn't I think it, man?" I sighed with relief. "You've pulled so many other things on me." Deep down, I believed he was capable of anything.

We had some good times together and I've always appreciated what Faron Young did for me. Some people are able to put their separatist notions aside quicker than others and he was one of them.

It seemed ironic to me that I later went to Faron's hometown of Shreveport to appear on a show headlined by Stonewall Jackson and almost found myself without a band to back me up. Stonewall's contract called for his musicians to be the house band, but he refused to let them play for me. It was not unusual for singers to not want their bands to back other singers.

At the last minute, the promoters had to scramble around Shreveport to find local musicians who would go on stage with me.

* * *

Getting acquainted with Nashville, I discovered, was largely a matter of satisfying the curiosity of other performers. From their comments, some seemed to be under the impression I was crossing over from blues or rock and roll or another field of music. A large part of becoming accepted was convincing people I was genuine, that I was not just passing through country music on my way to somewhere else but was there to stay.

Mel Tillis, whom I met about the time I first recorded his songs, asked me, "Have you ever met Brook Benton? How about B.B. King? Sam Cooke?" He was surprised to find out that I was a hell of a lot better versed in country music than rhythm and blues.

Ed Bruce, who wrote "Mamas Don't Let Your Babies Grow Up to Be Cowboys," did the same thing—quizzed me about country songs and singers to see if I was in my element.

"Damn," he said after we had talked for a while, "you're more country than I am."

One thing I was not going to do was affect the country look as it was defined in those days—a flashy rhinestone cowboy veneer at one extreme and cowboy boots and jeans at the other. I grew up on a farm in the South, not a ranch out west, and I would have felt out of place in Western duds. My taste in clothes ran to slacks, loafers, casual jackets, sweaters, or suits.

Jack Johnson took me to a Nashville clothing store and we loaded up on some good-looking suits. He and I were determined that I would look no different than Tony Bennett or Frank Sinatra.

The fans never made an issue of it, but the attire was duly noted by some people. In Las Vegas I was on my way to see Flip Wilson, and outside the casino hotel where he was playing I ran into Redd Foxx, who was also going to the show. Redd and I introduced ourselves and together we went backstage. Away from the cameras, Redd was the same gruff old codger you saw on television. His tongue spent most of its time in his cheek.

"Goddamn, man," he said to Flip, whose name was in small letters on the marquee, "why don't you tell these people your name ain't big enough out there in the lights. Hell, you can barely see the son of a bitch."

Before Flip could say anything, Redd turned to me and said, "Here's this young hillbilly . . . Charley Pride. You sing country and western music, don't ya?"

I said, "Yes sir."

"Why ain't you dressed like it?"

"Well, I'm not a cowboy . . ."

He said, "Listen, nigger, I've seen 'em come up and I've seen 'em go down. If you're going up you'd better look the part."

"Oh, yes sir, Mr. Foxx."

Redd died a few years ago, but I imagine he didn't mind that I didn't take his advice. I wore a cowboy hat now and then but I never took to the traditional western garb on stage.

In all honesty, it took longer for the Nashville crowd to become accustomed to me than I thought it would. I was a novelty, but I never allowed myself to feel out of place. Unless someone else brought it up—that I was *different*—I tried not to think about it much. To give you an idea of how little I thought about it, Rozene and I had never really discussed the fact that I was plowing new ground in this industry and she was surprised to learn that.

We received a copy of a press release RCA sent out and it noted that I was the first black country singer ever signed by a major label. Rozene read it, looked over at me, and said, "Pride, is that true?"

"I guess so," I said.

Once I was through the door, I considered myself no different than anyone else. But I was pretty much alone in that respect.

"Charley," Webb Pierce said to me after I had begun recording, "it's good to have you, good for you to be in our music."

I loved Webb, I truly did. But that statement made me bristle, even though I'm sure he had nothing but goodwill on his mind.

"Webb, it's my music, too," I said.

"What was that?"

"It's my music, too," I said.

"Of course . . ."

It didn't occur to him that putting it that way cast me in the role of an outsider, someone intruding on private property. It was something I would face time and again until people stopped seeing me as some kind of prepackaged curio.

Don Meredith, Brenda Lee, Joe Tex, Ferlin Husky, and I went up to Toronto to be in a pilot for a television show, and while we were waiting to rehearse I spent some time talking to Joe Tex's drummer, a black guy.

We were discussing singers—Jim Reeves, in particular—and music and various things and I noticed he was looking at me with a funny expression. Finally he said, "You really talk like that, don't you?"

"Talk like what?" I asked.

He had been sitting there sizing me up while I rambled on about Jim Reeves.

"I've heard you sing and I've heard about you but I thought you were just doing this . . . well, to make a dollar. I didn't think you talked like them, too."

"I just talk like me," I said.

He was so distracted by my speaking voice—the fact that I didn't talk the basic Southern black dialect—that we never got back to our conversation about Jim Reeves.

* * *

Looking back on it, I realize I was more of a curiosity to the older Nashville artists than the new ones. Waylon Jennings and I signed with RCA about the same time and we spent a lot of hours at the Capitol Park Inn, a place where all the artists and DJs and other industry people stayed when they were in town.

If Waylon was uncomfortable or felt there was anything remarkable about sitting in a booth with a *colored* guy in downtown Nashville, he certainly never showed it. Waylon is part Indian and I don't remember the subject of race ever being mentioned between us. We were just a couple of rookies trying to work our way onto the starting lineup.

I also met a lot of the younger artists at Tootsie's Orchard Lounge, which is just across the alley from the Ryman Auditorium. When *The Grand Ole Opry* was in the Ryman, Tootsie's was where everyone went to oil their gears before a show and cool them down afterward.

Tootsie's was a photographic museum of country music. Pictures and posters of country music legends—everybody from Cowboy Copas and Hawkshaw Hawkins to Minnie Pearl and Rod Brassfield—covered every square inch of the high walls, and I used to sit in there and stare with reverence at those photos and wonder if someday I'd find myself a place in Tootsie's gallery.

I met Mooney Lynn in there, and he and Loretta have been good friends to Rozene and me. Years later, when Loretta was picked to present me with a country music award, she got letters and phone calls warning her that she had better not hug me during the presentation. She not only hugged me, she kissed me.

George Jones, though a little older, is also from my generation of country singers and he didn't have any problems with my skin color. We once spent the night in the same bed.

I'd better explain that.

We were touring together around Texas and after a show—I think it was in Waco—we went over to the home of a local DJ to bend our elbows a little.

"Every time George takes a drink, you take one," the DJ said to me. George has a legendary capacity for whiskey and while I drank pretty hard in those days I couldn't keep up with him.

"I don't want to drink that much," I said.

George said, "If you're going to drink with me, you're going to drink when I do."

Well, I tried and, sure enough, got loaded. I barely remember lying across one of the beds and conking out. When I woke up, George was right beside me.

Our host woke us both up chattering about something that had happened during the night.

"Charley, they've been here," he was saying. "Look at your car out there."

"What do you mean they've been here?" Trying to match George drink for drink had left me with a hangover the size of the Astrodome.

"The Klan," he said. "You got KKK written on your car."

I jumped up and looked out the window. Then it hit me.

"No," I said. "If the Klan had been here they would have come in after me."

George and the DJ had written that on my car after I had passed out the night before.

The older artists were more aloof and standoffish, and I soon learned that if the ice was going to be broken, I would have to swing the pick.

Tex Ritter seemed leery of me the first time we were around one another. He didn't initiate a conversation but I would catch him looking me over while I was talking to someone else. Tex was another of my childhood idols, like the old radio stars that had been so familiar to me. But he was from the picture shows of my youth, the Saturday Westerns at the movie house in Sledge. Like the radio programs, most of those films were etched in my memory. Determined to talk to him, I ambled over and said, "How's Charles King?"

Tex raised his eyebrows. "Old Charles? He's dead now. You remember him?"

"Oh, yes," I said. "He played Big Joe. Poor guy. One week you whipped up on him and Bob Steele whipped up on him the next."

A wide smile crossed his face. I described some scenes from a couple of those old movies—one about a gunfight in a saloon.

"You remember that, huh?" he said. We talked for a long time about those movies. In time Tex and I became good friends and I am very fond of his widow, Katherine, and their son John, who followed his father into show business.

There were disc jockeys who balked at playing my early records. I couldn't name them, but I remember hearing at the time that a few stations were reluctant, mostly out of concern for how their audiences and advertisers would react.

But the guys at the big stations, the 50,000-watt window benders, not only played my records but they had me on their shows pretty early in my career. There was Charlie Douglass at WWL in New Orleans, Mike Hoyer at WHO in Des Moines, Bill Mack at WBAP in Fort Worth, Billy Parker at KVOO in Tulsa, and, of course, Ralph Emery at WSM in Nashville. They were all influential in getting me the kind of air play I needed and did a lot toward helping me get acquainted with country fans.

Ralph Emery was the overnight DJ for WSM and he had a reputation for asking pretty tough, direct questions, going right to the heart of the matter. I was warned to be prepared for that, but Ralph was gentle and gentlemanly with me.

Ralph was a gutsy broadcaster in more ways than just his questioning. He invited me on his afternoon show on WSM-TV, but before I arrived on the scene he had already broken that show's color barrier with another black singer, who was more of a pop artist. The guy sang two songs—"I Left My Heart in San Francisco," followed by the Patsy Cline classic "I Fall to Pieces."

After the show, Ralph got a call from a woman viewer who was incensed by the performance.

"Why did you have him on?" she demanded.

"I thought he was a good singer," Ralph said.

"But he sang Patsy's song," she said.

"Lady," Ralph asked, "why are you so prejudiced?" He hung up on her.

Neither Ralph nor I remember much detail about my appearance on his television show except that there was no adverse fallout for him and it did a lot to establish my credibility as a country singer.

Gradually I was getting past the influential people in Nashville. Faron Young. Ralph Emery. Webb Pierce. The next one I had to test was a prolific young songwriter and rising singer named Willie Nelson.

CHAPTER SEVENTEEN

Winning Over Willie

Since I was not personally involved in the planning and negotiations, I have to rely on secondhand accounts of how I got a spot on what has come to be remembered as The Willie Nelson Tour in 1967. If Detroit was a watershed concert for me, traveling with Willie through Texas and Louisiana was a milestone of a different sort. We would be working some hard-core segregationist turf—many of the small towns strung across southeast Texas and into Louisiana had active Ku Klux Klan chapters.

Originally it was a tour that Crash Stewart was putting together for Ray Price and he was in Nashville looking for some other acts to fill out the package. For some reason Ray had to back out, and Willie, whose biggest years were still ahead of him, persuaded Stewart to make him the headliner instead. He even offered to help out with some of the costs, such as buying radio advertising to promote the tour. It would be called The Willie Nelson Show and would feature four or five other acts—Jeannie Seely, Hank Cochran, Stonewall Jackson, and maybe some newcomer who wouldn't cost a lot.

To round out the program Crash Stewart proposed hiring

me. He liked my singing and at that time I did not yet command a big fee.

As Willie has told it, he was reluctant, purely for monetary reasons, to go along with the plan. "It's too big a risk," he told Crash. "We could piss a lot of people off and lose a lot of money."

Willie understood Texas as well as anybody and there probably was a good basis for his reservations. That tour would visit towns where it was risky for blacks to drive through in broad daylight, let alone spend the night. Vidor, a little town outside of Beaumont toward the Louisiana state line, is one of those. As recently as 1993, there was a big flap there because a black man moved into a public housing project. Until then Vidor had been all white. There were many places like Vidor along the roads the tour would be following.

But Crash argued with Willie and, to convince him, played one of my songs for him. It was "Snakes Crawl at Night." Willie liked it and said, "Okay, put him on the show."

The tour started in Houston and then came to the Convention Center Arena Theater in Dallas. Jack Johnson and I drove into town the night of the show. About all either of us knew about Dallas was that it was the city where President Kennedy had been assassinated. In our minds Dealey Plaza was a spooky place we wanted to avoid.

"We don't want to get lost and end up there," I told Jack.

We arrived in town after dark and immediately got lost. Downtown Dallas is laid out on a diagonal, and the way some of the streets meander around, it's easy to get confused about which direction you're going. We stopped to asked for directions and still had trouble finding the arena. We pulled over to the curb to get our bearings. I looked out the window and there was the Texas School Book Depository Building. We were in Dealey Plaza.

173

"Dad gum," Jack said. "We're pretty good at finding the places we don't want to be."

Things got spookier at the arena. It was a large place and was packed to the rafters. When we walked in, the promoter took me aside.

"You're not thin-skinned are you, Charley?" he said.

"Why?"

"We got about ten thousand people here . . . and . . . well . . . we . . ."

I thought he was concerned that someone would shout a racial slur and hurt my feelings or something like that.

"I don't think I'm thin-skinned," I said.

". . . we don't think anything's going to happen . . . but we got two fellas out here in case something *does* happen," he said, "and they're ready to get you off the stage."

My mouth went so dry it felt like it was stuffed with cotton. He's not talking about name calling. He thinks something really bad might happen in a room with ten thousand people, and he only has two guys to get me out?

From time to time people have asked me, "How could you go on stage and perform under those conditions?" I'll admit I was nervous, but somehow the Master gives you the courage to do what you have to do. Besides, all my experience up to then told me that the promoters were seriously misjudging the audiences. Not once had I had an unpleasant encounter with a country music fan. But everyone else—the promoters, club owners, the other entertainers—always seemed to be expecting the worst, and sometimes I had to take their fears seriously. After all, they understood country music crowds better than I—or so I thought.

Horace Logan was the emcee for the show. He, too, was edgy. He took Jack Johnson aside and said, "How should we bring him on?"

Jack remembered how Ralph Emery had handled my introduction in Detroit. "Just say here's a fellow from RCA Records and he has three singles out," Jack said.

Horace went out on stage but apparently felt he needed to alert the audience to what was coming.

"Here's a young man from RCA records and he's colored and has three singles out," he said. He slipped in "and he's colored" so fast you could hardly detect it.

In a way, the Dallas Convention Center was a repeat of the Olympia Arena, except it was a lot farther south.

When I was introduced and walked on stage, the reaction was the same. The applause started out boisterous and then softly faded when the lights hit me. It didn't stop, just fell in volume.

I remember walking to the microphone and glancing to my right and seeing Jimmy Day, the steel guitar player. His hands were tense and suspended above the strings, as though he were bracing for something.

My mouth was still dry but I managed to moisten my lips and speak words similar to the ones I had used in Detroit and many times since. "I guess you're surprised to see me comin' out here wearin' this permanent tan and singing country music, but I love country music and I just hope you'll enjoy it."

It worked. I did my part of the show and the audience was probably more enthusiastic than the one in Detroit. A lot of country music fans may have been racist in some ways, but when it came to music, skin color didn't seem to mean a lot to them.

I had always had confidence that if I could just get on stage, I could win people over. The hard part was winning over the promoters and club owners, convincing them to let me get on stage in the first place.

That tour with Willie opened some doors, partly because it dispelled a lot of anxieties about the race factor, proved that trouble didn't follow Charley Pride.

Willie even began to flaunt it.

We had a stop in San Antonio and we were all staying at the Roadway Inn. Jack and I drove up and there were a lot of people standing in front of the motel. Willie was there, along with some of the band members and a group of fans.

As I got out of my car I heard Willie yell, "Hey, Supernigger, come over here."

As I walked toward him, everyone looked around nervously, maybe thinking there was going to be trouble. When I got to where Willie was standing, he grabbed me and kissed me with the whole crowd looking on. That broke everybody up.

Willie called me "Supernigger" for a long time after that. I think it was his way of disarming any racists who might be around, a way of taking the language of rancor and throwing it back at them as humor, the way Redd Foxx often did. In the same way that profanity is enfeebled by overuse, the buzzwords of hate can be neutralized by mocking them.

After that successful tour, Crash Stewart asked me to sign a photograph. "Put on there, 'You took the chance,'" Crash said.

For most entertainers, I believe, there is a single experience, one defining moment, when confidence replaces the self-doubt that most of us wrestle with early in our careers. For me that happened on an autumn day in Phoenix, Arizona, when I was asked to substitute for Jimmy Durante at a state fair show.

A series of performers was booked for the fair, one for each day. I had played before about seventeen thousand people and Jack Johnson and I were getting ready to leave town the next day.

We got a call from Rex Allen, who was emceeing the shows. Jimmy Durante had done his first show but fell and hurt his head and was unable to keep his second engagement.

"Would you consider doing thirty minutes for the old man?" he asked.

I was flattered but a little uneasy about it. The people who had bought tickets to my show came to hear country music. Those who had paid to see Jimmy Durante were expecting something else. I had no reason to think they were hungry for my kind of entertainment.

But Rex was very persuasive.

"What do you think, Jack?" I asked my manager.

"Well, why not?" he said.

We accepted. Suspecting that it would be a tough audience to please, Jack and I sat down and put together the tightest show we could think of, packing into thirty minutes what we thought were my best songs.

Rex explained to the audience about Jimmy Durante's accident and how Charley Pride had kindly consented to substitute for him.

I walked on and said, "Ladies and gentlemen, a lot of you probably have never heard of me but I'm happy to fill in for Mr. Durante. Here's a song from my first album. I hope you enjoy it."

I introduced each song by saying, "Here's one from my second album. . . . Here's one from my third album. . . ." I only had three or four albums out, but I was trying to create the impression that I had been around a long time. Those people had come to see a legendary comedian and I didn't want them to leave thinking they had had to settle for an unknown singer.

About halfway through the show, a guy in the audience stood, cupped his hands to his mouth, and shouted, "I've never heard of you," and then added, "but I'm going out and buying them all."

When the show was over, I got a standing ovation, a *standing ovation* from a Jimmy Durante crowd.

"Tell you what," I said to Jack Johnson later. "I believe all

I need to do is to get in front of them—any audience—and I can make it."

The opportunities to get in front of them were improving. Not every club owner believed it yet, but booking Charley Pride was no more controversial than booking George Jones or Jerry Lee Lewis, who sometimes had trouble showing up for their dates.

In Conroe, Texas, I was scheduled to play at the 21 Club, which was owned by Larry Butler. I always made it a policy to get to town early, find the club where I was to play, and check everything out a few hours before the show. I showed up at the 21 Club that afternoon and started through the front door. A guy who was sweeping up put out his hand and said, "Whoa."

I stopped, but before I could say anything, Butler came over from the bar and asked, "What's wrong?"

"Do you let *them* in here?" the hired hand asked.

Larry laughed and said, "We'd better let *him* in or we'll have four hundred angry people here tonight."

J.D.'s, a club in Phoenix, signed me to play one weekend, but after learning that I was black, the owner had second thoughts.

Bob Sikora, who owned Mr. Lucky's, a big place on Grand Avenue, heard about it and told Jack Johnson, "Bring him over here. We'll take him."

Bob Sikora had won a large spot in my heart. Even after I had stopped playing clubs, I used to go by Mr. Lucky's when I was in town and play for a percentage of the gate. I couldn't really afford to do it, but you don't forget old friends.

CHAPTER EIGHTEEN

Out of the Red

The first house Rozene and I owned was in Helena. It was small—two bedrooms, a kitchen, one bathroom, and a utility room in back—but we couldn't have been prouder of it. We had two children when we moved in and Angie was born while we were there. Kraig and Dion shared one of the bedrooms and Angie slept in a crib in our room, which was fine with Rozene. She never wanted the babies very far from her.

We paid $7,500 for that house and figured we could live there a few years before we outgrew it. But after the Detroit concert, my bookings picked up sharply—and not just in Montana. Helena did not have a major airport, and to keep my engagements I had to drive to Great Falls, ninety miles away, and fly out of there. It was not only inconvenient, it was expensive, and money was still a big factor in our lives. Rozene was as frugal as ever and we scrimped as we always had. We planned ahead and saved for the smallest things, such as a movie or dinner out.

My third single had reached the Top 10, but the royalty checks still weren't coming from the first one. So I was running around the country playing places like the Cimarron Ballroom in Tulsa or Panther Hall in Fort Worth for $200 or

$250 a pop. It took a lot of shows to put together a decent paycheck, and driving 180 miles round-trip to the airport ate up a lot of time I could have spent singing.

I badgered Jack Clement about the royalties. "When am I going to start seeing something?" I would say. "I've got a lot of expenses and not much income."

"It'll come," he assured me. "Believe me, it'll come."

The travel schedule was becoming so hectic that Rozene and I decided we would have to move to Great Falls and we couldn't wait for the royalties. We found a five-bedroom house there we could buy for $48,000. It was more than twice as large as our home in Helena and gave our family a lot of growing room. But we didn't have much equity in our old house and selling it would not give up enough for the down payment on the new one.

About that time a guy in Hurst, Texas, wanted to put together a tour for me. He had seen how the audiences re-acted to me on the Willie Nelson tour and told me he could book $5,000 worth of dates in Texas alone. That was a lot of money for playing in little honky-tonks. Jack Johnson was dubious, but we decided to take the chance. Any exposure I could get was important.

With those bookings as our collateral, Rozene and I bor-rowed $5,000 from a bank in Great Falls—a very short-term loan. We were supposed to pay it back within a few weeks. We made the down payment and I took off for Texas.

"Don't you go on that stage until you get paid," my man-ager sternly advised me.

It wasn't that easy. In Texas I told the promoter I had to have some money up front but he finessed around it, telling me we would settle up later. I was riding with him from club to club and he kept stalling with the payment. My experience with that kind of thing was pretty limited. Up to that time I mostly had worried about putting on a good show and someone else had taken care of the finances. To say I was feeling the squeeze wouldn't do justice to the situation.

Every day that passed I became more apprehensive. I called Rozene. "I'm having trouble with this guy," I told her. "I'm unsure whether I should refuse to go on or go along and hope we get the money when the tour's over."

We decided there really wasn't much choice. If I walked away, we were out the money for the trip to Texas and would probably lose the house in Great Falls as well as the earnest money we had put up.

"Just don't let him out of your sight," Rozene said.

I didn't, and in the end everything worked out. I got paid for the tour, we paid back the $5,000 loan and moved into the new house. But that experience made me wonder how long we would have to live on the edge. It seemed that everything I did to advance my singing career put us deeper into debt.

I was turning out an album every six months or so, but with every recording session I sank farther into the hole with RCA. Musicians, technicians, and studio time cost a lot of money, and a singer doesn't get anything until all the bills are paid. Appearing on a radio or television show normally pays little or nothing, but it is something you have to do— *want* to do—to sell records and build a following, even though it means money out of your pocket, money you don't have.

The first syndicated show I was invited to appear on was a program Bill Anderson hosted. It originated in Charlotte, North Carolina. To make the trip from Nashville, I had to borrow fifty dollars from Jack Clement. As my producer, he had my future royalties as security.

He got his money back out of my first check from RCA. In fact, he brought that first check to me personally. *Pay to the order of Charley Pride, One Hundred and Thirty Eight Dollars & 00/100.*

"I want to keep that," I told him. "I'm going to frame it."

"Nah," he said. "You can't do that."

"But it's my first check from RCA."

"If you don't cash it, it'll mess up their books." He chuckled. "Besides, you owe me fifty dollars." He went with me to cash it and got his fifty dollars on the spot.

We still laugh about that check. Jack lives in Nashville and I saw him a few years ago. He invited me to his house for a breakfast of sausage and eggs and biscuits—he makes a good breakfast—and he hugged me and said, "You ain't ever going to forgive me for making you cash that check, are you?"

"Cowboy, I've forgiven you but I ain't going to forget it," I said.

A few months later, the next royalty payment came by mail to our home in Great Falls. Based on the size of the first one, we weren't sure what to expect. We probably would have been thrilled if it had been a few hundred dollars. I opened the envelope and looked at the amount.

Eighteen thousand dollars.

"Honey, look at this," I said, handing the check to Rozene. She said, "Whew!"

Just a couple of years earlier, my annual income had been $6,500, and now we were staring at a piece of paper worth three times that.

"I think we're on to something here," I said.

As excited as we were, we realized we had to sit down and talk about this. For the first time in a long time we were out of the red, but that much money can be a jolt. We decided we would just deposit the check and pretend we didn't have it. We would watch this singing business awhile and see where it took us.

My third album was released in December of 1967 and it contained several songs that had done well for other singers; Buck Owens's "Act Naturally" and Merle Haggard's "I Threw

Away the Rose" were among them. It sold pretty well, but the big cut for me on that one was "Does My Ring Hurt Your Finger," which followed "I Know One" into the Top 10.

I still hadn't had the monster hit, but Rozene and I learned where the singing business was taking us when the third royalty check arrived.

"Honey," I said, staring at it in amazement. "Sixty thousand dollars."

The road trips were getting longer and paying better and mile by mile I was learning a lot about the United States of America.

Jim Ames, who booked some gigs for me after the Detroit concert, flew to Montana to travel with me on a long trip through the West. With the third royalty check, I bought a new Oldsmobile and we were going in it to Seattle and Spokane, down through Milton and Freewater, Oregon, into Hayward, Sacramento, San Francisco, and San Jose, California, and over to Arizona and New Mexico.

It was a grind. Some swings like that one lasted a month. At each stop I played for a percentage of the gate. When the show was over, we drove all night to the next town, taking turns sleeping in the backseat.

Late one night, Ames was asleep and I was driving, coming out of some hills near Globe, Arizona, and saw lights flashing in the rearview mirror.

I pulled to the side of the road and the trooper approached the car.

"You were doing about eighty-five down those hills," he said. "And your brakes were smoking."

"Smoking, huh?" Jim was still sawing logs.

The trooper got out his ticket book and started writing. "I didn't think I was driving that fast," I said, hoping I could talk him out of what he was doing. "I'm from Montana

. . . just a little state . . . you wouldn't want to make money off us."

He kept writing.

"You going to give me a ticket?" I said.

"Yes, I'd like you to sign this." I glanced into the backseat, hoping Jim Ames was waking up. He wasn't. The trooper offered the ticket book for my signature.

"I don't believe I want to sign anything," I said.

"Well, sir," he said, moving back and putting a hand on his gun, "I'd like you to step out of the car."

"I believe I'll sign it," I said.

Arizona, I learned, doesn't mind making money off of Montana drivers, especially those tooling downhill at eighty-five miles an hour with their brakes smoking.

A few days later, we were leaving Phoenix headed to Albuquerque and spotted a couple of hitchhikers, a guy and a girl.

"Let's give them a ride," I said to Jim. I had hitchhiked a bit in my time and understood what it was like.

We pulled over and they hurried toward the car. They were hippies, with backpacks, love beads, and the whole works. The guy was wearing a German army helmet and had a swastika tattooed on his hand.

"I'll get in back and sleep awhile," I told Jim. "They can ride up here with you."

They were surly, bitter kids and nervous as hell about me being in the backseat. We had been on the road for a long time and I was tired. Getting comfortable in the backseat wasn't easy. Every time I shifted positions, the hippie guy would jump and look back at me.

Finally, I said, "Look, we picked you up because you needed a ride. We're not going to harm you. If one of you wants to sleep while the other keeps watch, go ahead. But you can both sleep. Nothing's going to happen to you."

He kind of went limp. He probably hadn't slept in days. Before long, they were both sound asleep.

Jim and I tried to be nice to them. We stopped at a little grocery store and bought food to eat along the way. They wolfed it down like they hadn't eaten in a month. But they still seemed full of hate and bitterness.

We let them out in Albuquerque and gave them five dollars apiece. They didn't say a word. Normally I don't get the urge to lecture anybody, but I got it then. What could two people so young have to be so resentful about?

"Can I say something?" I asked them, determined to say it whether they consented or not. "We've watched you all the way from Phoenix. We've talked and felt some of your anger. I can't even guess what you're angry about, but we just gave you some money. You took it but you never said thank you for the ride or thank you for the money. I can't figure out who you despise or who you dislike, but there must be somebody you like. Try to find them and say 'hi' or some kind word. The way your attitude is, you're not going to make it. I would hope someday I could see some happiness in you— if I ever see you again. I hope you can find some happiness somewhere in this world."

That little sermon probably accomplished nothing, but it made me feel better.

They listened until I was finished, mumbled, "Thank you," and walked away.

We could have put them out much earlier, but I didn't want to just dump them beside the road, so we took them as far as we were going. But it was a very unpleasant experience, one I didn't care to repeat. It was painful to see that much hate and anger in people so young.

They were the last hitchhikers I ever picked up.

CHAPTER NINETEEN

Bouts with Depression

The German countryside flitted past the car window but I was in no shape to enjoy it. Slouched down in my seat, exhausted from not sleeping the night before and nursing a severe headache, I closed my eyes and tried to doze.

"My head hurts," I moaned to Rozene. "If I could just sleep . . ."

We were driving to a USO show at one of the army posts with a sergeant named Pop Phillips, who was handling our bookings. Sergeant Phillips was as nice a guy as you would want to meet, but after a few days of playing for the GIs in Germany, I became suspicious of him.

"Don't trust him," I told Rozene. "He's going to do something to us."

She couldn't figure out what I was talking about, but it alarmed her. There were times when she had to ride with Phillips and I wasn't along. Because it was not my nature to be suspicious and fearful of people, she began to wonder, What if he is right?

Explaining to her why I feared Pop Phillips was impossible. He had done nothing, said nothing to provoke those feelings. But as the USO tour went on, it was as though a veil of dark gauze was drawn around me, wrapping me in paranoia, insomnia, confusion, and dread. I believed someone was putting things in my drinks and trying to harm me.

Under the best circumstances, it was a stressful time. We played two shows a day and, as I've already related, I was sometimes jeered by black soldiers who wanted me to sing something besides country music. Working too hard, drinking too much, and wrestling with the racial nonsense had worn me down.

But that didn't account for my behavior, the strange thoughts that were bouncing around in my head. Something alien, something I had no way of understanding, was going on inside me.

Rozene held my head all the way to the USO club that night. When we got there, I broke down and cried. Rozene had been puzzled by my conduct for a few days, but at that point she was convinced that something was seriously out of kilter.

"Pride can't work," she said to Sergeant Phillips. "There's something wrong."

"He'll be all right. Just let him sleep," Phillips said.

She ignored him and went to the band. "There's something wrong with Pride and he can't go on stage," she said.

They had no advice for her, so she found a security person and demanded, "Where's the hospital? We need a doctor."

Within a few hours I was in a hospital under the constant watch of a doctor or nurse or orderly. I was given tranquilizers and sedatives and still had trouble sleeping. I imagined things that weren't there. I talked nonstop, refused to take orders, and was determined to bust out of the place. It was as though a turbine engine were racing inside me. At times I had to be forcefully restrained and held in bed with nylon straps.

Oddly enough, I could often control the wild moods and emotions when I tried hard enough. During Rozene's visits,

I was relatively calm, almost normal. But as soon as she left, I lost control again.

I was impulsive and unpredictable. Walking to the cafeteria for lunch with a group of other patients, I saw a door and, unnoticed by the orderlies, I angled toward it, walked faster, and bolted through it in a full run. The orderlies gave chase but I had a good jump on them.

I ran past an open manhole where a guy was working in a sewer and considered for an instant trying to lose myself down there. Cutting across a street, I ignored the traffic and was nearly struck by a car. I could still motor pretty well but the orderlies eventually overtook me, returned me to the hospital, and strapped me to the bed. After that I was never more than arm's length away from an attendant.

In a week or so, I began to get back to normal and was released from the hospital. The doctors instructed me to find a psychiatrist when I returned home, someone who could provide the treatment I needed. Their diagnosis: manic depression.

That was in 1968 and we still lived in Great Falls, Montana. As ordered, I visited a psychiatrist, who tried to explain manic depression to me. My assumptions that the problems in Germany had been brought on by stress, fatigue, and alcohol, he assured me, were false.

It is a chemical imbalance, he explained, and can be completely controlled by medication, without which the problem will recur. The imbalance has something to do with the amount of salt and liquids in and around cells, but not a lot is known about what causes the imbalance. Drinking and exhaustion would aggravate it, the doctor said, but would not cause it.

"You will have to take medication for the rest of your life," he said.

Like hell I will. I've never liked taking drugs of any kind—

not even aspirin. I just didn't like the feeling of being medicated, of being controlled by chemicals. He gave me a prescription for tranquilizers. Lithium, the most common treatment today, was still experimental back then. I took the pills for a while and then threw them away. I refused to believe there was anything wrong with me.

Manic depression takes several different forms, I learned over the years, and is much more common than I realized.

In most people the moods swing from extreme highs to extreme lows. For me, the highs were more extreme than the lows. My highs appeared to be typical—sleeplessness, mind speeding like a cruise missile, talkativeness, restlessness, grand schemes and plans. I've been told that during those times, when the energy level is high and little sleep is required, many people become extremely creative and productive.

In a lot of cases the lows are debilitating and paralyzing. People are unable to work or even get out of bed. I was lucky. The dips took the milder form of headaches and weariness.

For many years after the episode in Germany there were no serious problems. I think I had mild experiences with the manic highs but was able to contain them. When I couldn't, Rozene usually recognized the symptoms before I did.

My second major bout occurred in 1982, long after we had moved to Dallas. I began sleeping less and made it difficult for Rozene to sleep, too. I would lie in bed and talk incessantly. I became distrustful of everyone around me except Rozene.

One common symptom of a manic high is lavish spending. I bought a limited-edition Stutz for myself and an expensive ring for Rozene. I was making a lot of money at the time so that wasn't excessive, it was just out of character—another clue to Rozene that my body chemistry was tilting again.

Slowly, it got worse. She wanted me to go into the hospital, but I refused. She talked to my agent and others who worked for me. They were against hospitalization, fearful that it would result in publicity that would affect my career, which was at a peak. Rozene allowed herself to be persuaded for a while and tried to cope with me at home until the crisis passed.

It only got worse. Small noises bothered me so much that I threw televisions and VCRs out the door. She hired order-lies and nurse's aides to come to the house. As before, I was obsessed with getting out of the house, getting in the car, and driving off. I tried to bolt through every door I passed.

At night Rozene put a belt around my waist and hooked her hand through it to keep me from slipping out of bed while she slept. She was exhausted most of the time.

Her mother came to stay with us and my brother Harmon, who lived in Dallas then, came by now and then to help out. While they were there, they later told me I became convinced that I was a preacher—not just any preacher, but Moses himself. With a staff in hand, I walked through the house preaching sermons. Some of what I learned growing up in the household and church of a Baptist deacon, I suppose, had lain dormant in my mind until aroused by skewed brain chemistry.

Rozene had contacted a psychiatrist, Dr. William Waltrip, about my condition. He prescribed lithium, but I refused to take it. Most of the time I gripped the pills in my hand, walked into the bathroom, and flushed them down the toilet.

The doctor wanted to treat me at home but Rozene over-ruled him and took me to Baylor Hospital. She was told she couldn't admit me without my consent. Fortunately for me, she can be very persuasive, and in those periods of confusion and paranoia, she was the only person on earth I trusted or would listen to. I checked myself into the hospital.

With the aid of lithium, my chemical balance was restored in a few days, in time to keep an engagement at Billy Bob's Texas in Forth Worth.

"Shouldn't we cancel that show?" Rozene asked.

"I can do it," I insisted. "I can do it."

Except for that one occasion in Germany, I never had to cancel a show because of manic depression. I've gone on stage halfway there, fighting to control it with willpower, and the audience never suspected a thing.

The show at Billy Bob's went off without a hitch and not long after that I stopped taking the lithium. I had developed a skin rash serious enough to send me to a dermatologist. He couldn't diagnose precisely what caused it, but I blamed the lithium and refused to take any more of it.

Lithium was not responsible, the doctor told me, but I was still convinced that I could whip the manic depression without pharmaceutical assistance.

We were in Albuquerque for a charity golf tournament. I went into one of my talkative spells and couldn't sleep. This time Rozene wasted no time.

One of the charities the tournament benefited was a Catholic hospital. Rozene went to one of the nuns and said, "I need the name of a doctor who can talk to Charley's doctor and give him some medication." After speaking to Dr. Waltrip, the Albuquerque physician prescribed thorazine and sleeping pills.

Rozene went to the tournament chairman. "Pride is manic and he's having a mini episode," she said. "I'm taking him home."

We were on a plane to Dallas the same day.

Those mini episodes were likely to happen at any time, but the severe bouts with manic depression occurred in the wintertime. There is a form of depression (seasonal affective disorder, SAD) that occurs mostly in the winter and is triggered by a lack of sunlight. That may or may not have been a factor in my case, but the fact that my worst episodes were seasonal, popping up during the winter breaks from my concert tours, prevented them from interfering in my career and, therefore, kept me from grasping the seriousness of the problem.

I finally came to terms with manic depression and lithium in 1989.

That episode began like the others—talking ceaselessly, insomnia—but grew much worse. I had attacks of panic, anxiety, and delusions. Dr. Waltrip prescribed lithium again, but I wouldn't take it.

Kraig and his wife stayed at our house to help Rozene— mostly to keep me from doing something harmful to myself. When I walked around the house, someone was always with me, usually positioned between me and the door.

I insisted on having access to the telephone. One night I called Travis Ward, who owned the company from which we leased our airplane.

"I need a plane right away," I said.

"Okay, Charley, we'll get it ready," he said.

"I want Air Force One," I told him.

He laughed, thinking I was making a joke.

The next morning Rozene called Dr. Waltrip. "I won't go through what I went through in 1982," she told him. "I want something done."

Dr. Waltrip arranged for me to be placed in one of the suites at Baylor Hospital, but we had to hire someone to keep me from leaving. That lasted one day before I was moved, strapped to a gurney, to the psychiatric ward, where I could be restrained to the bed. I wasn't aware of what town I was in or what planet I was on.

One of the down sides to celebrity is that people sometimes treat you differently than they do others when they shouldn't, deferring to you rather than demanding of you. Rozene felt that was the case with William Waltrip. He was my friend as well as my doctor and she believed he was being too gentle with me. If I refused to take the medication, he would coax rather than command. As often as not, I didn't respond to the coaxing.

Rozene waited while I was checked into the psychiatric ward and then confronted Dr. Waltrip. She was strained to the limit and broke into tears as they talked.

"I want the name of the best doctor in Dallas to treat a manic," she told him. "Pride doesn't need a friend, he needs a doctor. You're going to let him outtalk you. He doesn't need that. Why are you treating him, when *he's* telling *you* what he's going to do and what he's not?"

From that point on my relationship with Bill Waltrip changed. He was far less accommodating to me than he had been before. He administered medication whether or not I approved and he gave instructions for the nurses to follow, whether I protested or not.

A few weeks after I was released, Rozene and I went to his office for a check-up. He insisted that I stay on the lithium and maintain certain other routines that I found disagreeable. I argued with him but he wouldn't budge.

"But, Doctor," I said, "you're my friend."

He look at Rozene and back at me and said, "I'm not your friend, I'm your doctor."

In truth, he is both. I've only seen him professionally a few times since then and it is just to talk. I'm thankful for that.

Manic depression can be a nightmare for the sufferers and for everyone around them. I was probably hesitant to accept the fact that I was afflicted by it because it smacked of *mental disease* or *emotional disorder* or something just as horrible. It is neither of those. It is a medical condition like diabetes or any other malady over which the mind has no control.

My advice to anyone who suffers from it, or even suspects they do, is to get help. It is treatable and controllable.

I've taken the lithium regularly for the past few years and

have had no further bouts with manic depression. I've always been a hyper person, one who needed to be doing something physical all the time. I had difficulty sitting through business meetings or any other sedentary activity. I'm still that way, but I run on an even keel—no wild highs, no migraines, and no imagining things that aren't there. And I sleep very well.

CHAPTER TWENTY

Looking for a Home

Great Falls had been a great place to live but by 1969 it was obvious that we would have to leave Montana. Travel connections from there were simply too difficult and too time-consuming. That realization came to me when I was booked for a Saturday show in Dayton, Ohio. To get there I had to fly to Chicago on Friday, stay overnight, and catch an early flight to Dayton in the morning.

Flights out of Great Falls were not frequent. If you missed one, you might have to wait a day for the next one.

Rozene and I discussed several cities where we might want to live. Nashville would have been an obvious choice, but memories of segregation still weighed on both our minds. Our children were young and we wanted a different environment for them. It was 1969, after all—only a year after Martin Luther King, Jr., was killed in Memphis. It seemed to us that there was too much turmoil in that area and we did not want our children to be subjected to it.

Denver was high on our list. We loved the mountains and the city was centrally located, had a good airport, and was a good place for kids. But Denver was still a growing city and lacked certain amenities. There were no Denver Broncos or

Denver Nuggets back then and we both wanted access to professional sports.

We considered Phoenix. It offered easy access, but the climate was unacceptable. We wanted four seasons. If moving were necessary, it might as well be to someplace that could satisfy as many of our criteria and passions as possible.

On my way back to Montana after a show in Corpus Christi, Texas, early that year I made a connection through Love Field in Dallas. The layover was about two hours and I spent most of the time hanging around the departure lounge sizing up the passengers, playing the same guessing game I used to play while people-watching on the streets of Memphis. *Who are they? What do they do? Where are they going?*

Along came a guy in a blue-and-white seersucker pinstripe suit and dark glasses—a good-looking son of a gun in his thirties with thick hair that was already starting to turn gray. He had a certain air about him. *He's flying first class,* I guessed.

Sure enough, we got on the plane and he had the seat right behind mine.

"Is that a putter?" he asked me.

I was just getting into golf, and in Corpus Christi a fan to whom I had confessed that I was a terrible golfer had given me a gold-plated putter with a few unusual attachments to help me out. It had a horn, a light, and a device for measuring the distance to the cup. Obviously, it was not a standard golf club.

"Sort of," I said.

I was sitting by the window and the aisle seat was vacant.

"Do you mind if I move up there?" he asked.

"Come on up."

He introduced himself as Jerry Lastelick, attorney at law, and told me was on his way to do some legal work for either Lee Elder, a black golfer, or Lee Elder's first wife. Normally he probably wouldn't have said anything to me but I suppose he thought I was another black golfer and there weren't many of them around.

"Are you a golfer?" he asked.

"Oh, no. I'm just trying to be."

"Are you in sports?"

"I used to be a baseball player," I said, "but now I'm a singer . . . country music singer."

As we talked, I told him about our plans to move from Great Falls and the various cities we had considered.

"Have you ever thought about Dallas?" he said.

We hadn't. I had passed through Dallas a lot, had played there on the Willie Nelson Tour, but that was all.

"Tell me about it," I said.

He did, and before we landed in Denver Jerry gave me his card. "Call me if you want to come to Dallas and look around," he said.

Instead of putting the card in my shirt or jacket pocket, as I usually did, I put it in a clip with my folding money to be sure it wasn't misplaced. I called him within a few days.

The next week I was scheduled to do a show in Atlanta and Rozene and I decided that she would go to Dallas to look around and I would join her there after my Atlanta engagement.

"I want a place I can afford," I told Jerry, "but I don't want someplace where it's going to be a big deal about us moving in, like busting blocks."

He picked Rozene up at the airport and found a black real estate agent to show her some houses. They visited subdivisions around Richardson and places like that, neighborhoods with small tract-type houses. Rozene wasn't interested.

We were doing pretty well by 1969. I released three albums that year and the first one, *Charley Pride—In Person*, went gold. "All I Have to Offer You Is Me," a single off that year's third album, was my first number-one hit. The royalty checks were getting bigger and coming steadily. We were not bargain hunting.

When I got to Dallas from Atlanta, I met Rozene at the Holiday Inn just off Industrial Boulevard—the same hotel where I stayed on the Willie Nelson Tour—and Jerry picked us up and drove us to his house for dinner. He and Rozene told me about the houses they had looked at and what she didn't like about them.

"Jerry," I said as we were eating, "are there any houses for sale here in your neighborhood?"

He kind of sat back, crossed his legs, and looked at me for a second. "As a matter of fact," he said, "there's one right across the street. But you may not like it. It's got striped rugs and all that."

The first thing that crossed my mind was, *He's trying to talk me out of it.* That wasn't the case at all. Jerry, I think, had no idea of the kind of money that could be made singing country music. It was still early in my career and it hadn't occurred to him that we could afford a house in North Dallas.

"We can start looking tomorrow," he said. He set us up with Dottie Whitebread, of Ebby Halliday Realtors, a company that did not dabble in cheap property. She showed us one house with a pool in Russwood Acres. We turned it down. None of us swam and I had heard too many stories about people coming home and finding a son or daughter floating lifeless in the pool. We would consider a pool when the kids were older.

We walked up the street to Royal Crest, turned and went a block or so to Russwood Circle and a house that was just being finished by the builders. Rozene walked in, looked around and said, "Is this for sale?"

"Sure is," Jack White, the builder, said.

"This is what I want," Rozene said. "This is it. Can you add a playroom over the garage and have it ready by June?"

Ordering the extra room ran the price of the house up to about $130,000. That was high-priced real estate in 1969, even in North Dallas.

We moved in that summer. Before we arrived, word got around. *There's one moving in.* But the neighbors were gracious and welcomed us to the street. Some brought champagne over to christen the new house.

If there was concern about integrating the neighborhood, it may have had less to do with our race than with the fact that I was a country singer. It got back to us later than there had been some fretting over the lifestyle we might bring to the street. *Those show business people have rowdy ways . . . wild parties . . . throwing things through windows.*

Rozene and I were not given to boisterous revelry and to the relief of the neighbors—maybe the disappointment of a few— ours was one of the quietest houses in Russwood Acres.

This story has probably been told about every black man who ever moved into an affluent white neighborhood. I think it was told on Thurgood Marshall, the Supreme Court Justice; Carl Rowan, the syndicated columnist; Jesse Jackson, the civil rights leader; and Lord knows who else.

It was told on me, along with another that probably is a Pride exclusive.

The first one goes like this:

> *Charley Pride is mowing his lawn and a white woman drives by in a long, expensive car. Assuming him to be a yard man, she pulls to the curb and waves him over.*
>
> *"How much do you charge for mowing lawns?" she asks.*
>
> *"Well," Pride says, "for this particular one, I get to sleep with the lady of the house."*

The second version was customized to take my profession into account:

Charley Pride moves into an all-white neighborhood in Dallas. One day he is mowing his lawn and a woman comes from the house across the street.
"When you finish there, will you come over and mow mine?" she says.
"Sure," Charley says. They agree on a price.
He mows her lawn, but she is not at home to pay him. That evening he shows up at her house to collect and Elvis is with him.

Neither of those stories is true but my denials in the past have never stopped them from circulating. I've mowed a lot of lawns in my time, but since we have lived in Dallas the music business has been generous enough to allow me to employ others to do that for me.

Besides, Elvis never visited me in Dallas.

Besides good schools, a good airport, and the Cowboys, Dallas had golf courses, and golf was fast becoming a preoccupation—some might say an obsession—with me. I'm still not as good as I would like to be. I took lessons to learn how to do things the right way and can hold my own on most courses. Since Grand Rapids, Minnesota, in 1966, I have not lost a driver to a cottonwood, or any other kind of tree.

I've played in just about every kind of weather. I play for fun, for charity, for therapy, for fellowship, for just about any reason I can think up.

As we settled into Dallas, the Great Southwest Golf Club gave me membership and later I joined Brookhaven Country Club. Because of those two memberships, I wasn't really looking for another place to play, but in 1979, James Harrison, a neighbor of mine, suggested I join Royal Oaks Country Club, where he was a member.

"We only have about six hundred members," he said.

I said, "Well, I already belong to two."

"Why don't you fill out an application," he said. "We have thirty on the waiting list, so it'll take a while to get down to you."

I sent in the application, paid the $6,000 fee, and waited. It took some time for my name to move up the list. After a while, my check was returned along with a letter from Royal Oaks which said, "Article 12, section 3, states that if five or more members object to an applicant . . ."

Five or more had objected.

Word got out and right away camera crews and reporters from the three major Dallas network-affiliated television stations descended on my office.

"Charley, what do you think was behind this?" they asked.

"Jim Harrison asked me to fill out an application and I did. This is what I got back," I said, showing them the letter of rejection.

"Do they have any black members?"

"You'll have to ask them."

They kept pushing me, obviously wanting me to say, "Hell yes, I was turned down because of my skin color." That much was apparent. It would have been redundant for me to state it.

"What do you think, Charley?" a reporter asked for the fifteenth or twentieth time.

"Maybe my finger was too short or something," I said.

"We checked and found out there are no Jews or blacks in that club," a reporter said.

"Look," I said, "there's a possibility that is it, and in case it is, let me say this: First of all, I already belong to two clubs. I had no idea this would come up. Those five members who objected probably don't have enough money to pay their dues every month. It makes no difference to me. But it's not just them. That club has five hundred and ninety-five other members who let that rule exist. I don't want to be around them either—not just the five who objected, but the whole six hundred.

"I play golf all over the world. If I didn't belong to two other clubs and wanted to play bad enough, I'd go out and buy my own golf course."

If anyone really doubted that I was rejected because of my skin pigmentation, the proof wasn't long in coming. Another black guy went out there, as a member's guest, and somebody put a dead rat in his bag.

For a while I played occasionally at Preston Trails Country Club and there was a little flap over certain members taking me there too often. A few folks went to the club pro and suggested that there should be limits placed on how much I could play there. I heard about the complaints and never went back.

Mostly what I feel for those kinds of people is pity. If that's the way they believe, so be it, but I wasn't going to let them draw me into their moral swamp. If you're not careful, you can wake up some morning and realize you missed a lot of enjoyment because you spent too much time worrying about those people and what they think. There is little to be gained by letting yourself be saddled with that kind of demented mentality.

CHAPTER TWENTY-ONE

Banking on Business

Sometime around two in the morning, the telephone rang at my hotel on Prince Edward Island and I answered in a half stupor induced by fatigue and whiskey. We had had a good show that night and afterward, feeling good, I went to my room to unwind with a bottle of VO. The ringing woke me from the first stages of sleep.

"Yeah."

"Pride? This is Rozene . . ."

"Honey . . ." I started to ask if anything was wrong, but another voice broke in.

"This is George Jones." Not *that* George Jones. This one was an executive with Mercantile Bank, the correspondent bank of First Texas Bank in Dallas, of which I was the majority stockholder. I tried to clear my head.

"I'm on the line, too, Charley." It was Jerry Lastelick, my attorney and the guy who had introduced me to the banking business.

"What's goin' on?" I asked.

They proceeded to give me a rundown, which sobered me up and woke me up pretty quick. A kite—a bogus check scheme—had been run on the bank . . . major losses . . .

federal examiners may shut the doors . . . president tossed out and locked out . . . immediate cash required.

A lot of what they were telling me got lost in the fog, but I understood one thing: The bank had to have a $1.2-million cash infusion or the regulators would close it and I would lose everything—not just my investment in stock, but most of the half million I had on deposit.

If I could come up with $800,000 in cash collateral, another investor would chip in $400,000 in cash collateral, and Mercantile Bank would lend us the entire amount, Jerry and George explained.

"What you're telling me is that I have no choice," I said.

"Something like that," Jerry said.

There I was, at two in the morning, half asleep and half a continent away, trying to deal with a multimillion-dollar banking problem. It was a big leap from picking cotton for three dollars a hundred. Well, Pride, you wanted to be a businessman, I thought. At the moment, it was hard to remember why.

Early in my singing career I began to pay attention to those entertainers who seemed to have a talent for putting their earnings to work for them. Bob Hope was probably the ultimate one that I watched. Eddy Arnold, Roy Acuff, and, of course, Gene Autry were others who had done well in business. I didn't talk to any of them at length about their activities but I tried to pick up on what they were doing and file it away for future reference.

Buck Owens also made some very shrewd investments, particularly in real estate around his adopted hometown of Bakersfield, California. While I was touring with him, he talked to me a lot about what he was doing and what was good for him. I wish there had been time for me to learn more from him. I might have avoided a few of the potholes I stepped into along the way.

I've had winners and losers, but probably more of the latter. I'm not complaining. There is a learning process you have to go through and you have to pay for your education. You pay through the nose a lot of times before you learn.

When your career is hot and the hits are coming fast, you make a lot of money in a short period of time. There are only two things you can do with money—spend it or invest it. If you do either the wrong way, you're in trouble.

There is never a shortage of advice—a lot of it well meaning but misguided. Swindlers and con artists are also circling around you. Because you're performing all the time, you have to trust someone to help you with your financial affairs and that leaves you vulnerable. The more you expand yourself, widen your affairs, increase your holdings, the more dependent you become on others to manage things for you. You're not able to watch every angle and see every way you can be had.

Willie Nelson got $16 or $18 million in debt to the Internal Revenue Service that way. The people who were managing his money did a lousy job of it. Some of his money was put into tax shelters that turned out to be illegal. There were times when I was urged to do the same thing. "People with money use tax shelters," I was told. I never bit on that one. My attitude was, "I'll pay my taxes and keep what's left over and sleep well at night."

Consequently I've never had trouble with the IRS. They audited us five years in a row and couldn't believe we were paying that honestly. They kept coming back, costing me a lot of money by tying up my attorneys and my accountants, but the only big error they ever found was in our favor. We had overpaid one year and got a big chunk back.

My first business ventures were made jointly with Jack Johnson, my manager, and I'm not sure which was worse, our timing or our choice of partners.

We got into some oil and gas ventures and stayed in until the bottom fell out of the oil business. We got into the electric grill business and were taken for a ride by our partner.

Jack came to me with that deal. I don't blame him. It just went sour because we couldn't see how the company was operating until it was too late. For $200,000, he said, I could own 16 or 18 percent of a company called Lectra-Chef Grill in Nashville. We looked it over pretty carefully, we thought. Rozene and I sat down with Jerry Lastelick and our accountants, went over the numbers, and saw nothing to scare us away.

Lectra-Chef seemed to have everything going for it. The company produced a good grill, probably the best on the market, and had a national distribution system and good sales figures. On the surface it looked like a going enterprise. The assembly lines were busy, the trucks were running, and a lot of product was being shipped.

We found out later that a large number of grills were coming back because the salesmen were shipping on consignment and persuading vendors to take more than they could sell.

It worked like this: A salesman would tell a buyer, "Why don't you take this thirty-thousand-dollar consignment?" and the buyer might say, "I don't think I can move that many." The salesman would say, "Well, send back whatever you don't sell."

The retailer had nothing to lose and as soon as the consignment left the building, the salesman collected 18 percent commission on the full amount. Three months later, the dealer might send back $10,000 worth of grills, but the salesman didn't refund any of the commission. In fact, if he sold the same grills again, he collected another 18 percent on them, even though a few might come back yet again.

You can't stay in business for long at that rate.

We discovered what was going on after I got a call from

the company offering me another 30 percent ownership for another $200,000. If the money were not forthcoming, I was told, the company would go broke. That meant I had to put up more money to keep the company afloat or lose the $200,000 I had already invested.

I was about to become Lectra-Chef's cash flow.

Jerry Lastelick and I looked a little deeper into how the company was operating. It didn't make sense to keep putting money into a operation that was so poorly run that it bordered on fraud, so I borrowed $350,000 from First American Bank in Nashville and bought the whole company, moved it to Dallas, and installed new management.

At first the wheels were humming right along. We made a deal with Sears, Roebuck to sell our grills under their Kenmore brand name. That was an important account and we were glad to have it, but the profit picture didn't get much better. A trip to a trade show at McCormick Place in Chicago helped me understand why. There must have been nine thousand other grills on display.

"Everybody," I said to Rozene, "is in the grill business."

The decision to holler "Calf rope" on the whole venture was made when the guy who was running the company called and said we needed another $170,000 booster shot to get us over the hump. I had already been over a million or a million and a half dollars worth of humps with that company, so I elected to let it die a natural death. We managed to recover only $225,000 from the sale of our molds and equipment.

Jim Long was a guy with a track record in running successful radio stations. Until we got into the business together, I don't think he had ever had a loser and the deal he came to me with looked like another winner.

We bought two radio stations—WQAM and KEYN in Wichita, Kansas, and we hired a guy named Roger Dotson from Nebraska to run them for us. In a short time, KEYN became the number-one station in Wichita and was throwing off about $500,000 a year, net.

We thought, Okay, that's a keeper. We started looking for other stations, and because Roger had done such a good job, we even offered him an interest in the next properties we acquired. Jim Long found two stations in Beaumont, Texas, and we bought them.

Beaumont was in a booming oil and refining area and as good a place as any to park some money and let it grow. Politicians and oil companies had been saying for years that the world was running out of fossil fuels and the price of oil would keep going up until it was all gone. Like everybody else, we had no reason to doubt them.

So we went into Beaumont just before the oil business collapsed and took the Texas economy down with it. In the first couple of months of 1986, oil prices went from about thirty-two dollars a barrel to as low as eight dollars or nine dollars. Unemployment rates in the places where the economy depended on oil shot up to 30 percent or more. It set off a chain reaction. Real estate prices dropped, banks and savings and loans collapsed, and bankruptcy was as common as scrap iron—not a good environment for selling air time to advertisers.

We started taking profits out of Wichita and shoveling them into Beaumont, trying to keep those stations alive. Eventually even the transfusions from Wichita were not enough and we put all the stations up for sale. We found a buyer, a doctor from Boston.

Our only requirement of him was that he put $200,000 into escrow as earnest money toward $8 million worth of radio stations. He agreed and we took the stations off the market.

Two weeks before the sale was to take place, the doctor backed out. By then, our best people—salesmen and air personalities—had bailed out and everything was falling apart. Under those conditions it was harder to court buyers and the

Happier days at RCA: *(left to right)* Jerry Bradley, head of RCA in Nashville; Connie Bradley; Charley; Blake Mevis, who worked for Pride's publishing company; Joe Galante, who later became head of RCA in Nashville; Norro Wilson, Pride's producer

With father, Mack, in Mack's home in Lambert, Mississippi

Pride with Glen Campbell on CBS special *Country Comes Home*

COURTESY CBS

With quadruple platinum album *Best of Charley Pride,* released in 1983

With Loretta Lynn during taping of Conway Twitty special on Mississippi riverboat in late 1980s

At BMI awards show, 1983, with *(left to right)* Frances Preston, president of BMI Nashville; Blake Mevis, head of Pride Music Group; and Ben Peters, who wrote "Kiss an Angel Good Morning," Charley's biggest-selling single

HOPE POWELL

Charley and Rozene at reception in 1983, Wheeling, West Virginia, after Pride was placed in Walk of Stars in front of Wheeling Jamboree Theater. Behind them is John Daines, road manager.

Pride receiving honorary doctorate of humanities from Wheeling College in West Virginia, May 1985

Family at home, Dallas, 1985, *(left to right)* daughter Angela, Charley, Rozene, daughter-in-law Deborah, Kraig, Dion

Charley and Rozene celebrate thirtieth wedding anniversary, 1988

Charley holding grandsons Carlton and Malachi

Charley and Rozene with Gene Autry, ASCAP awards dinner, Nashville, 1989

Pride talks with Tom
Collins, who ran Pi-Gem
Publishing Company, which
Pride owned.

Charley and Rozene with
Memphis mayor Dr. W. W.
Harrington in 1992, for United
Music Heritage Music Pioneer
Award

ERNEST C. WITHERS

With Bob Hope, Houston, 1990

BRIAN W. PAINE

Charley and Rozene, 1991

HOPE POWELL

Pride with George and Nancy
Jones in recent get-together,
Nashville

JUDY MOCK

With Roy Clark on *Hee Haw,* 1991

BRUCE J. BERMAN

Pride in a recent portrait

HOPE POWELL

Pride, most recent portrait

BOBBY BADGER

Pride performing at the Grand Ole Opry when he
became a member, spring 1993

terms were more unfavorable, but we managed to get out of the radio business.

Unlike some other business partners I had, Jim Long and I remained good friends. Neither of us could blame the other for the collapse of oil prices.

In the grill business, Jack Johnson and I had been the victim of bad management. In radio, Jim Long and I wounded ourselves with bad timing. Were there any traps I hadn't fallen into? Of course.

I went into the sausage business. Using my father's recipe and my name recognition, we made a deal with the Potter Sausage Co. near Durant, Oklahoma, to process and distribute Pride's Sausage. It started out doing real well, and if my partner had devoted enough time to the business, it could have worked. But he got sidetracked with a divorce and, when that was settled, he went back to being seventeen years old again, spending more time socializing than selling sausage.

That business folded but I managed to escape without a loss; I even made a few bucks on that one. It just wasn't possible to keep it going.

Along with some other people I put about $300,000 into a restaurant called Ellington's Place in Dallas. The guy running it was, I thought, a friend. He turned out to be a con man. He took money from investors and didn't do what he said he was going to do.

That went down the tube, too.

While playing charity golf tournaments in Albuquerque, I became acquainted with Lloyd McKee, who had been in the car business there for forty years or longer. He had a company called McKee Motors and was interested in starting a Dodge dealership. I agreed to invest $180,000 and we would call it Pride Dodge. There were other investors, but my name was the most recognizable.

That could have been a successful company except for the people running it. They were ordering cars from the Chrysler

Corporation and not paying for them. Chrysler came in, took the company over, and the attorney general of New Mexico started an investigation. In 1991 the *Albuquerque Journal* told us how badly we had misjudged the people we had picked to run the dealership:

EX-MCKEE OFFICIALS
FACE FRAUD CHARGES

Two officers of a defunct Albuquerque car dealership were indicted Friday on charges of defrauding former employees of more than $20,000.

Named in the state District Court indictments were Kenneth B. Zangara and Alfred K. Hardin, former officers of McKee Motors.

Zangara and Hardin each face four felony counts: Fraud over $20,000, embezzlement over $20,000, conspiracy to commit fraud and conspiracy to commit embezzlement.

Zangara and Hardin are accused of defrauding employees of Lloyd McKee Motors and Pride Dodge of more than $20,000 in wages and benefits, said Assistant District Attorney Joe Paone. Zangara and Hardin were president and secretary-treasurer of the company that owned the dealerships.

The allegations cover a time period from late 1987 to the summer of 1989, Paone said.

Car Dealer Lloyd McKee sold Pride Dodge in late April to Zangara. In May, Lloyd McKee Motors closed abruptly, putting 81 employees out of work. McKee filed Chapter 11 bankruptcy for his defunct dealerships in August.

That same month, the State Labor Department ordered McKee, Zangara and Hardin to pay almost $90,000 in back pay to 33 former employees. The

*department also found that as much as $700,000 was
missing from the employee retirement fund.*

As part owner of the dealership, I was entitled to the use
of a new car each year. That much I got out of the investment:
a new car to drive for four or five years. I should have had
them stuffed and mounted and put on display—the most
expensive cars a country singer ever drove.

Looking back at what happened to the banking business
in the 1980's, I can say now that First Texas Bank might
easily have become my worst investment.

It was my best.

Jerry Lastelick and some another lawyers formed the bank
in 1975, six years after I moved to Dallas. They solicited
friends and clients to invest in it and I put in $25,000—a
modest sum, considering what I had been wagering on other
investments.

In 1977 some of the bank's founders wanted to sell their
interests and start another bank. They held about 50 percent
of the stock.

"Would you be interested in buying any of their shares?"
Jerry asked me.

"I'll just buy it all," I told him. The bank had good growth
in those two years, and because Jerry was involved and his
law offices were in the bank building, I felt more than comfortable with the investment. Banks were safe, well regu-
lated, and hardly ever failed. I bought out the lawyers who
wanted to sell and found myself with 52 percent of the stock.
It was only a $10 million bank, but it had a lot of potential.

It was just a few weeks after becoming the majority stockholder that I went on a tour of Canada and was in Char-
lottetown, Prince Edward Island, when the federal bank
examiners notified Jerry of the check-kiting scheme. Some
friends of the bank president, Jack Nunnelee, were involved

in the manipulation of accounts and the initial losses were $1.2 million.

We had just gone through our annual audit by an outside accounting firm *and* state banking examiners, and they hadn't detected it. The feds did, however, and because I owned controlling interest, I was the guy holding the bag.

Agents of the Federal Deposit Insurance Corporation swarmed over the bank like fleas on a hound dog. The regulators summarily fired the president. They took his keys to the building, his company car, booted him out of his office, and escorted him right out the front door of the building.

"How will I get home?" Nunnelee asked them.

"You can take a bus or a cab or you can walk," the regulators said.

At eight that evening the FDIC examiners determined that the majority owner—one Charley Frank Pride—would have to put up $1.2 million to satisfy them that the bank had adequate capital.

Mercantile Bank would loan us what we needed. The whole deal hinged on Charley Pride's $800,000.

"If I have no choice," I told Jerry and Rozene and George Jones when they reached me in Canada, "it's an easy decision."

Normally the drive-in bank opened at seven in the morning. Despite my commitment to provide the required cash, the FDIC wouldn't let First Texas open. Cars began lining up early as customers tried to transact business on their way to work. The shades were kept drawn at the drive-in windows and a chorus of honking horns couldn't persuade the FDIC to open them.

By nine o'clock the examiners were satisfied that the money was available to assure the bank's solvency and they allowed the lobby doors to be opened.

By the time I returned to Dallas, the crisis had passed.

Ron Cohen, a customer of the bank, was charged with a misdemeanor and U.S. District Judge Sarah Hughes, who was best known as the judge who swore in Lyndon B. Johnson as president after the assassination of President John F. Kennedy, sentenced him to two years in federal prison—the maximum penalty the law allowed her to impose.

The state bank examiners who missed the kite in their audit were transferred to Lubbock in West Texas. After recovering most of the money our losses amounted to $200,000 to $300,000.

First Texas, under sounder management, prospered. It has grown to a $100-million bank—one of the largest minority-owned financial institutions in the country. At one time there were nine or ten banks within a three-mile radius of us. Now there are only three, the others having fallen victim to the economic disaster that hit Texas in the 1980s. Rozene serves on the board of directors and my participation is mostly limited to attending annual stockholder meetings.

To be sure, I haven't batted a thousand in business, but that bank is as good as a home run with the bases loaded.

I still want to be as good a businessman as I am an entertainer, but I have grown more cautious. I don't need any more aggravation and grief.

Besides the bank, I have an office building in Dallas, one in Nashville, and a 248-acre ranch in north Texas. I believe you can't go too wrong investing in the right real estate.

Several years ago, I went back to Mississippi and bought the first land my father ever rented. Sometimes people have tried to suggest that I bought that farm to flaunt my success, to redeem my impoverished, sharecropping childhood or something.

The truth is less glamorous. It is good land. You could grow rocks on it if you planted them right. A black man who was almost like a second father to me owned it—120 acres—

and he got into trouble with creditors and needed to sell the property. I gave him top dollar for 119 acres and he left the other acre to his son.

It's leased out now to a guy who grows beans on it. It's kind of ironic, a black landowner leasing to a white farmer, but it is not a sharecropper arrangement. He can make as much as he can and I don't get a percentage—only the rent specified in the lease contract.

Daddy keeps a small garden out there and he oversees the property for me, but I didn't buy it to make some kind of statement. It was a good, safe investment and that's the only kind I'm interested in these days.

If someone comes to me now with a proposal, I'm willing to talk about it, but I tell them up front, "All I'm going to be out is my time. I'll invest my likeness and my marketability, but nothing out of my pocket."

CHAPTER TWENTY-TWO

Faces in the Crowd

The first time I realized that there were aspects to being an entertainer that I had not anticipated was when a woman came up to me after a show and asked where I was from.

"Sledge, Mississippi," I said.

"No, I mean where are you really from?"

"Sledge, really."

"You're not from this planet," she insisted.

At first, I couldn't tell if she was joking or if one of her tires was out of round.

"You've been sent here from somewhere." She wasn't joking.

"I've got a mother and a father," I explained. "I've got brothers and sisters. How did I get them if I was sent from someplace else?"

My best efforts to convince her didn't seem very successful and she eventually walked away.

Fans are what make a performer and I've always taken them seriously and treated them with courtesy and respect. A few have become friends to me and my family. Often, I'll look out across an audience and see faces I've been seeing at my shows for twenty years or more.

There was a woman from Hershey, Pennsylvania, who used to come to twenty or thirty of my shows a year. She had lost her legs and got around in a wheelchair. I guess she had money because she once flew as far as Hawaii to attend one of my concerts and brought a friend with her. She died several years ago and I received a letter from her daughter thanking me for years of enjoyment I had given her mother. In truth, whatever I gave to her was returned in full. The pleasure of seeing her at show after show was immeasurable.

Doris McNew of Nashville is another of those familiar faces. Just about every time I'm in that city for a recording session, a television show, or a concert she shows up with homemade cookies for me and the band. Among my crew and around Nashville, she was affectionately called the Cookie Lady. Recently, I made an appearance on *Nashville Now* and as soon as I walked into the studio the staff began asking, "Where's the Cookie Lady?"

She didn't show up that night and I was told later that she called the show's producers and complained because they had not notified her I would be there.

From time to time, I have received letters from fans with strange but heart-warming stories to tell. One was from a woman who had been hospitalized and suffered some form of amnesia. She played eight-track tapes of my songs and her memory began to return. Another was from a family with a sick child who could not eat or keep medication down except when listening to my songs.

It's a little scary to think you might have that kind of effect on people's lives but it is also gratifying to think that the good you do goes beyond the stage and the recording studio.

But there is another side to the artist-fan relationship that is sometimes troubling.

Early in my career I began receiving letters from a woman in the Midwest who claimed to be my mother. "I'm your white mother you don't know about," her first letter said. She explained that I was conceived in a haystack and that her family, unhappy about her union with a black man, insisted that she give me away. She wrote several letters and I suddenly stopped hearing from her.

Some people are more persistent.

A musician from New York, a black guy, approached me about being on my show. I told him there wasn't an opening at the time and that those decisions were made by my manager. He turned up at a couple of my performances and was stubbornly insistent and I tried to dissuade him as gently as possible.

One Sunday morning back in Dallas, while I was away, Rozene and the kids returned home from church and this guy was at our house and had his guitar with him. Our phone is unlisted, but it isn't too difficult to find out where someone lives. He had asked the police, neighbors, and various other people until he found our house.

Rozene sent him away but we began to get phone calls— always from the operator. She had not given him our number, but he insisted it was an emergency and asked her to put him through to me.

At first I wouldn't take his calls but he kept calling and calling. Finally, in anger, I told the operator to put him through.

He told me he was calling from a bar and wanted to see me.

"Leave my family alone," I told him. "Never come to my house again."

After I hung up, I was still seething. "I'm going down to that bar and beat the hell out of him," I told Rozene.

She talked me out of it and we didn't receive any more phone calls. Within a few days, though, we started receiving postcards with pictures of tombstones and graveyards on them. My lawyer, Jerry Lastelick, advised me to keep those cards as evidence in case it became necessary to go to the police. Fortunately, it wasn't. The guy never bothered us again.

Without a doubt, the most unusual experience I've had with a fan involved a woman who went so far as to hire private detectives to contact me to help bring her out of what she called a hypnotic trance.

It began with a series of letters.

She was watching *Hee Haw*, she wrote, and heard me sing "I'd Rather Love You." "You came out of the television and hypnotized me," she said. Over the next few weeks, she said, she was unable to function normally and began to lose weight. She wanted to meet with me in hopes that I could rid her of the spell.

I ignored the letters, but she then began to write to my manager, Jack Johnson, in Nashville. He, too, did not respond, and private detectives began showing up at my shows trying to persuade me to meet with her.

The seriousness of the problem became clear to me and Jack when I was in Nashville for a recording session. The detectives showed up at the studio and that frightened the RCA people so much that they canceled the session and sent me home.

Jack decided something had to be done and began to negotiate with the woman and her private sleuths. She wanted to meet with me alone, but Jack vetoed that. There were too many risks involved. Without witnesses, she could have made any outlandish claims about what transpired between us.

We were scheduled to be at the Iowa State Fair in Des Moines in a few weeks and Jack consented to my meeting with her there, but only if he, one of the detectives, a state fair security guard, and her husband were present.

It was an eerie meeting. We went into a little room backstage. The woman and her husband were very pleasant.

"What do you think about all this?" I asked her husband.

"Well . . . I don't like it much," he said. But he seemed to believe something really was affecting his wife and he was anxious to exorcise whatever it was. I couldn't tell if they expected me to perform some kind of ritual or what.

We sat for a while and made light conversation. The woman repeated what she had said in her letters. Even though I felt no responsibility for what had happened to her, I felt badly just the same. After a while, she and her husband went back out front and, I assume, stayed for the performance.

A couple of months later, I received another letter from her. After leaving the show, she said, she had blacked out for an hour and when she came to everything was okay. The spell was gone. Her thoughts, emotions, and eating habits had returned to normal and she gained back the weight she lost.

I've kept most of the fan letters I have received and I never tire of hearing from the people who buy my records and come to my shows. Fans are quick to tell you what they like and are about as quick to tell you what they dislike. To me, they are good barometer of audience tastes and attitudes toward music.

Sometimes I'm surprised by the depth of their loyalty. Recently in Branson, I spotted in the audience a guy I first met while playing USO shows in Germany in the late 1960s. I introduced him and he came forward and asked if he could say a few words, all of which, happily, were generous to Charley Pride.

Fans will praise you, scold you, and offer helpful advice. One woman wrote to tell me that she had a gap between her two front teeth closed and suggested I do the same.

Fans will also defend you when they think you are being mistreated. A few years ago, after I left RCA and was recording for 16th Avenue Records, I received a copy of a letter a guy in Oshkosh, Wisconsin, had written to *Billboard* magazine:

> *You are not scoring any points with the Master above by mistreating and shitting on Charley Pride the way you have been.*
>
> *That song, "Have I Got Some Blues for You," should be number one about now and I see you brought it down from 14 to 30.*
>
> *We both know this is honkie shit, and that you continue to mistreat and abuse him because he is a black person.*
>
> *The Lord don't like people like you, and he made Charley Pride the color he wanted him to be. You are not to mistreat him in any way because of his color. Is this clear to you?*
>
> *You will be held responsible if you refuse to treat him right.*

Of course, I appreciated the fellow's sentiments and efforts on my behalf, but I will admit that if I had been writing the complaint I would have phrased it a bit differently.

Any entertainer who tells you that the adoration of fans is not a heady experience probably never had the experience. But if you drift too high on praise, there are those moments, fortunately, that quickly bring you back to earth.

A couple of years ago, I received a phone call from an old friend, Dan McKinnon, whom I had met when he was running radio station KSON in San Diego. He later ran North American Airlines and was being appointed to the Civil Aeronautics Board. He was passing through Dallas and having dinner with Robert Crandall, the chairman of American Airlines. He invited me to join them.

Though we lived in the same town—practically in the same neighborhood—I had never met Crandall.

Dan introduced us and we sat down to wait for Crandall's wife, Jan, before ordering lunch.

Dan and Crandall talked for a moment and Crandall turned to me and said, "Now what is it that you do?"

Before I could answer, Dan said, "Bob, this is Charley Pride. He's a country singer."

Crandall said, "I'm sorry, but I run an airline."

My ego wasn't too bruised. It isn't reasonable to expect that everyone in the world is a country music fan. Not yet, anyway.

CHAPTER TWENTY-THREE

Music and Politics

In my motel room I watched the news reports and tried to decide what I would do—if I should go ahead and perform or cancel the show. My manager was not with me on that trip to Big Spring, Texas, so I had to make the decision myself.

The television networks had preempted their regular programming to cover the assassination of Martin Luther King, Jr., and the ugly mood that had quickly settled on cities across the country. I sat glued to the television set in my room, heartsick and unnerved by what had happened in Memphis that day—Memphis, where I had spent some of my best years playing baseball, courting the woman I would marry, learning about people and life.

Dr. King had gone there to lead peaceful demonstrations by striking sanitation workers. On the night of April 3, 1968, he made a speech that was later called prophetic, because it seemed to foretell the violence:

Like anybody, I would like to live a long life. . . . But I'm not concerned about that now. I just want to do God's will. And He's allowed me to go up to the mountain. And I've looked over. And I've seen the promised land. I may not get there with you, but I want you to know tonight, that we, as a people will get to the promised land.

In less than twenty-four hours, he was killed by a sniper as he stood on the walkway outside his motel room.

Guy Mitchell, who was supposed to have worked with me that night in Big Spring, had already decided he wasn't up to a performance. When he heard the news from Memphis, he became sick and went to his room and cried. I wasn't certain what to do and had no one to counsel me.

We each react to public tragedies in our own way, I suppose, and that afternoon I had to come to terms with my own limitations. *You're a singer*, I told myself. *You chose to be a singer. You were hired to sing. The show has been booked. You're just one man in a small town a long way from anywhere. What do you gain by not doing what you agreed to do?*

Refusing to perform would be a feeble political statement and could be misinterpreted as a gesture, not of respect for Dr. King, but of fear for my personal safety. Besides, once you start down the path of allowing your work to be an expression of political protest or endorsement, where do you draw the line? My decision was to sing.

Outside my room in Big Spring, a light wind was rolling across the drab expanse of high plains and the evening sun had turned into a crimson ball sinking into the earth. Feeling emotionally drained, I got dressed, walked through the motel lobby, and found a cab to take me to the show.

We drove in silence until the dispatcher's voice cracked over the radio.

"Did you hear about what happened in Memphis?" he asked the driver.

"Yeah."

"Well, they got that son of . . ."

"I heard," the driver said quickly. "And, uh, I got *one* with me now . . . right here in the cab. I'm carrying him out to a show."

The dispatcher said no more.

Big Spring is in the heart of the West Texas oil patch and has the usual transient population of roughnecks and jug hustlers, but it is not exactly an ethnic melting pot. There probably weren't enough black people there to form a softball team, so the cabdriver had something to talk about for a long time. The day Martin Luther King, Jr., died, he carried *one* in his cab.

I tried to sing my best that night, but it wasn't my finest hour. But what I gained from that experience was a determination not to allow my work to become mingled with the political and social backdrop of the moment.

A lot of celebrities relish politics and are eager to lend their names to candidates and causes. I never wanted to be a role model or a spokesman for anybody.

I even declined when my own father-in-law asked me to endorse a candidate for sheriff in his home county.

"I'm not going to endorse anyone," I said.

"Why not?" he asked.

"Because I don't do that. I'm not familiar with him or the other candidate," I said. "If he is good enough, he will win anyway." He did, with no help from me.

I'm no Martin Luther King, Jr., or Jesse Jackson or John F. Kennedy. What qualifies me to tell people what to think or how to act? I'm Charley Pride, country singer. Period. It has taken all of my time and energy to be just that. If I tried to be something else, allowed myself to be distracted by everything that's going on in the world, when would I have time to sing? When would I have time to be me?

But once your name becomes well known, politicians come courting, and it is not always easy to say no.

About midway through President Nixon's second term, I was asked to serve as a member of the American Revolution Bicentennial Committee. The way I was approached bothered me, but it seemed like a reasonably good cause and I saw no harm in associating myself with it.

How could you say no to being made a member of a nonpolitical group charged with planning the biggest birthday party in American history, a celebration of two hundred years of America? Committee membership was largely honorary, made up of men and women of all creeds and colors, reflecting the diversity of the country. We would be asked to make speeches or public appearances to raise money or drum up enthusiasm for the big event, but the detail work was being done by a full-time staff.

But I felt uneasy about it from the beginning. I was contacted by telephone by a guy named Jack Levant.

"Charley," he said, "we would like to ask you to be a member of the committee. We have checked you out and you fit the bill. You're the kind of guy we're looking for. We can tell you everywhere you've walked since you were five years old and—"

"Oh?" I said. "Is that so?"

"Yeah, we have a dossier on you that is nine feet long. We would like for you to join the committee."

"What is this dossier thing?" I said. "What is your name again?"

"Jack Levant," he said.

"Have you seen my dossier?"

"Sure."

"Well, I would like to see it."

"You can't see it," he said.

"Where is it?"

"It's in the White House."

"Do they have a dossier on you?" I asked.

"They sure do," he said.

"Since you have seen mine, can I see yours?"

"Oh, no," he said.

"That doesn't seem fair," I said. "You've seen mine but I can't see yours."

He said, "Look, all the Bicentennial Committee is doing is celebrating two hundred years of American independence. You don't object to that, do you?"

"No. I'm an American. I don't mind celebrating . . ."

"It's a nonpartisan thing," he said. Considering who was in the White House in 1974, it was hard to imagine anything in Washington being nonpartisan. "There's no politics involved. We have Democrats, Republicans, businessmen, entertainers, sports figures—all kinds of people."

He gave me the names of some others who had agreed to be on the committee, and as far as I could tell, they were all reputable.

Then Watergate hit. I didn't understand what it was about at first, but it smelled bad. I didn't like the idea of being associated with an administration that was involved in the worst political scandal of my lifetime. The newspapers were full of stories about the Nixon administration, stories about enemies lists, dirty trick artists, burglars, and assorted other lawbreakers connected to the White House.

"I was reluctant to join anyway, but I had no idea this would happen," I told Jerry Lastelick, my attorney. "I want to resign."

"Do what you want to do," he said.

"I just don't want to be a part of anything in that administration," I said.

"They can't stop you from resigning," he advised me. Jerry drafted a letter of resignation. I signed it and he mailed it to the committee. To this day I have never received a response.

Obviously I wasn't tarnished by Watergate, but the whole notion of being publicly identified with politics makes me uncomfortable. Sometimes you can do something as innocent as posing for pictures with a politician and it can come back to haunt you. I've played a lot of shows in Washington, D.C., and had my picture taken with such people as Robert Byrd, the senator from West Virginia—he's a pretty good fiddle player—and Howard Baker, who was a senator from Tennessee, and later President Reagan's chief of staff.

Most of the politicians I have met were good people, but I've tried to maintain an image of neutrality. I've got fans who are Democrats and fans who are Republicans. If I identify myself with one party, I run the risk of alienating half my fans.

In 1984 Dan Hexter, my agent, told me I had been invited to sing the national anthem at the Democratic National Convention in San Francisco. I told him to turn down the offer. "I don't want anyone to think I'm favoring one party," I said.

Through some of his contacts, Dan then arranged for me also to sing at the Republican convention in Dallas. It would be good exposure because millions of people watched those conventions on television and I couldn't be accused of trying to help one party or the other. I let myself be seduced into breaking with a long-standing policy of staying away from politics. I would just be singing a patriotic song, not endorsing Walter Mondale or Ronald Reagan. I reworked my schedule so I could be at both conventions.

After singing the "Star Spangled Banner" for the Democrats, I learned it had not been broadcast, but was preempted by a commercial or banter by the news anchors or something. Instead of singing for the millions watching television, I sang only for the few thousand who were in the convention hall.

When they learned I had appeared at the Democratic convention, the Republicans withdrew their invitation for me to be an official part of their program, even though they were meeting in my hometown.

But I was maneuvered by an old friend into being an unofficial part of the GOP convention.

227

One of the guys who came to town as a delegate was Sy Laughter, who ran a tool and die company that made a lot of its money from defense contracting. Sy was well connected. I had met him through a charity golf tournament, the Bogie Busters, he ran up in Ohio. He would have everybody from Dean Rusk to Duffy Daugherty playing in that tournament.

Sy called when he got to Dallas and invited Rozene and me to dinner. Afterward, we went down to the convention center and he took me up to his box overlooking the activity.

"Come on," he said, "let's go down to the floor."

"Sy, I can hardly walk." That was true. All year I had been suffering from a pinched nerve in my leg and was getting around with great difficulty. "I can see everything from up here."

He kept insisting, so finally we made our way down to the floor and up to the front of the hall. Lo and behold, in all that mob, there were two empty seats conveniently located right on the front row, right next to Jerry Falwell and all the seats held by George Bush and his family. As packed as the place was, how could two seats just happen to be available?

As soon as Rozene and I sat down, three or four cameras turned on us—Charley and Rozene Pride, in the front row, looking for all the world like two delegates to the Republican National Convention.

I looked up at Sy and said, "Well, you got me."

He grinned and tried to feign innocence. For weeks after that when I was on tour people came up to me and said, "I saw you at the Republican Convention. I didn't know you were a Republican."

I guess no harm was done. There are worse things than being thought a Republican.

Since I was at the convention and seated next to the Reverend Falwell, who was well known and controversial for the politics he preached from his television pulpit, I decided to talk with him.

"You're a Leo, aren't you?" I said.

"What was that?" he said. A lot of religious people don't believe in astrology. They think of it as demonic or somehow associated with Satanism. Being a fundamentalist Baptist, Falwell is, I imagine, among that group.

"You're a Leo. You were born in August," I said.

An uncomfortable expression crossed his face. "How did you know that?" he asked.

"I've been watching you . . . on television. I have three Leo brothers," I said.

He turned back toward the platform. If being seated next to an astrology buff shook him up, he was in for a bigger shock in a few years when he learned that the man he was here to nominate for another term as president was married to an even more devoted follower of the planets. Nancy Reagan, it was revealed, consulted an astrologer almost daily and relied on those consultations to help guide the president's decisions.

I've always approached religion the same as politics. I'm cautious and conservative about joining organizations, and that includes churches. I grew up in a Baptist home and was a member of a Baptist church for a while in Montana, so I'm a Baptist, but I don't belong to any church now.

All of my brothers and sisters also grew up Baptist, but now three of them are Seventh Day Adventists. Rozene was a Baptist until we moved to Dallas. Now she is a Catholic. That doesn't bother me too much. My son Kraig participates in the Institute of Divine Metaphysics. That's his preference. A person's beliefs are a private matter between him and his God.

I believe in God, too, but I never wanted to get caught up in organized religion and I wouldn't try to influence someone else's beliefs. I've been in just about every sort of worshiping place except Muslim, Buddhist, and Jewish temples, and I hope to visit those someday. I don't care what the religion is called; as far as I'm concerned, one God, the God I adhere to, is in charge of all of them.

No one church has all the answers or the perfect map to the Promised Land, and I prefer to work out my own faith and my own convictions in the seclusion of my own mind.

Everyone should believe in God—believe in something—but they shouldn't be forced. Too many religious organizations are in the business of enforcing beliefs. What happened in Waco, Texas, in the spring of 1993, after all, happened under the guise of organized religion.

My faith is simple: to believe and not to pretend to *know*. I choose to believe that I *know* nothing. Having said that, I further choose to believe or disbelieve what I see, smell, taste, hear, or feel. Having said that, I further choose to believe that there is but One who *knows* that he *knows* that he *knows*.

After that, I'm reaching.

CHAPTER TWENTY-FOUR

A Collision in Midair

The twin-engine Fairchild turboprop screamed across the Red River and began a gradual descent on a flight path into Love Field in Dallas. At 6,800 feet, we crossed over Bridgeport, Texas, and something hit us so hard that it knocked the plane sideways.

I looked out the window and saw nothing. The plane shuddered and swayed for a second and then more or less stabilized. We were about to resume the card game that had been in progress since leaving Rapid City, South Dakota, when the pilot's voice cracked over the intercom.

"Buckle up, we have a problem," he said.

In the cockpit Fred Acciardo, the co-pilot, was riding the rudder like a bronc buster, and the pilot, Bob Sowers, was talking to the control tower in Dallas. He thought he had left the intercom on so we would also be aware of the situation. Fortunately he didn't. Bobby Smith, who handled our concessions, Danny Hutchins, our keyboard man, and Ron Baker, my guitar player, always flew with white knuckles anyway. We would have had to handcuff them to keep them on board if they had heard the radio traffic.

"Yes, we definitely had a midair collision," our pilot said.

"Do you want to land in Bridgeport?" the air traffic controller asked.

"No, I think we can make it to Meacham Field [in Fort Worth]," Sowers said. He was aware that the runway at Bridgeport would not accommodate the Fairchild.

Sowers wrestled the crippled plane to Meacham Field, brought it down to a few feet over the runway, and cut the engines, letting it drop with a thud onto the paved surface. The tires squealed, and the plane rocked back and forth and coasted to a stop a few feet from the end of the runway.

When we got out I looked up at the tail section. The stabilizer looked as though it had been chewed off.

Three television camera crews and a gang of reporters ran toward us.

"What happened?" they asked.

"Beats me," I said. "We were playing poker and the pilot just told us we had a slight problem."

A newspaper headline the next day said: ENTERTAINER ALMOST DEALS HIS LAST HAND.

Almost. We later were told that we had been hit by a Cessna 172 that had taken off from Love Field carrying a student pilot and flight instructor. They were flying instrument hooded, meaning they were not in touch with the control tower. Their plane crashed and both were killed.

That night we played a concert for six hundred nuns at the University of Dallas.

"We were praying you would arrive safely," one of them told me.

"We needed all the help we could get."

"Will you ever fly again?"

"Not until tomorrow morning," I said. "We're taking a commercial flight to Canada."

Luck and prayers were with us, but I gave a lot of the credit for our survival to Bob Sowers. Somehow he brought

232

the plane in without a stabilizer, landed, and parked it safely.

A few months later, we were in Cheyenne, Wyoming, watching the Air Force Thunderbirds perform their synchronized flying routine and I was standing on a platform with General Buck Shuler. He looked down and said, "Is that Bob Sowers?"

"Yes, he's my pilot," I said.

"Well, Charley, you've got the best pilot that has ever been in the air force," he said.

"I couldn't agree more, General."

The only casualty to my crew from that midair collision was Ron Baker, the lead guitarist. And it was temporary.

"I'm through," he said, shaken by the experience. "I quit."
He later came back.

That fear of flying I felt on my first plane ride from Boise to Chicago by way of Salt Lake City had long since vanished. Even if it hadn't, I would have had to live with it. Flying was as necessary to my business as fiddles and footlights.

Having weighed the cost and time factors of getting around by bus, I decided that planes made more sense. Buses were fine if you could become accustomed to virtually living in one—eating, sleeping, showering, rehearsing—or if you were willing to spend more time traveling and less time entertaining each year.

I preferred a tighter schedule and less transit time, and figured the revenue from the extra shows we could work in would easily offset the higher cost of operating airplanes.

We started out flying commercial, but as we added more people to our show, going from four to six band members and adding backup singers, cost was a serious consideration. When we reached the point where we were paying $200,000 to commercial airlines every year, I thought it was time to buy a plane.

But first we leased the Fairchild. A leasing company in Dallas made us a good deal—$1,100 a day. Then it started creeping up: $1,300 a day, $1,400, then $1,500.

"Wait a minute," I told Rozene. "We're back over $200,000 a year. For that kind of money we could own a plane."

Big Sky Airlines in Montana had just gone belly up and had some 10-passenger Hadley Page Jetstreams for sale. The Fairchild had carried twenty-one. If I bought two of the Jetstreams, I would lose one seat and would have to have four pilots instead of two, but we could get where we were going faster using less fuel. And the price of the planes seemed right.

But the advice I was getting conflicted.

"I'm telling you, you might not want to buy an airplane," my pilot, Bob Sowers, said.

By then I had a new co-pilot, Ian Charman. He argued just the opposite, possibly because it would give him his own craft to command, one that could be put to other use when we weren't traveling. He convinced me that we could reconfigure the planes so that the seats went in and out easily. When we were not using them, we could charter the planes out for ski trips and things like that.

I probably should have listened to Sowers, but I bought two of the Jetstreams and flew them to a hangar at Meacham Field for the interior work. They were beautiful little creatures, sleek as dolphins and quick as hummingbirds. I ordered telephones and galleys installed and a few other luxuries.

"Charley, what are you going to do with these planes?" the guy who was doing the refurbishing work asked when I stopped by to check on the progress.

"Fly my crew and myself to engagements," I said.

"How are you going to travel?"

"Just like in the Fairchild, except ten in each plane." His questions were leading somewhere.

"I mean, where will you be going?"

"All over the country. Chicago, Louisville, L.A. . . ."

"Oh, boy," he said. "Let me tell you something. You can put people on the plane or you can put fuel in it. It's called weight. You can put ten people on this one and ten on that one, but you're going to be refueling in Memphis just to get to Nashville. Start to Seattle and you'll be landing three, four times."

That was the one factor that no one had pointed out to me before I bought the aircraft. But I couldn't very well complain to Sowers, since he had discouraged me from buying them in the first place. I confronted Charman about it, but the damage had been done.

"Jerry," I said to my attorney, "we've been had. We've got to have a plane and those two won't cut it."

We decided that I would have to buy one plane that was adequate and unload the other two. As it happened, there was an industrialist in Fort Worth named Eddie Chiles, whose oil field service and equipment business had been hit hard by the oil bust of the 1980s and he was selling his fleet of four planes.

He had a Falcon 50, a Grumman One, a King Air, and a Convair 580, his personal plane. The Convair, with a cabin as big as a DC-9, would carry thirty-six passengers, all of our equipment and baggage, and would reach either coast from Dallas without refueling. I bought it.

All of a sudden, I was up to my rump in airplanes and the expenses that go with them—insurance, maintenance, storage. I had $3 or $4 million tied up in airplanes with two of them up for sale in a soft market. My memories of flying commercially grew fonder each day.

We finally got rid of the Hadley Page Jetstreams. The Convair served us well, but I sold it a few years ago when I scaled back my show. Dropping the backup singers reduced the entourage enough that commercial air travel made more sense. It also gave me a chance to indulge in one of my favorite diversions—watching and studying people.

On a flight to Los Angeles, I was seated next to an elderly woman.

"Going to California for a visit?" I asked her.

"Oh, yes, I'm going to see my son," she said.

After talking for a while I said, "You're a Leo, aren't you?"

She said, "What was that?"

"You're a Leo."

"Why, yes."

"You were born in August."

"Yes."

"Like, August the fourth?"

She was sitting on the outside, in an aisle seat, and she drew away from me. She looked between us, as though she suspected she had dropped her driver's license or some other identification.

"How do you do that?" she said.

I laughed and said, "I'm an amateur. Some astrologists who really study people can tell you what kind of food you like or what you did to your sister when you were sixteen years old."

She was dubious, I suppose, as a lot of people are, but I believe it is possible to tell what sign some people were born under by watching their eyes, watching how they walk, how they talk.

Johnny Duncan was one of the first opening acts I hired for my show and he is the one who initiated me into astrology. He had a fascination with the subject and one day he gave me a book entitled *Sun Signs* by Linda Goodman. I got hooked, too.

On airplanes and during idle time between shows I read the book and it made a lot of sense to me. The theory that people are somehow marked by the planetary alignments at the instant of their birth was intriguing and there was a certain symmetry and logic to it: twelve signs—three of fire, three of air, three of water, and three of earth. Each one is essential to life, each has an opposite and opposites attract.

Astrology isn't like a religion or some belief that controls my life, but I think it has practical applications. If nothing else, it hones my ability to remember people's birthdays and other dates. But mostly it helps me understand people and myself a little better. To me it is just another clue to human nature.

Capricorns, for example, often walk with a little hitch in one knee. They are practical and don't care about the pot of gold at the end of the rainbow. They want something they can get their hands on now. They believe it's all right to dream but not to be frivolous.

I'm a Pisces, the twelfth sign, the sign of the Fish, the sign of death. Sometimes people recoil at that, but death is a part of life, too.

When I was younger, I wondered why people thought I was a kook, but after I was introduced to astrology it wasn't such a mystery: That's the way Pisceans are and I was what I was supposed to be. After reading the book Duncan gave me, I thought, I'm okay, I'm not a kook after all, although there are people who might argue with that.

There was a time when I had to back off from astrology a little. I had people looking sideways at me. I used to get on airplanes and tell the stewardesses, "You're Aquarius . . . you're Aries . . . you're Libra . . ."

It seems that I'm sharper at figuring out people's signs in the mornings. At one point I was good enough that my percentage was fifty percent or higher, which is a pretty good batting average. But a lot of people reacted as though I were practicing some kind of voodoo. It was scaring them.

I still have fun with it. If I pick up strong signals from someone or see something that blatantly telegraphs their sign, the temptation to speak up is irresistible.

When I'm around Ralph Emery, he always brings up astrology. He was born March 10 and I was born March 18, so we are both Pisces. He doesn't put much stock in sun signs and he doesn't understand how I can remember dates. But once I'm told someone's birth date I don't forget it because I associate it with their astrological sign.

Ralph took his *Nashville Now* show to San Antonio a couple of years ago and invited me to be on. Juice Newton was also there. The three of us were onstage, broadcasting live, and Ralph mentioned my passion for astrology and asked me about Juice, who was sitting next to me.

"What sign do you think she is?" he said.

"I don't think, I'm certain. She's Aquarius, just like my wife."

"Is that right?" he asked Juice.

She said, "Yep."

Ralph thought we had cooked that up backstage, that she had told me her birth date before we came on. We didn't. But I didn't just guess it on the spot. I had learned Juice's sign years ago and hadn't forgotten it.

CHAPTER TWENTY FIVE

The Boys in the Band

I was standing near a bus at the IFCO (International Fan Club Organization) show at Fanfair in Nashville and a short, plump, middle-aged man with a beard and a gimmie cap was bearing down on me. He was wearing a T-shirt with a picture of a young, attractive woman printed on it—like one of those souvenir shirts that are plentiful in Music City.

As he got closer, I could read the lettering. It said "My Woman—Don't Touch," or something to that effect. He come toward me in a hurry and threw his arms around me.

Thinking he was a fan, I hugged him and then looked closer.

"Gene?" I said.

He said, "How you been, Charley?"

I almost didn't recognize Gene O'Neal. It had been several years since I had seen him. He told me he had a new baby with his fourth wife.

"That's her," he said, pointing to the picture on his T-shirt.

"How old is your wife, Gene?" I asked.

"She's gettin' old now," he said. "She's twenty-seven."

He'd married her when she was twenty.

"And you've got a four-month-old?"

"Yeah, and she wants more," he said. "I ain't shootin' no blanks, buddy."

Except for his looks, Gene O'Neal hadn't changed. I'm indebted to him for teaching me that, without question, steel guitar players are the squirreliest musicians in the lineup.

He was the first guy I hired when I began putting a band together for what became The Charley Pride Show in the late 1960s. Gene may have had a serious moment in his life, but I never saw it.

But then, we were only together for eleven years.

When I first began touring, opening for people such as Ernest Tubb, Buck Owens, and Faron Young, I used their bands. Until I was sure the music business was going to be permanent for me, I saw no reason to create a lot of expenses for myself. That had been my approach from the beginning. Move slowly and cautiously—do things one step at a time.

Instead of running out and buying a tour bus the way I had seen other newcomers do, I bought an Oldsmobile and traveled and slept in it. When it came time to grow a little, I hired my first band member, Gene O'Neal, but I stayed with the Olds and bought a small trailer, painted to match the car, for carrying clothes, instruments, sound equipment, and other gear. Gene and I spent a year or more crisscrossing the country in the Olds with the trailer in tow.

He was as impulsive as a bear cub and as unpredictable as a funnel cloud. After a show in Detroit one weekend, I had to catch a plane to Nashville and Gene was going to drive the car back to Dallas. Somewhere along the way he spotted a church, tooled into the parking lot, and walked in carrying his steel guitar and amplifier.

"Can I play?" he asked.

With the pastor's permission, he hooked up his gear, played gospel songs awhile, and continued on his way to Dallas.

Being from Nevada, Gene did not have a fine ear for the Southern accent. In some small Southern town he went through a yield sign without slowing down and crowded another car. A policeman pulled him over.

"Didn't yew see that yale sign?" the officer asked.

"Yale sign?" Gene asked.

"Yeah, that yale sign back there."

"What's a yale sign?" He didn't understand what the cop was talking about and the cop thought he was being insolent. I don't remember if he got a ticket, but he figured out what a yale sign was before the cop lost his patience and hauled him to jail.

I've had several steel players and they had one thing in common—they can be flakier than piecrust. Maybe to play that particular instrument, the brain has to work in weird ways.

A young guy named Joe Wright was with me for eight years and he was a case study. At the point in our show where we introduced the band members, we had a routine worked out for Joe to clown around and put a little humor into the act. After introducing him, I would turn back to face the audience and Joe would gesture for more applause or do something goofy to get a laugh behind my back, and of course I wasn't supposed to catch him at it.

It was supposed to go on for a few minutes, but Joe would improvise and add a little to the routine. He got a lot of laughs and he loved it, but we had to keep a clock on him. He'd go on for forty minutes if we let him.

Generally there's a fair amount of turnover among band members. It is not uncommon for musicians to go on to individual careers as singers after they've been around for a while, or they just want a change of scenery, so you have to keep finding new talent. I was lucky because so many of my musicians stayed with me a long time. The second guy I hired was Rudy Gray, a Hispanic drummer from San Antonio, and he was with me nearly as long as Gene O'Neal.

The longevity record, though, belongs to Preston Buchanan, who has been my bass player since 1969. I've always felt loyalty to people who were loyal to me, and early in my career we organized our operation like any other business with a regular payroll, pension plans, and insurance benefits for the band, as well as everyone else.

I think I have a reputation for being pretty easy to work for. If I weren't, Preston probably would have been gone a long time ago. He used to drink his share, as most of us did in our younger days, and his feelings, lubricated with whiskey, always spilled out of him easily.

We were in a bar in St. Louis one night after a show and none of us was feeling any pain. I have no idea what triggered it, but all of a sudden Preston was telling me exactly what he thought of my picking and singing. To put it nicely, he thought I still had some things to learn.

Naturally I didn't agree with him, but I wasn't going to fire a damn good musician for speaking his mind. There is a risk in surrounding yourself only with people who stroke your ego. You lose the benefit of their honest opinions.

Over the past twenty-five years, the average tenure of my musicians has been about ten years. I've been proud of the hires I've made, but the most memorable was a kid named Danny Hutchins.

When musicians contact me about a job, I usually ask them to send a sample of their work. At any one time I may have a backlog of several tapes lying around.

In 1977 I was looking for someone to play keyboard. A day or two earlier, a package had come in from Tom Collins, who ran my publishing company in Nashville, and I hadn't gotten around to listening to it. I was getting ready to leave the office and Hortense asked if I had reviewed the tape. I decided at the last minute to check it out.

I opened the envelope, put the tape in the player, and heard a whole band-guitar, keyboard, the works. I looked at the cover letter and the picture of five young men that accompanied it.

"That's me in the middle," Danny wrote of the picture. Referring to the tape, he said, "That's me on all the instruments."

Is this for real? I wondered.

"Hortense, get this guy on the phone," I said to Rozene's sister, who runs my office.

She placed the call and I got on the line.

"Danny Hutchins?"

He said, "Yeah."

"This is Charley Pride in Dallas. You sent me a tape." "Yeah ... yeah." He suddenly sounded nervous. "That's you on all those instruments?"

"Yeah."

"Do you think you could get into Dallas tonight? We're hurting for some keyboard help."

"Tonight?"

"Yeah. I'd like for you to get here tonight, if you can," I said.

He said, "I don't know. My dad doesn't get home until about five-thirty or six."

"How old are you, Danny?" "Seventeen," he said.

"Tell you what," I said. "I'm going to make plane reservations for you and your dad. Where do you come out of?"

"Knoxville."

He and his father arrived in Dallas at ten o'clock that night. I picked them up at the airport and we went to rehearse with the band. We went through a few of my songs and he stayed right with us. I thought, Well, he's surely heard them and he might have brushed up on them before he got here.

We decided to do a medley, which he hadn't heard. He might have heard the individual songs, but not the transitions and the lead-ins, the way they were put together.

We played it one time through and the kid didn't miss a damn turn. He hit every note—sharp, flat, augmented, everything.

I looked at Preston and the others and their faces showed how impressed they were. There was no way to hide it. This was a seventeen-year-old kid. His daddy was sitting there beaming. He could read our reactions, too.

I hired him on the spot and he's been with me ever since. I feel as though I've practically raised him. When we're on the road, Danny is usually the one who roughs out the first outline for our shows. He's been a big asset.

When I was starting out, I had a lot of help from established singers, who took a chance by taking me onstage with them and nudging me along when they thought I needed nudging.

Willie Nelson and Faron Young are two I've already told you about. Ernest Tubb and Buck Owens were two others. I toured with Ernest early in my career. The first show we did, I opened. Ernest went to his band leader and said, "Tell that young man he's going to close the next show."

Closing the show is a treasured position in the lineup. A lot of artists feel that if they have status and longevity, it would be demeaning to go out in front of a young upstart. When you're tapped to close, it suggests that the promoter or the show's featured performer is confident that you will put the proper icing on the cake. It is a big step up from being a warm-up act.

Buck Owens did the same thing for me. We were at the

Medina Temple in Chicago and Buck said, "You're going to close the next show."

"Buck, wait a minute . . ." I said, not sure I was ready for that slot.

"No, it'll work," he said. "I've watched the crowd. It's time. You close the show."

After I became established and had The Charley Pride Show, I wanted to develop new talent whenever I could—by taking them on tour with me and helping them get recording contracts. Many times I sat in clubs in Nashville listening to aspiring artists and recognized someone who deserved a break.

Gary Stewart, Earl Thomas Conley, Johnny Russell, Johnny Duncan, and Janie Fricke each opened for me early in their careers. Stewart, Conley, and Fricke were at one time clients of Chardon Booking Agency, which I owned.

For one of my early tours of Australia, I hired three backup singers named Dave Rowland, Vicki Baker, and Jackie Frantz. They had people jumping out of their seats down there.

When we got back to the States, I called Jerry Bradley at RCA.

"We haven't just put together a backup," I said. "We've got an act here, man. I'd like you to come and take a look at them."

We had a gig in Belle Vernon, Pennsylvania, not long after that and Jerry showed up. At my insistence he did not tell the backup singers he was coming. I didn't want them to be nervous because the president of RCA was in the audience.

They put on one of the finest shows you've ever seen. They knocked people's hats in the creek. Jerry watched the show and afterward came backstage.

"Hello," he said to the trio, "I'm Jerry Bradley from RCA and I'm going to sign you to a record contract."

They all stared at him, not sure they had heard him right.

"And we're going to record one of the songs you did up there tonight," he said.

It wasn't long before "Queen of the Silver Dollar" was a major hit, and my backup singers were known as Dave & Sugar and had their own show.

Jack Johnson and I had gone to the King of the Road in Nashville to hear a singer named Ronnie Milsap, who did mostly rock and roll on a small label called Chips Records. That night he did a little bit of everything—rock, pop, country, R&B—and played piano. Watching Ronnie onstage, it was hard to believe he was blind.

"That's our man right there," I told Jack.

We talked to him about signing with us to manage him. I told him I would talk to the people at RCA about giving him a record deal and would hire him to open my show.

Ronnie slid into country as easily and as successfully as any rock singer I had ever seen and I like to think I was of some help to him. Not long after we recruited him, someone brought me a song called "Pure Love." I liked it, but I had one hit out at the time and several songs in the works, so I told them, "Give it to Ronnie."

He did very well with it—so well, in fact, that he wasn't long for The Charley Pride Show. Within fourteen months he was on his own and well on his way to becoming a star. In time he would win six Grammy awards and become a permanent fixture on the country charts.

One of Rozene's favorite stories is about the time Ronnie came to visit us in Dallas. I had to leave for a while and Ronnie asked Rozene to show him around the house. They went to each room and she described things to him while he touched the furniture and different items.

After Ronnie has walked through a place once, you don't have to worry about him. He has a map in his head that tells him where everything is and he can get around fine by himself.

The television was on and Ronnie walked over and tinkered with the knobs a bit. "Rozene, isn't that better?" he said.

Our housekeeper, Hattie, was introduced to him and she had watched him walking around the house. Later, when she needed to change a light bulb, Hattie asked Rozene, "Mrs. Pride, would you ask that gentleman if he would put this bulb in for me?"

Rozene said, "Hattie, he can't see. He's blind."

"What?" Hattie said. "He been walking all through your house. He adjusted the TV."

"He was playing with me," Rozene said.

It is a good feeling to find someone talented and help them get on their way, but a couple of bad experiences discouraged me from getting too involved with someone else's career. Dave & Sugar got into a squabble over who was going to get how much. When they started out, Dave Rowland was going to own 50 percent of the act and Vicki Baker and Jackie Frantz would have 25 percent apiece. Then Dave wanted 100 percent of everything. You can't have a successful act with that kind of fighting going on, and because my company was booking them, I was frequently drawn into their spats. It wasn't something I enjoyed dealing with.

Gary Stewart was one I just couldn't figure out. He had all the ability in the world, but he got on the stuff, as they say, and it was affecting his career. I tried talking to him, telling how big he could be if he just got straight and worked at it.

"Maybe I don't want to be that big," he said.

Why someone would squander a God-given gift is beyond me, but it has been known to happen in this business. Some get drawn into destructive vices but are able to pull themselves out in time. George Jones, Johnny Cash, and Waylon Jennings have talked pretty openly about their problems with booze and drugs, but they figured out in time that they would have to whip those problems or be destroyed by them.

I drank my share of the nation's liquor supply in my younger days but I never got drawn into any other chemical vices. Tiny Stokes, the Montana disc jockey who introduced me to Red Foley and Red Sovine, gave me some good advice and I never forgot it.

"If you ever get tired, don't take uppers or any kinds of drugs to keep you going," he said. "If you get tired, rest. Always lay your head on a pillow and you will always be able to sing."

Tiny had spent his life watching entertainers come and go, had seen what they do to themselves just to keep up the pace the business demands. His words made a lasting impression on me.

I quit drinking when I realized the booze was liking me too much and I was a little too fond of it, also. I was in Reading, Pennsylvania, and after a show I fell and hit my head. I was loaded at the time but wasn't seriously hurt. That fall knocked some sense into me. I decided that someone was trying to tell me something. I never took another drink.

About ten years earlier, I quit smoking just as abruptly. I had smoked just about everything—Prince Alberts, unfiltered Lucky Strikes, cigarettes with nicotine so gooey you could taste it. I was in Hawaii when I got tired of the cigarettes that felt like they were sawing on my throat. I thought, I don't believe I like this. What the hell am I doing messing around with this? The Lord has blessed me with a voice. I don't need this to destroy it. I put out the cigarette I was smoking and never lit another one.

For someone who came from a hardscrabble childhood, I

found that fear can play a big part in keeping you on the straight and narrow—fear of going back to what you were before you were a singer. I've heard Waylon say that life only presented him with two options—sing or pick cotton.

Believe me, singing is better.

CHAPTER TWENTY-SIX

Going My Own Way

Splitting up with Jack Johnson was one of the most agonizing ordeals of my career. For a time we were one of the best teams I had ever seen, but what started out as an exciting adventure ended up in a heap of acrimony and ugliness.

When I first sang for Jack in that downstairs room at Cedarwood Publishing, we were both trying to get a toehold in the business. In a sense, we got into the music business together and went to the top side by side.

He saw potential in me and his confidence was strong enough that he left Cedarwood as soon as we signed our first contract to work together. After I got past the initial shock of having to split 75–25 with a manager and booking agent, I was confident that I had signed on with the right guy. He had never managed an entertainer on his own but he had good connections in Nashville and he was savvy about the music business.

We spent a lot of time on the road together and that gave us plenty of time to plan and analyze and generate ideas. Career moves have to be plotted carefully. If too much is left to chance, you'll find yourself skidding backward. Jack's instincts were excellent. He helped me pick out the right clothes to project the image we wanted. Together we worked out that "permanent tan" line that broke a lot of ice in the early concerts. He had a good sense of which levers to pull and which doors to knock on next.

Timidity wasn't one of my weaknesses to begin with and Jack encouraged my brashness. While I was having initial success with country music audiences, Jack was scheming for broader exposure. He tried long and hard to get me on *The Tonight Show* but wasn't making any progress.

"Why don't you just go to their offices and introduce yourself to the talent coordinator?" he said.

Why not?

The show was taped in Burbank, California, and at the first opportunity I paid a visit to NBC. There wasn't exactly a welcoming committee waiting. I talked to receptionists and secretaries and couldn't get much higher. The talent coordinator wasn't in, they told me. Sorry.

"Is there anyone else I could see?"

"Well, you need to see the talent coordinator. Would you like to make an appointment?"

I had no intention of leaving the building until I spoke with someone above the level of receptionist. I stood around awhile, planning to ambush the first person who looked vulnerable. The victim was a guy I had never seen before and I cornered him as he was heading toward the restroom.

"Hey!" I said, getting his attention. "One of these days y'all are going to be wanting me. I'm Charley Pride, the first black country singer."

He said, "Wait a minute." When he came out of the restroom, he said, "Come on in here," and led me into an office.

We sat down and I did most of the talking, giving him a rundown of who I was and where I had been. The more I talked, the more interested he became. He asked for my manager's phone number and said he would get in touch. I had heard that before, but for some reason I believed him.

The next week I was on *The Tonight Show*. Joey Bishop was the guest host that night, so I never appeared there with Johnny Carson. When Johnny was getting ready to retire I thought about trying to get on before he left, but I suppose time had erased some of my audacity.

My first contract with Jack was for five years with a one-year option, and when the time came to renew it I still had reservations about the split. My records and public appearances were starting to generate generous revenue, but expenses were pretty extravagant, too. I wanted to think about it awhile and talk it over with Rozene.

Jack and I were driving to Atlanta and he handed me the new contract.

"Let's talk about this percentage," I said. "How about an eighty–twenty. Then I can give five percent to my father. He's getting old and everything . . ."

"Listen, Elvis and the colonel split fifty–fifty," Jack said.

"But I ain't Elvis."

The discussion got testy and I felt uncomfortable closing the deal on the spot.

"Before I sign again, I want to take it back and let Rozene see it and talk it over with her," I said. That angered him.

"I don't manage Rozene!" he screamed.

"Look, man, you've been to college," I said. "You've got a degree in journalism from the University of Tennessee . . . a minor in accounting. I don't. I've got an eleventh-grade education. Don't I get a chance to talk to someone?"

He said, "You've got to sign it now."

Before we got to Atlanta, I had signed the contract but was unhappy with myself for doing it. We were friends, partners, a team, and I felt he should not have pressured me, but at the same time, he hadn't held a gun to my head. I was an adult and could have drawn the line wherever I wanted.

Whatever resentment I felt passed. I still had faith in Jack, still believed in what the two of us were doing and could do.

We started a publishing company called Pi-Gem, a combination of my astrological sign (Pisces) and his (Gemini). We bought some office buildings in Nashville and we were going to develop a stable of talent to manage under the umbrella of Pi-Gem. All of our activities would be tied to the publishing company and we would split fifty–fifty on those.

That should have been a good, workable arrangement, but it developed into a wedge between us.

If I balked at one of his ideas, Jack would try to bring me around by going to Rozene. He knew that I trusted her judgment and he figured if he could recruit her as an ally, he could get me to go along. She saw through that fairly quickly and began to question the ways that our money was being spent.

Jack wanted me to have an office in Nashville, although I was only there for recording sessions and industry social events.

"Why do you need an office in Nashville?" Rozene asked me. "You live in Dallas. You have an office here."

I said, "Well, Jack and I have gone over some things . . . and we decided to do it."

At first it irritated me when she questioned the way our money was being spent. My loyalty to him, my dependence on him, made me defensive.

After one of his overtures for her help in changing my mind, Rozene got fed up.

"He doesn't think you have any sense at all," she said.

"Come on," I snapped. "You're just jealous of him."

But my doubts about some of the things that were happening grew as our activities broadened. For every joint venture we entered, whether it was real estate or electric grills or entertainment, Jack borrowed his half from me, so I was putting up 100 percent of the money. He paid it back, but without interest. It slowly occurred to me that there was something inequitable about that arrangement. Jack usually made the decisions about our investments, but I took all the risks.

Still, I honestly felt that I needed him. He needed me, too, but he needed me in my place. Jack had grown into his role as manager but I don't think he wanted me to grow beyond my role as singer.

That seems to be a prevalent attitude in the entertainment business. The handlers want the artists to perform and not get too interested in the business side of things. Jack Clement, my producer, said to me once: "I'm producing your music and everything . . . but a colored guy singing country . . . who are you, anyway? What do you want?"

"I just want to sing, like everybody else," I said. "I want to be a good singer. Someday I want to write songs, have my own publishing company . . ."

He interrupted: "I've got a publishing company."

"Yeah, and I'd like to have one, too."

"Well, that might be your downfall."

What he was saying was, Don't get too big for your britches, don't get too smart. Just do what you do—sing—and we'll take care of the rest. You just take directions.

Like a lot of artists, I took directions for a long time. The thing that started to change that for me was meeting Ronnie Milsap.

When we formed Pi-Gem, Jack and I agreed that 50 percent of the profits would go into finding and developing new talent. If we found someone promising, we would manage them through Pi-Gem and therefore share equally from handling their careers.

Jack had found a few people he liked and wanted to invest

in them. I didn't share his opinion of their potential and declined to go along.

"Is it all right with you if I do it on my own?" he said.

"Sure. If you want to do it on your own," I said, "go ahead. Put your own money behind them."

He did and they flopped.

Milsap was a winner, however—certainly the best talent I ever happened across.

The money from managing Ronnie was supposed to go into Pi-Gem, and Jack Johnson and I would share equally in the profits. The money was coming in, all right, but Jack had decided to manage Ronnie on his own.

"Well, look, two people can't manage somebody," he told me. "I'm going to manage him, just the way I manage you."

"Wait a minute, that wasn't the agreement," I said.

"That's the way we're going to do it."

Jack and I had made some bad investments, but I didn't blame him. You take the bad with the good. But if Pi-Gem was going to be a stash house for the sour deals, it seemed to me that there should have been room there for the sweet ones as well.

Jack had guided my career for twelve years and I couldn't quarrel with the success I had found. In just my first six years with him, I turned out fourteen albums, had a steady stream of number-one hits, and among country singers my fee for concerts was second only to Johnny Cash's. I'd been voted Entertainer of the Year and Best Male Vocalist by the Country Music Association.

The next six years had been just as good, but my second contract with Jack was about to expire and I was beginning to wonder if I could live without him.

Rozene's sister Hortense and her husband came to visit in the summer of 1969, just a couple of months after we moved from Montana to Texas. They were both teachers and they liked Dallas so much that before leaving they picked up job applications from the Dallas school district.

While Jack Johnson was managing my career and investments from Nashville, Rozene was handling a lot of the business in Dallas. We had set up a small office in Dallas to handle such things as the band payroll, expenses, and the like. Somebody had to answer the phones and handle correspondence and keep the books, and as the job became more demanding Rozene wanted to hire Hortense to help her out.

Family and business don't always mix and I reminded Rozene of that. Fortunately she was persistent. Hortense and her husband moved to Dallas the following spring and in a short time she was running our office. At first there wasn't a lot to do, but the leisurely pace gave Hortense time to prepare for the day when things would get hectic, which was five years later, on the expiration of my second contract with Jack Johnson.

As that time approached, I was in constant turmoil on the inside. Jack and I had been together for nearly twelve years and we had been through a lot together. But somewhere along the way, it had all broken down. As we became more successful, it was harder to tell which tail was wagging which dog, which was the most important—the manager or the artist.

Ours had ceased to be a joint effort. We had disagreements, sometimes over silly things. If I told him I was hearing something on stage I didn't like, he would argue. "You're not hearing what you think you're hearing," he'd say. At times I felt as though his ego had reached out to annex mine. Once he said to me, "When you go out on stage, that's me up there singing." He wanted my power of attorney and I refused to go along with that.

For me the conflict was miserable. Rozene watched me fretting over it for a long time and said, "Pride, you've got to do something about this. You can make it without Jack."

Jerry Lastelick, my friend and attorney, gave me the same counsel.

My career was running under a pretty good head of steam. My singles routinely were going to number one on the country charts and "Kiss an Angel Good Morning" had crossed over to the pop charts and made it to the Top 20. The novelty of a black country singer had worn off and few, if any, doors were closed to me. Concert invitations were coming so fast I was having to turn many of them down, simply because my schedule would not accommodate them.

Hortense, like Rozene, had a thorough understanding of my business and had become an excellent administrator. I had an attorney, accountants, a booking agent, a road manager, and an office building in Dallas to house everything I was involved in. Why did I need a manager?

On the way to Mississippi to visit my father, I made a side trip to Nashville to talk to Jack about our situation. It seemed that he had not considered the possibility that I might dissolve our partnership.

"I want to up the percentage of what I get," Jack said.

"I'm not going to sign another contract with you," I said, although I wasn't sure I wouldn't.

We had a long, serious talk. I expressed my feelings about a lot of things and Jack tried to convince me that I couldn't make it without him. I wavered back and forth. Part of me wanted to make a clean break, another part was apprehensive about doing it.

Jack went to his secretary and had her type up a short statement. He handed it to me. It wasn't a contract and I was uncertain what to make of it.

I went into another room and called Rozene. "Jack wants me to sign this piece of paper," I said. "It isn't a contract."

"What does it say?"

I don't recall the language now, but I read it to her and she and I agreed that it would probably have the effect of keeping me tied to him, at least for a while.

"Don't you sign anything without letting Jerry see it first," she said.

"Jack is gonna be mad if I don't sign it," I said.

"What do you care? You're saying you don't want to get tied up with him again but you don't want to make him mad."

She was right. I still hadn't made the hard decision.

I left Jack's office and went over to RCA. Chet Atkins had climbed up the RCA ladder since he first persuaded the company to sign me. He was running the Nashville office.

"Charley, why are you letting this drive you crazy?" Chet said. "Why don't you go back home and turn it over to your lawyer. You can make it without Jack Johnson. You're the singer."

By the time I got back to Dallas, I felt as though a big burden had been lifted from me. Jerry Lastelick looked at the paper Jack had given me to sign and confirmed what Rozene and I had concluded. It would have tied me to Jack for a while longer and I had already decided that he and I were not going to make it together.

As far as I was concerned, the split could be amicable. But after Jack realized that my decision was firm, he became very hostile. My younger brother Ed was singing professionally at the time and Jack tried to play us against each other.

"I'm going to manage him and we're going bury you," he said.

Amid all that bitterness, we still had to dissolve our joint businesses. He took one of the Nashville office buildings and I took the commercial building that was later leased to a television station. My main concern was not letting go of the publishing company and Jack agreed to let me buy out his interest in that. He charged me every penny it was worth. I had to borrow $300,000, but I managed to keep Pi-Gem. I didn't have the time to run the company personally, so I turned the management over to Tom Collins, who had been working for us quite a while.

"You run it," I said.

He ran it very well. It was one of the most active publishing companies in Nashville until we sold it a few years ago to Lawrence Welk for $4.8 million.

Financially the split with Jack was fair to us both and I saw no reason for us to be enemies.

But not long afterward, I was back in Nashville and went to Skulls, a club in Printer's Alley, with Glen Keener, who had been my lead guitar player for a while, and Elroy Kahanek, who was with RCA. Jack was there with a group of people and apparently he had been drinking a little too much.

Jack asked us over to his table. He was upset and unusually hostile. I don't remember what triggered it, but we had been there just a short time, and Jack was letting his dissatisfaction spill out.

"You ignorant nigger son-of-a-bitch," he said, glaring at me.

His voice ricocheted around in my head, which was not at its clearest. Glen, Elroy, and I looked at each other, got up, and walked out.

"Why didn't you knock his head off?" Keener asked me when we were outside.

"That's probably what he wanted me to do so he could sue me," I said.

"I thought of doing it myself," Glen said.

I have no regrets for walking away. The words hurt, but I felt sorry for him more than anything else. Jack later tried to blame the outburst on liquor.

"No," I told him. "It was there all the time. The liquor just helped you say it."

* * *

After an awards show in Los Angeles, I took a flight to another engagement and Rozene boarded a plane back to Dallas. She was riding in first class, assigned to a seat in the same row with Jack. Several years had passed since our breakup and he was still trying to patch things up.

"Do you want the window or the aisle?" he asked Rozene.

"I want the one that my boarding pass says is mine," she said.

Jack tried to make small talk but Rozene ignored him. She read or pretended to sleep the whole flight.

Later, Rozene and I were in Nashville, where I was appearing on Ralph Emery's show, *Nashville Now*. I was backstage, but Rozene was out front and ran into an old friend of ours, Billy Deaton, who had come to see the show. Billy had booked some of my earliest shows when I was still playing small clubs, and he and I had traveled together a lot.

They talked for a while and Rozene took out pictures of our grandson to show him. Jack Johnson walked up and she quickly put the pictures away. Jack sensed her antagonism and walked away.

"Jack wanted to come out to see you," Billy said to her. "He told me about the plane ride and how you ignored him all the way from California to Dallas."

"Billy, has Jack ever told you what he said to Pride when they broke up?"

"What do you mean?"

"Has he ever told you about the incident at Skulls?"

"No."

"Pride won't tell you but I will," she said.

After she had finished relating the incident, Billy said, "My God, no wonder you were so cold to him."

Over the years Jack called many times to try to make amends. I've accepted his apology because I believe he offered it in sincerity. When I'm in Nashville for Fanfair or something he still comes around and wants to talk to me.

"I wish you would call me," he said once. "We need to make things right before I meet my Master."

"Jack, I've forgiven you. What else do you want me to do?"

CHAPTER TWENTY-SEVEN

"Say You Love Me"

Mack Pride still has his barbershop in Sledge, the same little frame building where he first went into business fifty years ago. I doubt that much hair gets cut there these days, but he opens it up now and then and his buddies come by to hang out. I still like to sit around that shop listening to them swap stories.

Ten or more years ago, I was in town and a television station in Jackson sent a reporter and camera crew up to Quitman County do a feature story. The barbershop was one of the places they wanted to film. Daddy was cutting somebody's hair and while the cameras were rolling I bent over him and said, "Dad, I don't think I deserved all those whippings and spankings I used to get."

He snapped, "Yes you did." Then he looked right into the camera and asked the reporter, "You goin' to finish this thing?"

How many times have I wondered if this old man was ever going to mellow? Why was it impossible for him to laugh or show any but the severe side of himself?

He was not indifferent to his family. The walls of his house are covered with photographs of his children and grandchildren and great-grandchildren, and people who have visited him have told me that he talks expansively and proudly about each one. Yet I can remember a time when one of his sons tried to hug him and he pushed him away.

My relationship with my father began to change after I married Rozene. Having grown up in a different environment, one with an affectionate and tolerant father, she couldn't understand why my brothers and sisters and I remained afraid of our father even after we were grown and out of his house. She caused me to wonder, too.

"You know, Pride, your dad is a little man," she said to me early in our marriage.

Mack Pride? A little man? What was she talking about?

It was impossible for me to think of him as small. In my mind he was a giant, just as he had been when I was young. He was only five foot eight or nine, but he had long arms and huge hands and a toughness that magnified his physical stature. Something intense—power or will or fury—seemed to flow from inside him and made him larger than he was. When I thought of Daddy, I thought of someone seven feet tall. Even after I had grown taller than he, I still felt that I was looking up to him.

As his children became adults, he made no allowance for our sizes and ages. We were still his to control, by rod or fist or otherwise. When Rozene became part of the family, he tried to treat her as he treated the rest of us. He was as brusque and domineering with her as with his own children, but she was not in the least intimidated.

They had an exchange of words soon after we were married and Daddy said something to the effect that he didn't care about her or what she thought.

"I don't care if you don't love me," Rozene said calmly. "When I married Pride I wasn't looking for a father or mother. I've got a mother and father just up the road who love me and I don't care if you don't."

On one of our visits from Montana, Daddy told us that my brother Joe L. had come to his house recently and had been drinking.

"I told him the next time he came over here like that I was going to knock him down, flatten him," Daddy said.

"Mr. Mack, you'd better not hit Joe L.," Rozene said.

"Why not?" he said.

"He might hit you back," she said. Joe L., too, was bigger than our father.

"What do you mean, hit me back?" Daddy said. "If your dad hit you, would you hit him back?"

"You're darn right I would," Rozene said. "If my dad hit me, he would either be crazy or something would be wrong with him. If he's normal, he wouldn't hit me. He would be out of his mind and I would do anything I could to get him off of me."

Daddy gave her a hard stare and let the discussion end there. No one had ever talked back to him that way in his own house and he may have been a little daunted by this sassy new daughter-in-law. Rozene didn't argue with him; she just stood her ground. If he raised his voice, she would say, "Don't holler at me. I'm not your daughter, I'm your daughter-in-law."

He complained to her once because she hadn't called in quite a while.

"Wait a minute," she said, "that phone works both ways. You can call as easily as I do."

Gradually I realized that he was becoming genuinely fond of her despite her brashness toward him—maybe even because of it.

After she had stood up to him on some minor point or another, he grumbled to me, "That girl is just like me. She's always right."

In dealing with him Rozene did one thing that seemed to completely disarm him. She always made it clear that she cared about him. At Christmas or birthdays or other special occasions, Rozene sent cards to him and my stepmother, Ena, whom my father had married in 1957, and she called to check on them as often as we could afford it.

After my stepmother died, Rozene would go to the store and buy cleaning materials and tidy up his house. He always protested, of course. "I don't need that," he'd say. "Don't move that table." Don't do this or that. Later, he'd tell my brothers and sisters everything Rozene had done for him.

She also insisted that he show affection—something akin to asking him to bench-press a Buick. When we left his house, she would say, "I'm not leaving until you say you love me." She would walk over and hug him. I doubt that anyone had ever done that to him.

To this day, when they talk on the phone, Rozene ends the conversation with, "I love you, Mr. Mack."

"Uh-huh."

"What are you supposed to say?"

"You know I do."

"I don't know anything. Tell me."

"Uh-huh."

"Say you love me or I'm not hanging up."

Somehow she usually coaxes it out of him.

Watching her handle him taught me that he could be handled, or at least that I could speak up to him at no physical risk.

On one of my visits to Lambert, my brother Harmon, who lived in Seattle at the time, was also there. We drove Daddy to Batesville one afternoon and on the way back he wanted to swing by Crowder and see his girlfriend. When we left there, Harmon, who was in the backseat, mentioned a particular road and said it would take us to Lambert.

"That goes right out to the Food Mart in Lambert," he said.

"It does not," Daddy said. Daddy had driven a school bus

265

in Quitman County until he was in his seventies and he was familiar with every back road and byway. But his memory failed him that evening.

"Go this way," he said, pointing to another road.

We drove for a while, looking for a turnoff we never found. We wound around and ended up by a little bayou. We turned around, backtracked, wound around some more, and weren't getting any closer to Lambert, but Daddy insisted on giving directions. The moon was rising and I tried to judge from it which direction we were going.

"Turn here," Daddy said.

"That's a driveway, Daddy, not a through road." A lot of years had passed since he had driven the school bus in those parts.

We turned, looped, backtracked, drove west, north, every which way, and crossed a familiar-looking road. I turned onto it.

"I believe this is the road Harmon wanted to take out of Crowder, Daddy," I said.

"No it's not," he said.

"Well, let's just see where it goes," I said.

Harmon said, "Dad, I do believe this is the road."

"It is not," he said, turning around to face Harmon. "You're crazy."

I said, "Well, Daddy, what if he is right?"

Harmon probably would have preferred that I drop the matter, but I had been doing that all my life and I wanted to somehow try to help Daddy realize that his adult children deserved to be treated with dignity and respect. "What if we get on down this road and it takes us into Lambert? Are you going to apologize to Harmon for calling him crazy?"

"What do you mean? No, I'm not going to apologize," he said. It was the answer Harmon and I both expected.

A few miles down the road, I said, "Daddy, there's the store Harmon was talking about. Are you going to apologize for calling him crazy?"

He said, "No," and stared straight ahead.

I said, "Look, I'm your son and he's your son. We are both extensions of you. You are the tree and we are the acorns. If the acorns are crazy, what does that say about the tree?"

It didn't quite register on him at first, but when it did, he blew up.

"I'm gettin' out," he said, reaching for the door handle.

I had had my say, but I didn't want him to get out of the car. It was two in the morning and we were at least a mile and a half from his house.

"All right," I said. "I won't say anymore."

Daddy had never roamed very far from the Delta in his lifetime and I thought a trip to Nashville would be good for him—for both of us. If he could see me in my element, maybe he would respect what I had become and our relationship would be different. Maybe he would see me as an adult and treat me as one.

I was flying down from Montana to record my third album and I asked him to meet me in Nashville. He accepted.

"Do you want to fly from Memphis?" I asked.

"Nah, I'll take the bus," he said.

"A plane will only take about twenty minutes," I said.

Mack Pride had no intention of getting on an airplane, but he was not about to admit to his son that he was leery of flying.

"I'll take the bus."

"That'll take three, four hours, maybe more," I said.

"That's okay," he said. "I'll look at the scenery."

I gave him directions, told him which hotel to go to, and when I would be there.

"Has Mack Pride checked in?" I asked the desk clerk later at our hotel in Nashville.

"Room two-twelve."

"Can you get me a room close by?"

He handed me the key and said, "Right across the hall."

I put my bags in my room and knocked on Daddy's door.

"Yes? Who is it?" he said.

"It's me, Daddy."

"Who is me?" He was in the big city and he wasn't taking any chances.

"Me. Charley," I said.

"Just a minute."

I heard *clink . . . rattle . . . chink . . . clang*. He had every lock on the door bolted tight and was trying to get them unlatched.

"Why are you locked up so tight?" I said, when the door finally opened.

"Well, you gotta be careful."

We talked for a while, went out for dinner, and made plans to go shopping the next morning before I was due at the studio. I wanted to buy him some clothes, some suits he could wear to the studio and to church when he got back home.

We went to the store where I bought most of my clothes. I found the suit racks with his size.

"Pick one out," I said. He was looking at the price tags more closely than he was looking at the clothes. We found a suit that fit him and then picked out a shirt, tie, hat, and a pair of shoes. He turned over every shoe looking for the price. "These cost forty-four dollars," he said.

"Pick out another suit," I said.

"Another suit?" he said. He looked at the price tag. It was sixty-five dollars or seventy dollars, which was a lot of money in 1968. "Boy, don't you think you're overdoing this?"

We didn't get into the studio until six that evening and we recorded until two the next morning. He gave up early and went back to the hotel. He caught a bus back home the next day and I suspect he was happy to be out of the big city, where people work all night and you can't sleep well without the doors locked.

*   *   *

Daddy turned eighty-four years old in 1991 and is as stubborn and cantankerous as ever. He still gets on top of his house and fixes the roof, tills his garden through the sweltering Mississippi summers, and, against the wishes of all his children, drives a car.

He doesn't judge distances well and Harmon told me he had seen Daddy more than once nearly have a head-on collision while passing another car or tractor on a two-lane highway.

When I mentioned it to him, he became angry with Harmon. "What's he telling lies on me for? He ought to take care of himself. He ought to get a job."

"Daddy, have you ever thought that Harmon was just concerned about you?" I said. "Your reflexes—"

"Reflexes, shit—I don't care about reflexes. I can drive."

Not long after his eighty-fourth birthday, he wrecked the Chevrolet Impala I had bought new for him in 1977. Two semis were parked on the side of a narrow road and the drivers were talking. There wasn't room for two cars to pass beside them, but Daddy started through and didn't see that an oncoming car had got there first. He was forced into one of the truck trailers but was not hurt.

I was in Nashville for Fanfair, getting ready to go on stage, and just happened to call my office in Dallas. Daddy was on the phone trying to find me. Hortense gave me the number of the insurance office he was calling from.

I called and the insurance agent gave me the lowdown on the car. It was pretty badly damaged but could be fixed for $1,400. Or, if Daddy wanted, they would total it for $950. I didn't really have time to deal with it right then. He put Daddy on the phone.

"What do you want to do?" I asked him.

"I don't know. It looks a mess," he said. "The frame's bent. I don't know if I want to drive it anymore."

"You can take the $950 or let them fix it."

"I'll just take the money," he said.

Later, he talked to me about my getting him another car and I did not want that responsibility all to myself. I wasn't sure he should be driving at his age. He lives just a couple of blocks off the main street in Lambert and everything he needs—grocery stores, pharmacy, clothing and variety stores, cafés—is within walking distance of his house.

I talked to my brothers and sisters and suggested that if we agreed he should have a car, we would all chip in to pay for it. That way I wouldn't get the flack if he had another accident.

Before we could make up our minds, he went out and bought a car himself. He called Dallas to tell us about it. Rozene answered the phone. "You bought a Dynasty?" I heard her say. "How much is the note? No note? You paid nearly twenty hundred dollars for it?"

Several years earlier, Rozene and I had set up a trust fund for him and her parents. That, with his Social Security income, allows him to live comfortably. If he wants to spend his money on a car, it's his decision. Talking back to my father is one thing—influencing him is another.

To my surprise, Mack Pride did mellow. Ours is not yet the warm father-son relationship I have always wanted, and it may never be, but he talks to me now about personal things, reminisces about the past, and he'll occasionally tell a joke or funny story and laugh. I like to hear him laugh. I can even hug him now. I've wanted to do that for a long time.

He has become thinner, almost frail, and it saddens me to see him deteriorating that way. Sometimes he talks to me about dying, as though he is trying to prepare me for the day he passes on. As unpleasant as the thought is, it makes me feel good for him to talk to me about things that are intimate and personal.

It is still hard for him to show emotion, but he is learning as the years goes by. We were together recently and Daddy was in one of his softer, reflective moods.

"I remember one time I was standing there looking at you and thinking, There's that little curly-haired boy of mine," he said. His neck muscles tensed and emotion came over him.

All the time I was growing up I was never aware of him noticing me except when I misbehaved or did something to provoke him. I would have given anything to hear him say, "Hey, little curly-haired boy, I love you."

"Why didn't you tell me at the time?" I asked him.

He looked away and didn't answer. I didn't ask again. I had waited a long time to hear words like that from my father and I didn't want to spoil the moment.

CHAPTER TWENTY-EIGHT

"We Ain't Dead Yet"

On a show that was televised nationally in the spring of 1993, George Jones received the Pioneer Award from the Academy of Country Music, that organization's version of a hall of fame. A year earlier, he had received a similar award from the Country Music Association.

No one was more deserving of the recognition.

In one way or another George has probably influenced just about every country singer who has come along in the last fifteen or twenty years. In 1992, *Country America* magazine and *USA Today* did a poll of fans, asking them to pick the greatest country song of all time. They chose "He Stopped Loving Her Today," sung by George Jones.

When George and I were touring together, I loved jamming with him, just sitting around pickin' and singin' in a motel room. He had a voice that was timeless—classic country— and I don't think he's lost anything with age.

But in accepting the Pioneer Award, George felt the need to tack on to his thank-yous a message to the radio moguls.

"Don't write us old-timers off," he said. "We ain't dead yet."

Not dead, just silent. If you listen to radio in major markets across the country, you'll rarely hear the likes of George

Jones, Merle Haggard, Waylon Jennings, Johnny Cash, Loretta Lynn, Willie Nelson, Tammy Wynette, Ronnie Milsap, Mel Tillis, Charley Pride, or anybody else in the business over the age of forty-five.

A couple of years ago, I was in Bentonville, Arkansas, for the John Phillips Golf Tournament benefiting various cancer organizations and ran into Jay Worth, a disc jockey for a Little Rock radio station. He told me his station was not playing anything recorded before 1985.

Why? I didn't ask Jay and he didn't volunteer the reason for that policy, but I can tell you what Billy Parker, a DJ at KVOO in Tulsa, told me.

"It's the consultant syndrome. Some marketing or programming company in New York or someplace comes up with a format and everybody in Podunk, U.S.A., buys into it. It's a short playlist. They repeat the same old thing over and over. They bring in DJs from rock stations and they don't know what real country music is."

Billy, who is a singer as well as a DJ, is one of the few mavericks in the business. Bill Mack, who has the overnight show on WBAP in Fort Worth is another. They play what they like but, more important, they take requests from their listeners, so they have a strong sense of what the audiences like. That's the way radio used to be everywhere—each station determined its own format, which was dictated more or less by what the community wanted.

I was listening to Bill Mack's show recently and he played a song by Waylon Jennings and one by McBride and the Ride. "Call me and tell me which one you like the most," he told his listeners. It had been a long time since I'd heard a DJ do that.

Billy Parker's station, KVOO, is owned by Great Empire Broadcasting, which also has stations in Wichita, Kansas; Omaha, Nebraska; Springfield, Missouri; and Shreveport, Louisiana. Avoiding the canned programming is a companywide policy, Billy says, and the stations apparently are doing well in each market.

"If I was told I had to do what the consultants tell me or leave, I'd leave," Billy told me. "I'll play the older guys because I believe people want to hear them. I'd play Hank Snow if he came out with a new record."

I believe what happened to the country music industry was this: The Urban Cowboy craze of the 1970s brought a lot of young fans over from other forms, but when that fad died down, country music swung back to the more traditional sound, to people such as Reba McEntire and George Strait and Randy Travis.

Having seen what the Urban Cowboy mania did for the industry, the moguls were looking for that kind of surge again—maybe a bigger one, something on the scale of an Elvis Presley. They wanted to appeal to the folks who were tired of rap and heavy metal and the lyrics of violence, sex, drugs, and politics.

Along came some good young artists—Garth Brooks and Alan Jackson and Clint Black and Vince Gill, to name a few—who helped broaden the appeal of country music and created an even bigger audience, which could only be good for the industry.

But the problem, at least for the George Joneses and the Charley Prides, was that the people who produce the records gained too much control over what's played on the air. They were putting their money behind a small group of singers and influencing the DJs to play nobody else. To me it smacks of the Alan Freed days of payola, when a handful of powerful people determined what everyone else would hear.

It used to be that if you had a pretty good record, you could stop by a station in Little Rock or Atlanta and let the DJ listen to it. If he liked it, he would play it and see what his listeners thought. Many of us got started that way. There's no way something like that can happen now.

I had a glimpse of what was coming several years ago in England. While there for a series of concerts, I stopped by a radio station to see Tim Rice, a DJ I had met several years earlier. I had just released "Is Anybody Going to San Antone," and it was doing well in the States.

"Hello, Charley, nice to see you," Tim said when I walked into his studio. "I like 'Is Anybody Going to San Antone,' but I'm playing this record right now. It's a piece of shit, but it's going up the charts."

"Why don't you play my song?" I asked.

"It's not on the format." He shrugged.

The mentality of country music has become a lot like that of rock—you grind out as many new artists as you can. If one makes it a year or two, great. You get all you can get out of him and then find someone else. It's like the clothing or automobile industries—the designers keep changing the models and styles, increasing sales by creating new tastes and fads.

You can only put so many songs on the air waves and a lot of good material is being lost, never being heard because it's not on the format, not on the short playlist. Waylon Jennings came out with a new album in 1992. It got terrific reviews from the country music critics and he did a couple of numbers from it on *The Tonight Show*. But radio shunned it like spoiled meat. I read later that Waylon had said he probably would never cut another album.

Jerry Bradley left RCA in 1983 and was replaced by Joe Galante, a man with a plan that did not include Charley Pride and a lot of other established singers who had done pretty well by that label.

Galante was one of the major forces behind the so-called youth movement in Nashville. The signals I received were loud and clear. The label quickly lost interest in me and the snubs came in a lot of forms. I had trouble getting RCA interested in recording my songs or in promoting the records it did cut. At an awards show in Los Angeles, RCA provided limousines for most of its artists, including some who were new and relatively unknown, but not for Charley Pride.

Both Rozene and my attorney, Jerry Lastelick, urged me to consider changing labels. I guess I was a little slow to recognize that was what I needed or what RCA wanted. Why should I suspect something like that?

In twenty years I had sold more records for RCA than any artist except Elvis Presley. In *The Book of Lists*, the fifteen all-time best album-selling artists were listed. I was fifteenth and the only country singer on that roster. For RCA I had thirty-five number-one singles, twelve gold albums in the United States, and thirty-one gold and four platinum albums worldwide.

In all, I think I had sold about twenty-five million records for that company. All of a sudden I was a nonentity there.

"They're not giving you your due," Rozene and Jerry said. "You should ask for a release."

"I don't think they'll grant it," I said.

Was there any reason to think I was washed up, that nobody was interested in my music anymore? I saw no evidence of that. During that time period I had drawn a record-breaking crowd to the Astrodome in Houston. I could go to England, Scotland, Ireland, Australia, New Zealand, or Canada, and sell out as many concerts as I wanted to schedule. That hardly struck me as the track record of a has-been.

Sure, there were new artists coming along, good talent that needed to be developed and given exposure. That was true when I was trying to break into the business. But when I came up, there was room for the new and the old. For every new artist that came along, an old one didn't have to be pushed out.

"Go ahead and draft a letter requesting a release," I told

Jerry. If nothing else, maybe it would jolt RCA in New York into paying more attention to its established artists. Joe Galante paid attention, all right—long enough to release me from my contract.

It was a shock and it made me realize that something more radical than I had imagined was going on in the industry. It had to do with new marketing areas—mainly television. Videos were fast becoming a major sales tool, a quick way to promote fresh talent.

Until the success of MTV, television had not been a huge influence on music because, except for a few variety shows and occasional specials, there were few showcases even for established performers. But cable television had a lot of time to fill up and music videos were not just inexpensive programming, they were popular with a huge audience of younger viewers.

To compete with MTV, the country music moguls felt they had to appeal to the same young audience and do it the way MTV did—not just with music, but with youthful theatrics and sex appeal. A good song and a good voice weren't enough anymore.

With the release from RCA in hand, I sat down to figure out what I would do next. That was 1985 and I learned that E. K. Gaylord, who owned Opryland USA and The Nashville Network, was starting a new label called 16th Avenue Records and that my old RCA friend, Jerry Bradley, was going to run it.

I signed with 16th Avenue right out of the chute and the first record I cut on that label, "Have I Got Some Blues for You," got into the Top 10 on the *Billboard* chart and was number one in *Cash Box*. I was happy to be working with Jerry Bradley again and had high hopes for the new label.

It only lasted three years, though. 16th Avenue was trying to work out a distribution arrangement with Capitol Records, and when that fell through, I was without a recording contract for the first time since walking through the door of Cedarwood Publishing on Music Row a quarter of a century before.

In my time I've tried to help a lot of young artists get started and I would be the last person to knock any of the new guys who are coming along. I think there's enough room in country music for everybody, but there is something wrong with programming that cuts out everyone who doesn't fit a particular mold.

One effect of that has been to create a division that shouldn't exist. Whenever I'm interviewed by reporters these days, the first thing they ask is what I think about the old guard versus the young crowd. What I tell them is this: There's only one country music, and whoever is trying to divide us into two camps is not doing us any favors. The moguls or the media may be doing that, but not the artists. Nobody sings the praises of George Jones louder than Garth Brooks, and Garth is the biggest of the young crowd.

We've all been through this before, back when singers such as Kenny Rogers and Olivia Newton John and John Denver were crossing over to country. Before them it was Ray Charles and Dean Martin and Al Martino. There was all this friction about who's country and who's not, who's a traditionalist and who's not.

Some country artists even formed a new organization to try to combat what they saw as pop's infringement on us. They were saying, "They're crossing over into our music but they won't let us cross over to theirs. They get played on country stations, but the pop stations won't play us."

There was some truth to that. There was a DJ in Dallas named Ken Dow who worked for a station that played mostly pop and MOR (middle-of-the-road) music. "Kiss an Angel

Good Morning" was not only my biggest country hit, but it was my first crossover, reaching the Top 20 on the pop charts. But Ken Dow wouldn't touch it.

"I won't play your records as long as you have steel guitars on them," he said.

"It is in the Top Thirty now," I said.

"I don't care."

I told him, "Thanks" but I would stick with the steel guitars. And the fiddles. And everything else that was "country" in my songs. "Kiss an Angel" continued its rise on the pop charts, but with no help from Ken Dow.

I've always thought that drawing those fine lines was ridiculous. When Elvis came along with a sound heavily influenced by gospel and blues—the so-called black music of the South—people said he had no business trying to sing like *them*.

Why is it so important?

The basis of all American music is country, gospel, and the blues. We are the product of an intermingling of people and music. We have evolved by influencing each other, but we keep trying to separate ourselves with labels and clichés. Now we're divided again—the "hats" on one side and the "traditionalists" on the other.

One of the biggest phenomenons to hit country music in years was a song called "Achy, Breaky Heart," and it stirred up the friction all over again. That song went quadruple platinum but it seemed like everyone in Nashville was panning it, including some of the young "hat" set. The lyrics weren't the most profound I've heard, but the song worked for a lot of people. Why knock it?

What we don't need in country music is divisiveness, public criticism of each other, and some arbitrary judgment of what belongs and what doesn't. The fans have been making that decision for years and they are the proper arbiters.

* * *

"Country music," said John Daines, my road manager, after we had made a few trips to Branson, Missouri, "is becoming like the PGA. You have the regular tour and the seniors' tour. Branson is the seniors' tour."

If that is true, it proves the point I have been trying to make—that the tastes of country music fans are not limited to the narrow range defined by consultants and programmers and record company moguls.

Until the late 1980s, Branson was just a small town in the Ozark Mountains where people went to fish, camp out, water ski, and take in hillbilly jamborees. It is now one of the major entertainment centers in America and was made that way by the dozens of *senior* artists who go there to sing and the throngs—twenty-five to thirty thousand a day during the eight-month season—of fans who come to hear them.

I began playing Branson during the 1992 season and was a little amazed at what I found. The "strip" is five miles long and most days it is so jammed with cars that you can walk it faster than you can drive it. There were about thirty celebrity theaters there that year and more are being added all the time, along with the motels and restaurants to accommodate the crowds.

Mel Tillis has one of the larger theaters—it seats about two thousand. He performs there five days a week but books other acts so he can have some time off. I signed on to do about thirty dates, matinees on Sundays and two shows on Mondays.

Those are not considered choice days in Branson. Too many people are packing up to leave on Sunday and too many are arriving and settling in on Monday. But we found that we could pretty well fill up the house both days. That's how serious the fans are about the music. After two seasons of playing Branson, I decided to open my own theater there.

The season runs from March through October and in the

spring and fall the crowds tend to be older. But during the summer months, when schools are not in session, you see faces of all ages in the audience. There is an unwritten rule to playing Branson: You stay after each performance and sign autographs until the last fan has left.

I've seen people there who have been coming to my shows for twenty-five years. I go around to the other theaters to catch some of the acts—Glen Campbell, Loretta Lynn, Melba Montgomery, Ferlin Husky, Dick Curless. A lot of them are people who helped me get started.

But I see something else. Long lines at the ticket booths and sold-out performances—people who have driven in from Ohio and Nevada and Florida and just about everyplace else in America to hear Mickey Gilley and Roy Clark and Ray Stevens and Willie Nelson and all the rest.

I'd like to second George Jones's message to the moguls: Don't count us out. We ain't dead yet.

CHAPTER TWENTY-NINE

A Whole Lotta Things
to Sing About

Fresh flowers were on the table when I arrived and the dressing room had the glow of soft lighting and the warmth of old friends.

Billy Deaton, who booked some of my first gigs and now laughs about how he used to get me for two hundred dollars a night, was there. So was Jack Clement, my first producer, the guy who chose the songs of Charley Pride's vintage years. Tom Collins, who once ran my publishing company. Gene O'Neal, my first steel guitar player. Names and faces that reach across the decades brought a special touch to a special moment—my induction into an elite club, the official membership of the Grand Ole Opry.

Nearly twenty-five years had passed since I first played the Opry. That night I had waited offstage at the Ryman Auditorium, nervous as a jenny in a traffic jam, to hear Ernest Tubb call my name and to walk on those hallowed boards. In my mind the Ryman was something of a magical cathedral. From there the voices of Arnold, Snow, Acuff, Tubb, and Williams had been beamed all the way down to the Mississippi Delta of my childhood, to an old Philco radio on a table in a sharecropper's shotgun house.

That night I sang "Snakes Crawl at Night" and a mournful Hank Williams number, "I Can't Help It If I'm Still in Love with You." In those early days I sang Hank's songs so often that a rumor began circulating that I was his illegitimate son. The fact that Hank was only fifteen or sixteen years older than I was not a deterrent.

A few years after that, the Grand Ole Opry moved out of the Ryman, out of downtown Nashville, and into a theme park called Opryland USA. But the soul of the show—the singers and musicians and comics and storytellers—moved with it. As a memorial to the past, a section of the old stage was transplanted into the new theater.

The Opry is actually four shows spread over two nights, all of which are broadcast live over WSM Radio. The first show begins at 6:30 on Friday evening. After an intermission, during which the audience leaves and new patrons are seated, the second show runs until about midnight. The same procedure is followed on Saturday night, except that one half-hour segment of the first show is televised live on The Nashville Network, a cable channel that reaches more than fifty million homes.

Becoming a member of the Opry is usually unceremonious and is sometimes called an "induction." An invitation is extended. New members are simply introduced on stage.

This night, I arrived at the theater well before I was scheduled to go on and hung around the dressing room, greeting old friends and associates who had come by to offer their encouragement and congratulations. A special reception and a buffet of hors d'oeuvres were planned for me.

"It's about time," someone said to me, as though Opry membership had been closed to me before this May evening in 1993.

In truth, I've had a standing invitation to join the club since the mid-1960s and had not accepted purely out of financial and scheduling considerations. Members must commit to a certain number of appearances each year. The Opry is rich in tradition and prestige, but spare in stipend.

When I was first invited to join, the commitment was to play more than twenty Saturdays a year and the pay was eight dollars a song.

"We've got to look at it from an economic standpoint," Jack Johnson, my manager said. "We can't afford to give up that many Saturdays."

Now the time was right. Although I still maintained a full work schedule eight or nine months out of the year, the itinerary was such that the commitment to the Opry family created no hardship. Rather it was an opportunity to snuggle closer to the roots of country music.

I left the dressing room for a short time to join Porter Wagoner in a balcony booth looking down on the stage, where the Opry already was in progress. We taped a short interview to be telecast later. I went back downstairs, dressed, and walked down a short hallway to the backstage area. The televised part of the show had begun and during a commercial break my band members took their positions.

Jimmy C. Newman introduced me. I took the microphone and through the footlights and the spotlights I could see the faces of the audience. There is an intimacy about the Opry Theater that gives an entertainer a special charge. I love performing in places were you can see people, look into their eyes. Every person has an aura and you feel it. All those auras coming from all those people seem to build from the start to the finish of a performance. You become one with the crowd, and I'm as addicted to that sensation as the next guy.

A time or two in my life I've been accused of being egotistical and I'm not even sure what that means. If it means that I'm satisfied and gratified to spend my life before an audience, then I'm guilty. If it means I take pride in the industry I've been a part of, I'm guilty. If it means I thrive on the appreciation of fans, then I'm guilty.

But I will share this with you: Performing is an experience, for me, that is as humbling as it is energizing. There's never a time on stage when I'm not aware that any one of those faces looking up at me just as easily could be in my place and I could be sitting down there watching them. I was blessed with an ability to sing and for that I am thankful, but it made me nothing special. It did allow me to be touched by the hearts of those who come to hear me sing.

Each year, late in autumn, I sit down with my road manager and my booking agent and start filling up the calendar for the coming year. When I'm weary, looking at that schedule causes me to wonder if it is worth the galloping at high speed year after year. What is it getting me? What do I have that's paid for, that I really own? My clothes, my car—they're paid for. What else? My guitar. What's not paid for? My home, the office building, everything else that I'm involved with—all have notes that are forever coming due. At those times, I tell myself, All right, I'm backing off. I'm going to just smell the roses. I'm not going to do anything.

Then I think, How can you not perform, how can you not go on stage and feel that rush and look at those faces and feel the auras?

After a show, you meet with people, take pictures with them, sign autographs, and often make lasting friends. Every now and then I see people who have been coming to my shows for twenty years or longer and we reminisce like family. A fan will grab you and hug you and not let go. When that happens, you wish it could be that way all over the world. You'd like for everyone—your kids, your parents, the whole of mankind—to enjoy that feeling of warmth and appreciation and affection.

Before going on stage as the seventieth member of the Grand Ole Opry, I received a letter from Minnie Pearl's husband, Henry. Minnie was in ill health and unable to take part in the show as she had done for as long as I could remember. I read the letter and put it in my pocket.

I sang "Kiss an Angel Good Morning" and dedicated the second song, "On the Wings of a Dove," to Roy Acuff, who had passed away a few months earlier. I decided to share with the audience the letter from Henry.

Dear Charley and Rozene,
   Minnie and I are so happy and proud of you. We've always loved you. What would I give if Roy and Minnie could be there to welcome you.

                                                               Henry

A lump lodged in my throat halfway through the reading. The theater seemed as hushed as a cornfield. With the TNN cameras carrying the picture across the country, I stared down at Henry's words through watery eyes, trying to find the composure to complete them. *Yeah, Henry, what I would give to see Roy and Minnie right now.*

Stumbling a little, I finished reading the letter, folded it, put it back in my pocket, and ended the show with "Kawliga," whose upbeat tempo helped restore my emotional equilibrium. Porter Wagoner embraced me as I left the stage. Stonewall Jackson took his guitar from around his neck and hugged me.

We had both come a long way, Stonewall and I, since that night in Shreveport when he wouldn't let his band back me up.

So had country music and so had the country.

A few years ago, I was at the TNN studios just across the parking lot from the Grand Ole Opry to appear on *Nashville Now*. Tanya Tucker was there and was telling everyone she was expecting a child but was keeping the father's identity secret.

"It should have been me," I kidded her.

She was at Billy Bob's in Fort Worth a couple of years later and I went to her show. From the stage she mentioned her child and said, "Everyone wants to know who the father is, so I'm going to tell you. It's Charley Pride."

I flinched. Robert Gallagher, who manages the club's entertainment productions, ducked his head. I guess we half expected her to be thrown off the stage and me to be run out of the building. There was a time, after all, when it was deemed unsafe for me to sing "Green, Green Grass of Home" because it was about a condemned prisoner dreaming of his woman with "hair of gold."

Nothing. The audience laughed and Tanya went on with her show.

We're not color blind yet, but we've advanced a few paces along the path and I like to think I've contributed something to that progress. Five years after I cut my first record, I was given *Billboard* magazine's Trendsetter Award for "removing the color line in country music." It still puzzles me that more black singers have not followed and that there are so few blacks at country music shows. But if a barrier exists now, it is most likely in their own minds and in their own tastes and preferences.

The Grand Ole Opry was still going on when we left the theater and drove over to the Opryland Hotel. We had an early flight to Branson for a matinee the next day. The plane would carry us west over the green hills and croplands of Tennessee, across the Mississippi River.

Somewhere to the south—too far to be seen but in the mind's eye—the cotton fields of the Delta would be freshly planted and washed with dew. Mack Pride would be in his garden, tending the young sprouts of beans and tomatoes. New grass would be growing on the grave of a wise and tender woman who died too soon, but not before teaching a restless child to see the good in the world and face life without fear or resentment.

Then the plane would bank north, away from the Delta. It would pass over Kentucky and into the Ozark Mountains of Missouri. *You've got a show to do, Charley, and you've got a whole lotta things to sing about.*

INDEX

CHARLEY PRIDE INTERNATIONAL FAN CLUB

P. O. Box 670507
Dallas, TX 75367-0507
(214) 350-8477

RECENT CHARLEY PRIDE ALBUM RELEASES

"A Tribute to Jim Reeves"
Music City Records

Available
Wal-Mart
Best Buy

www.charleypride.com